Heinemann History Scheme

THE EARLY MODERN WORLD

BOOK 2

Judith Kidd
Rosemary Rees
Ruth Tudor

Heinemann Educational Publishers
Halley Court, Jordan Hill, Oxford, OX2 8EJ
a division of Reed Educational & Professional Publishing Ltd
Heinemann is a registered trademark of Reed Educational & Professional Publishing Ltd

OXFORD MELBOURNE AUCKLAND
JOHANNESBURG BLANTYRE GABORONE
IBADAN PORTSMOUTH NH (USA) CHICAGO

First published 2000

ISBN 0 435 32595 7

02 01 00
10 9 8 7 6 5 4 3 2 1

Designed and typeset by Visual Image, Taunton

Illustrated by Paul Bale, Jane Durston and Ian Heard

Printed and bound in Spain by Edelvives

Picture research by Thelma Gilbert

Photographic acknowledgements
The authors and publishers would like to thank the following for permission to reproduce photographs:

Cover illustration: © AKG

Art Archive: pp. 27, 146 (bottom left), 203; Ashmolean Museum: p. 202; Bodleian Library: p. 178 (bottom); Bradford Central Library: p. 119; Bridgeman Art Library/Giraudon: p. 99; Bridgeman Art Library/India Office Library: pp. 164, 166; Bridgeman Art Library/National Gallery: p. 21; Bridgeman Art Library/Staatliche Gemalde-Galerie, Berlin: p. 25; Bridgeman Art Library/Victoria and Albert Museum: p. 162; Bridgeman Art Library: pp. 82, 104, 172, 187, 204 (top); British Library/India Office Library: p. 177; British Library: p. 175; British Museum: pp. 18, 29, 93; Professor Rex Cathcart: p. 65; Jean Loup Charmet: pp. 88, 102; Corbis: p. 100; Mary Evans Picture Library: pp. 132 (bottom left), 146 (top), 146 (bottom right), 200; Fotomas: pp. 16, 38, 49, 54, 198; Fotomas/Marques of Salisbury: p. 7; Hulton Getty: pp. 105, 149, 204 (bottom), 205; Giraudon: p. 90; Granada Television: p. 192; Ronald Grant: p. 80; Robert Harding: pp. 50, 168;; Illustrated London News: p. 132 (bottom right); Imperial War Museum: p. 4; National Portrait Gallery: pp. 11, 13, 19, 23, 30; Robert Opie: p. 185; Pearson Television: p. 125; Phototheque des Musee de la Ville de Paris: p. 87; Punch: pp. 179, 197; Chris Ridley/Channel 4: p. 154; Roger Scruton: p. 81; Science and Society: p. 132 (top right); The Royal Collection © 2000: pp. 60, 78; University of Reading Rural History Centre: p. 132 (top left); Victoria and Albert Museum: p. 161.

Maps and realia
Bradford Central Library, Local Studies Section: pp. 113, 114, 130; Hertfordshire Record Office: p. 131; Reproduced from Ordnance Survey map with permission of The Controller of Her Majesty's Stationery Office: p. 111; Reproduced from the 1851 1:10,560 Ordnance Survey® map with the permission of Ordnance Survey on behalf of The Controller of Her Majesty's Stationery Office: p. 112; Public Record Office: pp. 138-9, 142-3; Perry: *A Geography of Nineteenth Century Britain*, B.T Batsford: p. 144

With thanks to Colin Johnston of the Bath & North East Somerset Archives and Records Office for the use of the material on pages 136, 137, 140, 141, 147, 148, 150, 151

Written source acknowledgements
The authors and publishers gratefully acknowledge the following publications from which written sources in the book are drawn. In some sources the wording or sentence structure has been simplified.

G Burnet, *A History of my own Time*, Oxford University Press, 1833: p.62; P Goalen, *India: from Mughal Empire to British Raj*, Cambridge University Press, 1992: pp.159, 163, 164, 165, 166, 168, 172, 174, 179 (Source 5), 187, 188 (Sources 5 and 6); J Godechot, *La Prise de la Bastille*, Longman, 1965: p.93; C Hanman (ed.), *Collected Poems of Sylvia Townsend Warner*, Carcanet Press, 1982: p.153; T Hepplewhite, *The Making of the UK*, Causeway Press, 1992: p.37; Thomas Saunders application to join the Sparrows Herne Turnpike Trust, Hertfordshire Record Office: p. 120; G Hetherton, *Revolutionary France*, Cambridge University Press, 1992: pp.97, 101 (Source 9), 105 (Source 4); C Hibbert, *The Days of the French Revolution*, Penguin, 1989: p.105 (Source 3); E Hobsbawn and G Rude, *Captain Swing*, Penguin, 1973: p.127 (both sources); D Hunt, *A History of Preston*, Carnegie Press, 1992: pp.75, 77; L James, *Rise and Fall of the British Empire*, Little, Brown and Co, 1999: pp.176, 179 (Source 6); N Kelly, R Rees and J Shuter, *The Making of the UK*, Heinemann, 1998: p.57; R Kelly, *The Making of the UK*, Stanley Thornes, 1992: pp.33, 54, 59; C and P Lane, *KS3 History*, Letts, 1995: p.96; C MacDonald, *The French Revolution and Napoleon*, Collins, 1994: p.100 (all sources); J Prebble, *Glencoe*, Penguin, 1969: p.67; J Mason, *Expansion, Trade and Industry*, Longman 1993: p.198; S Schama, *Dead Certainties*, Granta, 1991: p.202; R Strong, *The Story of Britain*, Pimlico, 1998: p.9

The publishers have made every effort to trace copyright holders of material in this book. Any omissions will be rectified in subsequent printings if notice is given to the publishers.

Contents

Unit 7: Images of an age – what can we learn from portraits 1500–1750?

In this Unit you will find out about the history of the period 1500–1750 by using portraits. Portraits were used at the time for very different reasons, sometimes for entertainment, sometimes to remember a loved one, sometimes to impress or frighten others. Many of the stories behind the portraits are about fear, power, murder or love. They also show changes in fashion and architecture, sources of wealth and sources of ruin. They will get you thinking about interesting questions – for example, why one famous person looked younger as she got older, or why it was more fun to be young in the 1700s than in the 1600s. And one mystery that nobody has been able to solve...

WHY DO POWERFUL PEOPLE TAKE GREAT CARE ABOUT THE WAY THEY ARE SHOWN IN PORTRAITS?

The picture in Source 1 is called a 'portrait'. It was painted in 1937 when Adolf Hitler was leader of Nazi Germany. Hitler took great care about the way he was shown in all images, including this portrait.

Like all rulers, Hitler was interested in power. He used many different ways to keep and increase his power. The use of images through film, photography, painting and sculpture was a particularly important way of keeping and increasing his power. In this portrait, Hitler's body language sends strong messages about him to anyone who sees it. These messages were all intended to be propaganda in support of Hitler. Find out what 'propaganda' means.

SOURCE 1

This portrait of Hitler was painted by Heinrich Knirr in 1937.

Question Time

1. Why do you think Hitler cared about the way he was shown?

3. Look carefully at the portrait and think about the following:
   a What is his pose in the portrait? Why do you think he has chosen to pose in that way?
   b What is his facial expression? Why might he have chosen to look like this?
   c What happens to his eyes if you look at the portrait from a different angle? Why do you think he wanted his eyes painted in this way?
   d What is in the background of the portrait? Why do you think this background has been chosen?
   e Why should people seeing this image be careful about how they use it to find out about Hitler?

2. Why do you think the use of images might be a more effective means of creating an impression about someone than the written word?

You are now going to look at a number of portraits to see what they tell us about the period in which they were painted. To understand the meaning of the images in them we need to know the context in which they were made. To find this out we need to answer a number of important questions.

1 WHY WAS THE IMAGE MADE?

Propaganda was just one purpose of portraits in the period 1500–1750. Other purposes could be:

- To remember a loved one, especially when away from them or after their death.
- To give information about what a person looked like. In the sixteenth century, most upper-class married couples met for the first time at the wedding. Portraits could help marriage negotiations by showing prospective partners the face of their future wife or husband.
- To entertain and follow fashion. Francis Drake, for example, was very famous and popular. Many rich people in England and overseas wanted portraits of him, rather like someone might put up a portrait of a pop star or football hero today!

The purpose of a portrait is important because it affects the way the sitter is painted. In marriage portraits, for example, sometimes the sitter wanted to look much more attractive than they really were. Philip II of Spain was said to have 'cursed the painters and envoys' when he first saw Queen Mary.

2 HOW WAS THE IMAGE MADE?

This question is also important. There are a range of media for portraits, such as oil, watercolour, drawing, sculpture, miniature and mural. Each medium affects the image. For example, what might be the difference between an image of you in oil paints and an image of you as a piece of sculpture? Size can also send different messages. A miniature was small enough to be held in the hand, while murals are usually larger than life! The choice of size would send different messages about the sitter.

Question Time

1. Why might Philip II of Spain have cursed the painters when he first met Queen Mary?
2. In the twenty-first century, unlike the period 1500–1750, we can take photographic images of ourselves. Why do you think some people today still want to have portraits painted?

3 WHO IS IN THE IMAGE, WHO PAINTED IT AND WHO COMMISSIONED IT?

Information about the people involved in the portrait is very important for interpreting the messages. The person who commissioned the portrait often had considerable power over the image it showed. If they were the sitter, this could be to their advantage. They could direct the artist to make them look more powerful, more attractive or younger.

It can also be very useful to know about all the people in the portrait and their relationship to each other. Who is the most powerful? Are they family or friends or rivals? How does the portrait help us to understand their relationships?

The artist is also very important! Some artists had messages about the world around them that they wanted to send. Sometimes the message was a moral one – the portrait is being used to say something about good and evil in the world. This can have a big effect on the way people are shown in portraits.

Activity Time

What does your body language say about you?

In pairs, use pose and expression to send messages about your 'mood'. For example, you could be 'angry', 'happy', 'sad', tired, brave, etc.

1. Can your partner work out what messages you are sending about your mood?
2. Now do the opposite 'mood'. For example, happy and sad, brave and cowardly, etc. Describe how each other's body language changes with different moods.

4 WHEN WAS THE IMAGE MADE?

When we are using portraits to find out about people and their lives, we need to know when the portrait was done. Many portraits were painted after the death of a person. For example, portraits of the Catholic Mary, Queen of Scots were painted after her execution. These portraits were commissioned by Catholics who did not want people to forget her life and death.

It can be useful to know dates for other reasons. You will find one portrait in this unit that is very flattering to the sitter. It shows her as a much younger woman. We would not know this without knowing and thinking about the date that the portrait was made!

SOURCE 2

The so-called 'Rainbow Portrait' of Elizabeth I was painted by an unknown artist in about 1600.

HOW DID ELIZABETH I WANT HERSELF TO BE PORTRAYED?

Look carefully at the portrait of Elizabeth I in Source 2.

Does it remind you of anything? Now look back at the portrait of Hitler in Source 1. What do you notice about the two portraits? Hitler was not doing anything new! By using images as propaganda, Hitler was using a very old technique. Elizabeth I was the last Tudor Monarch. The Tudors were a royal family who became very skilled in using images of themselves to keep and increase their power.

Question Time

1. For no more than ten minutes, write down everything you notice about the Rainbow Portrait. Compare your notes to others in the class. Add their observations to your own.
2. Now write a list of questions about the portrait. Look back to pages 5–6 to give you ideas.
3. Elizabeth was 67 when the Rainbow Portrait was painted. Why do you think she looks much younger in this portrait?
4. Find the serpent on her dress. The serpent is a symbol of wisdom. This is called symbolism. Symbolism is when a simple sign, such as a serpent, is used to represent a particular meaning, such as wisdom. What messages was she sending to the people?
5. What is hanging from the mouth of the serpent? What do you think this is supposed to symbolise? Which looks the most important - the serpent or the object hanging from its mouth?
6. Find her wings. Why might she want to be shown with wings?
7. Look at her eyes. What happens when you move your head? Why do you think she wanted her eyes to be painted in this way?
8. Look at her orange cloak. A cloak is worn to protect the person. What shapes are sewn into the cloak? What do you think these shapes symbolise?
9. The bodice of her dress is covered in embroidered spring flowers. Find pansies, cowslips, honeysuckle. Can you suggest reasons why Elizabeth might want to be seen with spring flowers on her dress?
10. In her hand, Elizabeth is holding a rainbow. In the Christian story of Noah's Ark, what do you think the rainbow might symbolise? What messages was Elizabeth trying to send?
11. Why do you think Elizabeth wanted this message to be in the portrait?

MORE ABOUT ELIZABETH I

In order to understand the Rainbow Portrait, we need to look at it within the context of Elizabeth's history.

Read Source 3. When Roy Strong stresses 'what the people saw' in 1558, he is making a very important point. We know today that Elizabeth was a successful queen. We know that she survived all rebellions and wars to die peacefully in 1603. But in 1558 nobody knew this! Elizabeth had many reasons to feel nervous and scared when she succeeded her sister, Mary, as queen. When she came to throne, England was a defeated, bankrupt and demoralised country.

WHAT CHALLENGES DID ELIZABETH FACE DURING HER REIGN?

- **Religion:** There were many changes in religion during the sixteenth century. Over 300 people were burnt at the stake because of religion. Elizabeth was a Protestant, but not keen to promote Puritanism. She tolerated Puritans and also tolerated Catholics, as long as they were peaceful and did not threaten her.
- **Succession:** Elizabeth had been declared illegitimate by her father on the execution of her mother, Anne Boleyn. Therefore, some people said that she was not the rightful queen. Elizabeth was not married and another problem for her was who would succeed as monarch after her death. Mary, Queen of Scots, a Catholic, had a very good claim.
- **Money:** Inflation rose rapidly during the middle decades of the sixteenth century. This meant that prices of food and other goods increased. People therefore needed more money to pay for food. Some people could not manage and there was famine and starvation. Elizabeth also had to save money, especially towards the end of her reign.
- **Foreign Policy:** France was the biggest threat to England at the start of Elizabeth's reign. Mary, Queen of Scots was married to the French king in 1558 and France was a Catholic country. However, by the 1580s Spain had become England's greatest enemy. Spain, too, was a Catholic country. Even after the defeat of Spain in 1588, England was not safe. It faced constant invasions and threats of invasions from Ireland, the Low Countries and France. All these problems cost money for ships, weapons and armies.

SOURCE 3

Elizabeth I was twenty-six when she came to the throne, a tall young woman of commanding presence with auburn hair and piercing grey-black eyes. She was to reign longer than any other Tudor, forty-five years in all. That lay in the future. In 1558 what the people saw was an inexperienced, unmarried woman assume control of England.

This was written by a modern historian, Roy Strong, in 1998.

Question Time

1. Did Elizabeth have any financial problems in 1600? How wealthy does Elizabeth look in the Rainbow Portrait? How can you explain this?
2. As Elizabeth got older, her portraits made her look younger! Read the section 'What challenges did Elizabeth face during her reign?' Why might Elizabeth have wanted to look younger as she got older?

THE VIRGIN QUEEN

In the Rainbow Portrait, Elizabeth's hair is worn loose around her shoulders. This was a deliberate sign of virginity. The legend of the 'Virgin Queen' was deliberately spread about Elizabeth during her reign through poems and books, as well as through portraits. For example, John Foxe's *Actes and Monuments* portrays Elizabeth as the heroic virgin queen who saves the country from the dark evils of Catholicism. It became a very popular book. Catholic images of the Virgin Mary, which people used to carry around with them, were banned. Instead, many rich people carried around miniatures of the Virgin Queen Elizabeth. They wore her picture in gold lockets attached to their clothes. Elizabeth was compared to other 'heroines' like the goddesses Venus and Diana.

WHAT CAN WE FIND OUT FROM THE RAINBOW PORTRAIT?

As you have worked out, by 1600 Elizabeth would have looked much older in real life. Written sources of information about Elizabeth confirm that she was not quite how the portrait shows her! But the portrait is still useful to us.

Activity Time

1. Why might Elizabeth want to be likened to goddesses and biblical heroines? Find out what Venus and Diana were goddesses of. Why were these two chosen?
2. The printing press was invented at the end of the fifteenth century. How does the information on this page suggest it was used to spread propaganda?
3. Sketch an outline of the Rainbow Portrait. Using different colours:
   a Choose four *descriptive* points and write them around your sketch.
   b Choose four *interpretive* points and write them around your sketch.
4. Add a thought bubble to your sketch. Suggest what Elizabeth is thinking and put it in the bubble.
5. Compare your ideas with others in the class. What do you notice about the interpretations you have reached?

Question Time

1. Make a list of all the things that we can find out from the Rainbow Portrait. Remember to include things about Tudor times, as well as about Elizabeth herself.
2. One very important way we can use a portrait is to find out about the sitter's personality. For example, we could use this portrait to argue that Elizabeth was an intelligent woman. Why is this?
3. What other conclusions might you reach about her?

SOURCE 4

This painting of Elizabeth I, known as the 'Ditchley Portrait', was made by Gheerhaerts in about 1592.

UNDERSTANDING THE PUBLIC AND THE PRIVATE STORIES

Look carefully at the Ditchley Portrait of Elizabeth I in Source 4. Now look back at the portrait of Hitler. What do you notice about the two portraits?

The Ditchley Portrait also has some similarities with the Rainbow Portrait. Why do you think Elizabeth wanted to repeat certain messages about herself? Like the Rainbow Portrait, the Ditchley Portrait contains symbolism (see page 8).

FEELING PROUD TO BE ENGLISH IN THE 1590s

In order to interpret the Ditchley Portrait more fully and understand its symbolism, we need to know what was going on at the time. In 1588 England had won a great victory against the Spanish Armada. For many Europeans this victory was seen as the judgement of God, who must have supported Elizabeth. It led to greater patriotism among English people. It was also seen as a victory of Protestant light and goodness over Catholic darkness and evil.

There were other reasons to feel proud to be English at this time. English seamen and ships were expanding trade and exploration all over the world. Under Elizabeth, England became one of the most powerful countries in the world.

THE PRIVATE STORY

There is another story that lies behind the Ditchley Portrait which is much more personal. The painting was commissioned by Sir Henry Lee, who may have been Elizabeth's lover. In 1590 he went to live in Oxfordshire with his mistress, Anne Vavasour. Anne had an illegitimate child by Henry. This birth led to a feud with Thomas Knyvett, Anne's guardian. It caused a duel, three fights and two murders! Elizabeth was very angry. It is likely that Henry Lee commissioned the portrait to mark Elizabeth's forgiveness of him.

Think about why forgiveness from Elizabeth would be very important to Sir Henry Lee. Look again at the portrait. How does it show that Henry was forgiven?

Question Time

1. Look carefully at the Ditchley Portrait and list all the symbols that you can find.
2. Why was symbolism used in portraits?
3. Use your knowledge of England in the 1580s and 1590s to interpret the symbolic messages of the portrait. What messages are being sent by:
   - the jewels on her clothes
   - the wings on her back
   - standing on a globe of the world
   - standing in the middle of England
   - the bad weather behind her
   - the good weather in front of her?
4. Elizabeth is wearing a rose. What do you think this might symbolise?
5. A historian has said that 'Elizabeth was England'. How does the symbolism of the Ditchley Portrait support the view that Elizabeth 'was England'? What was the advantage for Elizabeth in being England?
6. How would the victory against Spain increase patriotism? Why was it important for Elizabeth to be seen to 'have God on her side'?

Activity Time

What do you think Elizabeth's admirers would have said if someone had suggested cutting portraits and using the money for more soldiers to protect the queen instead?

IMAGES OF AN AGE: WHO WAS POWERFUL?

SOURCE 1

This painting of Henry VII (1457–1509) and Henry VIII (1491–1547) was made by Hans Holbein the Younger (1497-1543) who became a court painter in the service of Henry VIII.

GETTING THE MESSAGE ABOUT THE TUDORS

Look at the portrait of Henry VII and Henry VIII in Source 1.

The portrait is part of a drawing called a 'cartoon'. It is made up of many sheets of paper joined together. It was used to make a mural in Whitehall Palace. The outlines of the cartoon were pierced with tiny holes. The cartoon was then stuck on to the wall and charcoal dust brushed over it. The artist, Holbein, then joined up the dots left by the charcoal to make a copy of the drawing. Many copies were made and circulated on the continent as well as in Britain.

Question Time

1. Look at the date of the painting on page 13 and the dates for Henry VII and Henry VIII. What do you notice? Who do you think commissioned the portrait?
2. The size of the painting meant that Henry VIII was shown 'larger than life'. Why do you think he would have wanted to be shown this way?
3. Describe the pose and expression of Henry VIII. What messages is he sending by being shown in this way?
4. Describe the pose and expression of Henry VII. What messages were being sent about him?
5. Who do you think is the more important person in the portrait? Use at least three observations about the portrait to support your choice. (Note: There is no 'right' answer!)
6. Look at the portrait and see if you agree with the views of the historian quoted in Source 2.

PUTTING IDEAS INTO THE HEADS OF THE PEOPLE...

By using portraits as propaganda, Elizabeth was building on the work done by her father. Under Henry VIII, there was a change in royal power and control. No longer did monarchs rely heavily on armed lords and knights in local areas, as they had done in medieval times. Instead, power shifted to the royal court. Weapons became less important and images

SOURCE 2

Under Henry VIII there was a deliberate attempt to be more visible to the people. He was the first monarch to be called 'His Majesty'. He deliberately made himself look grand and powerful.

A modern historian said this about Henry VIII.

became more important as a way of controlling the people. In other words, the idea that the monarch was the most powerful person became very important.

WHO SAW PORTRAITS?

Portraits of monarchs needed to be seen by as many people as possible. Many copies were made and sent overseas, as well as all over Britain. Most people never saw Elizabeth in person. However, each Sunday in church they could look at her image on the title page of the Bible. The nearby great house would have a portrait of Elizabeth in its gallery. Towards the end of the century, more and more large wealthy houses had 'long galleries' where portraits were hung. It became very fashionable to have such portraits.

Elizabeth wanted to have control of all images of her. Just as she could use portraits as propaganda to make her more powerful, so her enemies could use unflattering portraits to try and damage her. Elizabeth issued orders that images that were unflattering were to be destroyed. In 1563 a proclamation was made that all images of the queen had to be approved by her.

Activity Time

An ambassador from a foreign court visits England to find out as much as he can about Henry VIII and his power. The first thing he sees is the Holbein mural of Henry VII and VIII in Whitehall Palace.

Write a letter from the ambassador to his monarch on the continent. What might he say about Henry VIII and his power after looking at the portrait?

Question Time

You have been contacted by a historian who is writing about:

a father and son relationships in the sixteenth century

b how Tudor monarchs got their power

c differences between Henry VII and Henry VIII

d the personality of Henry VII.

What information could you give her about these things, using the portrait of Henry VII and Henry VIII in Source 1?

SOURCE 3

This painting shows Edward VI and his council in 1549. It was painted by an unknown artist in about 1570.

In 1547, Edward VI succeeded his father, Henry VIII, as king. He was ten years old and needed the help of 'Lord Protectors' to rule. Edward VI was a very devout Protestant. In his reign, there was great support for the Protestant religion over Catholicism. In 1549 the first Book of Common Prayer, an English Protestant publication, was introduced into all churches and in 1552 a law was passed punishing those who failed to use it. An order of 1551 removed all images from churches. People were no longer able to light candles in prayer. Images and candles were recognised Catholic symbols.

These changes were very far reaching. For hundreds of years, English people had worshipped in the same way in churches that looked the same. Protestantism under Edward VI did away not just with papal authority (as under Henry VIII), but also with relics, saints, pilgrimages and the cult of the Virgin Mary.

Question Time

1. Find the following people in the portrait in Source 3:
   a Edward VI
   b Henry VIII
   c Edward Seymour, Lord Protector
   d the Pope.
2. Why is Henry VIII pointing at his son? What message is being sent?
3. What impression of Edward VI do you get from this painting?
4. Describe the way the Pope has been portrayed.
5. What is happening outside the window? Why do you think this image has been included in the portrait?
6. How does the portrait support the Protestant religion over Catholicism?
7. Edward died at the age of fifteen and was succeeded by his Catholic sister, Mary. This portrait was not painted during Edward's lifetime, but commissioned by his sister, Elizabeth. What religious reasons might Elizabeth have had for commissioning the portrait?
8. The Tudor family were all worried about succession. Henry VII had become king by force and there were other families who had better claims to the throne. How could this portrait be used as evidence that the Tudors were worried about succession?
   Think about:
   - what is shown in the painting
   - who commissioned the painting.

JAMES II AND PROPAGANDA

Using art for propaganda could work both ways. Kings and queens could be victims of it as well as benefiting from it.

In 1685, Charles II was succeeded by his brother, James II. James was a Catholic and had a Catholic second wife, Mary of Modena. It was James' commitment to Catholicism which was to be his downfall. By 1688, James had lost the support of many important people. They were worried that he would try and make England Catholic again. James had two daughters by his first marriage, but no sons. His daughter Mary had been brought up a Protestant and was married to the Protestant Prince of the Netherlands, William of Orange.

By the end of 1688, James had fled to France and Parliament had replaced him with his Protestant daughter Mary and her husband William. The flight was provoked by the birth of a son to James and

Mary of Modena on 10 June 1688. This was very important. It meant that James could be succeeded by his Catholic son. Rumours spread that James was not really the father of the child, who had been smuggled into the queen's bedroom. Some people said that the child was really the son of a miller. Parliament sent a letter to William asking him to invade and take over as king. James decided to send his wife and son to France, and then followed them into exile. There is a more detailed account of this story in Unit 9, pages 56–7.

SOURCE 4

A Dutch print about the birth of a son to James II and Mary of Modena

Question Time

1. In what ways is the painting in Source 4 propaganda for William of Orange and against James II?
2. What symbol is used in the portrait to send messages about James' son?
3. What else do you notice about the way the child is portrayed?

ONE FOR THE FAMILY ALBUM: THE CAPEL FAMILY

Source 1 is a portrait of the Capel family. It was painted in 1640 shortly before the outbreak of the English Civil War. Arthur Capel, First Baron Capel (1604-49), head of the family, was a Royalist.

The people in the portrait are (from left to right):
Arthur Capel, 1st Earl of Essex (1631-83)
Arthur Capel, 1st Baron Capel (1604-49)
Henry Capel, 2nd Baron Capel (1638-96)
Elizabeth, Lady Capel (died 1661)
Charles Capel (died 1657)
Elizabeth, Countess of Caernarvon (1633-78)
Mary, Duchess of Beaufort (1630-1715)

SOURCE 1

The Capel Family by Cornelius Johnson, painted in 1640.

Question Time

1. Find the baby in the portrait. The gender of the baby can be worked out from a very important clue. Look carefully at the clothing of **all** the children to work out the gender of the baby.
2. The Capel family were very wealthy. What evidence is there in the portrait that they were wealthy?
3. Who do you think is the most important person in the portrait? Give reasons for your choice.
4. Who do you think is the second most important person in the portrait? Give reasons for your choice.
5. Rank all the sitters in the portrait according to how powerful they are.
6. What messages does this portrait send about the power of men and women at this time? Do you think these messages were deliberate or not?
7. Look at the figures of Arthur Capel (1604-49) and his son Arthur (1631-83). What are the similarities between the two figures? What messages were being sent by portraying them in this way?
8. Find the figure of Mary, Duchess of Beaufort. She was the eldest daughter and shortly to be married. In this portrait, she is also the 'odd one out'. Look carefully. In what way is she the 'odd one out'? Why do you think she has been portrayed in this way?
9. Try to work out the ages of all the children. What impression of childhood do you get from this portrait?

HISTORICAL BACKGROUND

Between 1500 and 1640 there were major changes in architecture and landscape design. Many new and bigger houses were built in a building boom. Rich people started to spend their money on comfort and luxury within their own homes. They also used their homes to show off how wealthy and powerful they were. Unlike in the Middle Ages, rich families had private rooms with huge fireplaces, ornate plaster ceilings, panelling and rich furnishings. Glass windows were introduced. Houses were built in parkland for hunting parties to rest in.

Question Time

1. How does the evidence of the portrait in Source 1 support the evidence given in the paragraph called Historical Background?
2. Look carefully at the garden shown in Source 1. In reality, the garden could not be seen from the house in this way. Why do you think Arthur Capel wanted the artist to include it?

The portrait below shows Mr and Mrs Andrews. It was painted just after their marriage. Mrs Andrews is sixteen years old. Her education has prepared her for running a big house and for drawing, dancing and French. This portrait is particularly useful for telling us about the lives of wealthy landowners in the eighteenth century. We can also use it to find out about change by comparing it with the Capel Family portrait on page 19.

SOURCE 2

Mr and Mrs Andrews painted by Thomas Gainsborough around 1748.

Question Time

1. What do you think Mr Andrews had been doing just before posing for the portrait?
2. What can we learn about Mrs Andrew's lifestyle from her clothes?
3. Look carefully at the background of the portrait. Why did Mr and Mrs Andrews want their land to be included? What evidence is there in the portrait about farming in the eighteenth century?
4. In reality, the landscape would probably have contained farm workers and servants. Why do you think they have been left out of the portrait?
5. Using the Andrews and Capel family portraits, how did fashion change between the 1640s and the 1740s?
6. Look back at the Capel family portrait. Many historians think that the position of women did not change very much between the 1640s and the 1740s. How much do these two portraits support that view?

Activity Time

1. Collect images, including photographs and sketches, of your family or a famous family. You could do the royal family or a fictional family from a soap opera.
2. Use the images to make a montage that tells the story of your chosen family. You could mount the pictures on maps, advertisements, business information or street plans, to help tell the story of your family.
   Use what you have learned about positioning in portraits to send messages about relationships, and power if appropriate, in your chosen family.

MORE FOR THE FAMILY ALBUM: THE NEVILLE FAMILY

Look at the portrait in Source 3 on page 23. Record all your first reactions to it. For example, who do you think they might be? When was it painted? Why was it painted?

A STORY OF DISGRACE AND RESPECTABILITY

The portrait shows Lady Mary Neville and her son, Gregory Fiennes. Lady Mary's first husband and father to Gregory was executed during the reign of Henry VIII. He was caught poaching and a gamekeeper

SOURCE 3

was killed in the incident. His family were disgraced by his actions and execution. As a result, they lost the title of 'baron', but they had it given back to them in 1559. This portrait was painted very shortly afterwards.

Art historians believe that the portrait was commissioned by Mary Neville to celebrate the restoration of the title of 'baron'. Think about whether the appearance of Lady Mary and her son supports this view.

A STORY OF MOTHER AND SON

The portrait is very unusual for its time because it shows a mother and a son. Most family portraits showed husbands and wives. Written sources show that Mary Neville had a lot of power over her son. His wife Anne complained about it! Gregory himself was apparently easy to influence and described as a 'little Crack-brain'd'.

This information shows how important it is to use other sources, as well as portraits, to find out about people in the past.

PORTRAITS AND MEN OF POWER: THE SIXTEENTH CENTURY

In the sixteenth century, the majority of powerful and wealthy people made their money from the land. Most people were born either wealthy or poor and there was very little possibility of change. There were, however, minority groups who were not typical. Georg Gisze was one of these people.

Look carefully at the portrait in Source 4. There are clues that Gisze was a wealthy and powerful man. Think about how the portrait tells you about the type of man that Gisze was.

MORE ABOUT GISZE

Georg Gisze was a merchant. He made his money from buying and selling, not from owning land. The portrait shows him at his desk in the London Steelyard. He was thirty-two at the time. The inscription on the wall gives his motto in Latin, 'No joy without sorrow'.

Gisze came from the Hanseatic city of Danzig (now in Poland). European immigrants like Gisze made vital contributions to the English economy. Their skills in the techniques of metals, mining, engineering, farming and crafts were generally more advanced than those of the English. They also provided capital (money) to invest in business, manufacturing and trade.

In 1440 about 1 per cent of the English population was 'foreign'. Some of them, like Gisze, were wealthy and had influence in the royal court. This led to anger and hostility from some people and there was pressure to restrict their entry into England. Between 1556 and 1598 merchants from the Hanseatic League, like Gisze, were squeezed out when the London Steelyard was closed down.

Question Time

1. Use the portrait in Source 4 and the information above to answer these questions:
   a What evidence is there that Gisze was a powerful man?
   b What evidence is there that Gisze was not a powerful man?
2. The portrait was painted by Holbein, court painter of Henry VIII. Why do you think Gisze wanted to have this portrait painted? Look back at pages 5–6 to give you ideas.

SOURCE 4

A portrait of Georg Gisze, painted by Holbein around 1526.

PORTRAITS AND MEN OF POWER: THE EIGHTEENTH CENTURY

By the 1750s Britain's first empire had been created. Colonies in North America, the West Indies, India and Africa and the emerging slave trade were vital to English trade. Forty per cent of English products were sold to the colonies. Imports from colonies to England included tea, coffee, sugar, tobacco, rice and timber. African people were taken as slaves to the West Indies where they were exchanged for sugar, which was then taken to England. These changes made England the richest country in Europe and the world's largest empire.

This growth in England's power also meant that the way money was made had changed dramatically by the early eighteenth century. Great wealth no longer came only from land, but also from commerce and from holding office in the civil service, including the army. Up to the 1700s, monarchs had been able to govern by using just a small group of noblemen. But as the business of government became more complicated, a civil service was needed to carry out the increasing workload of government. It was at this time that the Post Office, the Navy Office and Customs and Excise were set up. From this time onwards, it was easier for men to make their fortunes themselves. They didn't have to inherit wealth.

LAWRENCE DUNDAS: THE NEW RICH

Lawrence Dundas was one of the 'new rich'. He made his fortune as a merchant and as a senior army officer during the Seven Years' War (1756–63). He was made a baronet and had four large houses.

Family life had also changed since 1500 and even since 1650. Family life was now seen as something to be enjoyed. Fathers like Dundas were less strict and more relaxed. Compare the family portrait in Source 5 to the Capel family on page 19 and think about how they could both be used to show changes in family life.

As England became the most powerful empire in the world, pride in English culture increased. Furniture makers like Chippendale, pottery makers like Wedgwood and architects like Robert Adam gained international reputations. Notice how these changes are reflected in the portrait of Dundas and his daughter.

SOURCE 5

A portrait of Sir Lawrence Dundas and his daughter.

Question Time

1. Look carefully at the portrait in Source 5. What evidence is there that Dundas was a very wealthy man?
2. Why do you think Dundas wanted to have this portrait painted?
3. How is his portrait different from that of Mr and Mrs Andrews on page 21? Can you suggest a reason for the difference?
4. What sorts of activity might have happened in this room? Use information from the portrait to support your ideas.
5. The furniture in the portrait is Chippendale and the house was built by Robert Adam. What does this tell you about:
   a English arts and crafts
   b Lawrence Dundas' attitude towards English arts and crafts?

WHAT DON'T PORTRAITS TELL US?

Look back over all the portraits in this chapter. What sort of people have you not been able to use portraits to find out about? Make a list of areas of life from 1500 to 1750 that cannot be found out about by using these portraits. What types of evidence would you use to find out about these areas?

The print in Source 6 does show poor people in the eighteenth century. The artist, William Hogarth (1697-1764), produced many prints showing the lives of poor people. Hogarth, like many other upper-class people, was terrified of the lower classes and the risks of crime. His prints tried to draw attention to the problems of poor people, especially in the cities. The prints carried strong moral messages. They were cheap to buy and could be found in the homes of the less well off as well as the wealthy.

Question Time

1. Look carefully at the Hogarth print *Gin Lane*. Choose three scenes from the print and describe each scene. What messages about good and evil are these scenes sending?
2. What sort of feelings and emotions did Hogarth want viewers of this print to have?
3. Cities, especially London, ports and industrial towns in the north, were growing rapidly at this time. What impression of city life does this print give?
4. Why did Hogarth call the print *Gin Lane*?
5. There was no police force in the eighteenth century. Does this help to explain why Hogarth produced this print?
6. The messages sent by *Gin Lane* are very clear and simple. How reliable do you think this image is about the lives of the urban poor in the eighteenth century?

SOURCE 6

Gin Lane by William Hogarth, printed in 1751.

WHAT DON'T PORTRAITS TELL US? A HISTORY MYSTERY!

The portrait in Source 7 is shown at its actual size. It was painted by the man on the left, Gerlach Flicke. Flicke was from Germany. The inscription above his head says: 'Such was the face of Gerlach Flicke when he was a painter in the city of London. This he himself painted from a looking glass for his dear friends. That they might have something to remember him after his death.'

The man on the right is Henry Strangwish. The portrait was painted while the two men were prisoners in the Tower of London. Strangwish was a gentleman pirate eventually forgiven and released by order of Elizabeth I. We do not know why Flicke was in prison. There are some questions about the past that cannot be answered!

SOURCE 7

Gerlach Flicke (left) and Henry Strangwish (below), painted in 1554.

Question Time

1. Look carefully at top the portrait in Source 7. What clue in the portrait suggests that Flicke was an artist?
2. Why was the portrait painted?
3. Why do you think it is so small?
4. What can we learn about Strangwish from his portrait?

IMAGES OF AN AGE: PORTRAITS, MUSEUMS AND AUDIENCES

In 1856 the National Portrait Gallery was set up to collect images of British men and women who have created British history and culture. The gallery cannot show all its portraits at once, but must always select from its huge collection. In addition, curators at the gallery have to write captions for portraits in their catalogues.

You have been commissioned by the National Portrait Gallery to design a travelling exhibition for secondary schools. The exhibition is called 'Important and Powerful People in England 1500-1750'.

Out of all the portraits in this chapter, you must select no more than six pictures for your exhibition. You must also write a caption for each portrait.

First you need to summarise all the portraits. Use a table like the one below and fill it in for each portrait. One row has been completed for you.

TITLE	DATE	PURPOSE	NUMBER OF SITTERS	NAME OF SITTER	IMPORTANT POINTS
Rainbow	1600	Propaganda for Elizabeth	1	Elizabeth I	Looks young, succession worries, Virgin Queen

Use the table to help select your six portraits and to write your captions. Each caption should be no longer than four sentences. It should, as far as possible, give names of artist, sitter(s) and the date it was painted. It should also point out why the portrait is important and/or interesting. You will need to decide what information to leave out as well as what to leave in! Remember that your audience is made up of secondary school pupils like yourself. Your choice of portraits is to help the audience learn about powerful people.

Activity Time

A

Now you need to make different choices for different exhibitions.

Below is a list of exhibition titles. Choose three and select portraits for each one. This time you have much less space and can only use four portraits for each exhibition.

1. England as a European and World Power
2. Change between the Sixteenth and Eighteenth Centuries
3. Continuity between the Sixteenth and Eighteenth Centuries
4. Ethnic Minorities in England
5. Position of Women and Men in Society
6. History of Family Life
7. Propaganda and Power

Think about how your selections and captions change according to the exhibition title.

Give some examples of how you used your knowledge of the period to choose particular portraits.

Unit 8: The Civil Wars – was England 'turned upside down' in the seventeenth century?

In Britain in the mid-seventeenth century there was a major struggle over power and control of government. Important questions were asked, such as:

- Who should have power?
- How much should they have?
- Should the king share power with Parliament, and if so, how?

Many different answers were suggested. Different groups had different ideas about power and who should have it. This led to power struggles, and as in most struggles, there were winners and losers and some of the winners used very dirty tactics indeed. In the end, the losers became 'winners' and the winners became 'losers'!

THE WORLD TURNED UPSIDE DOWN?

The picture in Source 1 shows the 'world being turned upside down' and was on the front page of a pamphlet printed in about 1647. It was all about the very shocking and dramatic events of the past few years. The world had become a very strange and frightening place for most English people.

For the first and only time in English history, the king and Parliament were at war with each other. They were fighting for control of the country. It was called a 'civil war' because English people were fighting other English people. In fact, there were two civil wars. They stopped fighting in 1646 and then they started again in 1648.

SOURCE 1

The World Turned Upside Down, the front cover of a pamphlet published in about 1647.

THE

World turn'd upſide down:

OR,

A briefe deſcription of the ridiculous Faſhions of theſe diſtracted Times.

By T.J. a well-willer to King, Parliament and Kingdom.

London: Printed for John Smith. 1647.

Question Time

1. Look carefully at the picture. Find:
   a the mouse chasing the cat
   b the rabbit chasing the dog.
2. What other things have 'turned upside down'?

FAMILIES AT WAR

In the month of May 1642, Mrs Eure wrote in a letter to her friend Ralph Verney:

> 'We are so many frightened people; for my part if I hear but a door creak I take it to be a drum, and almost have no courage left at all...'

Mrs Eure was frightened of the noise of a drum because that would mean soldiers were coming. Soldiers could mean that a battle would be fought nearby. Sometimes the soldiers looted private homes, stealing food and clothing. Some communities were torn apart by being involved in the war.

There were other reasons to be frightened and shocked. Many people did not want to 'take sides' with king or Parliament! They did not want to fight at all, but were forced to support someone.

Sir Edmund Verney, father of the Ralph that Mrs Eure was writing to, was one of those people who did not want to take sides. When the war started, he wrote in a letter to a friend:

> 'I do not like the quarrel and do heartily wish that the king would agree to what Parliament wants. But I have served the king nearly thirty years, and will not do so bad a thing as to abandon him. I would rather lose my life, which I am sure I will do.'

Sir Edmund was in a dilemma. What he wanted most was for the king to 'give in' to Parliament, but it didn't seem as if this was going to happen. It was his loyalty to the king, his old employer, that decided him. Edmund became a 'Royalist' fighting on the side of the king, Charles I.

Edmund had ten children. Not all of them took the same side as him. Mun Verney, one of Edmund's sons, wrote to Ralph, his brother:

> 'Brother, what I was frightened of is true - you are against the king. It hurts me to think that father and I are now your enemy. I am so troubled to think of you being on their side that I can write no more, only pray for peace.'

Ralph had chosen to fight on the side of Parliament. Like all civil wars, people were forced to take sides against each other – even if this set neighbour against neighbour, father against son, sister against brother.

THE ENGLISH CIVIL WARS

THE FIGHTING BEGINS

The first major battle was at Edgehill. Prince Rupert, nephew of Charles I, commanded the cavalry. He was a brave and brilliant soldier. Rupert had trained the cavalry to charge very fast at the enemy. This could be very effective, but at Edgehill, the cavalry went out of control. They galloped off the battlefield and into a village nearby which they looted. Neither the Royalists nor the Parliamentarians were able to win this battle. It was a draw. Despite the fact that neither side won a victory, there were many deaths. It was here that Edmund Verney, who had agonised to his friend about the coming conflict, was killed.

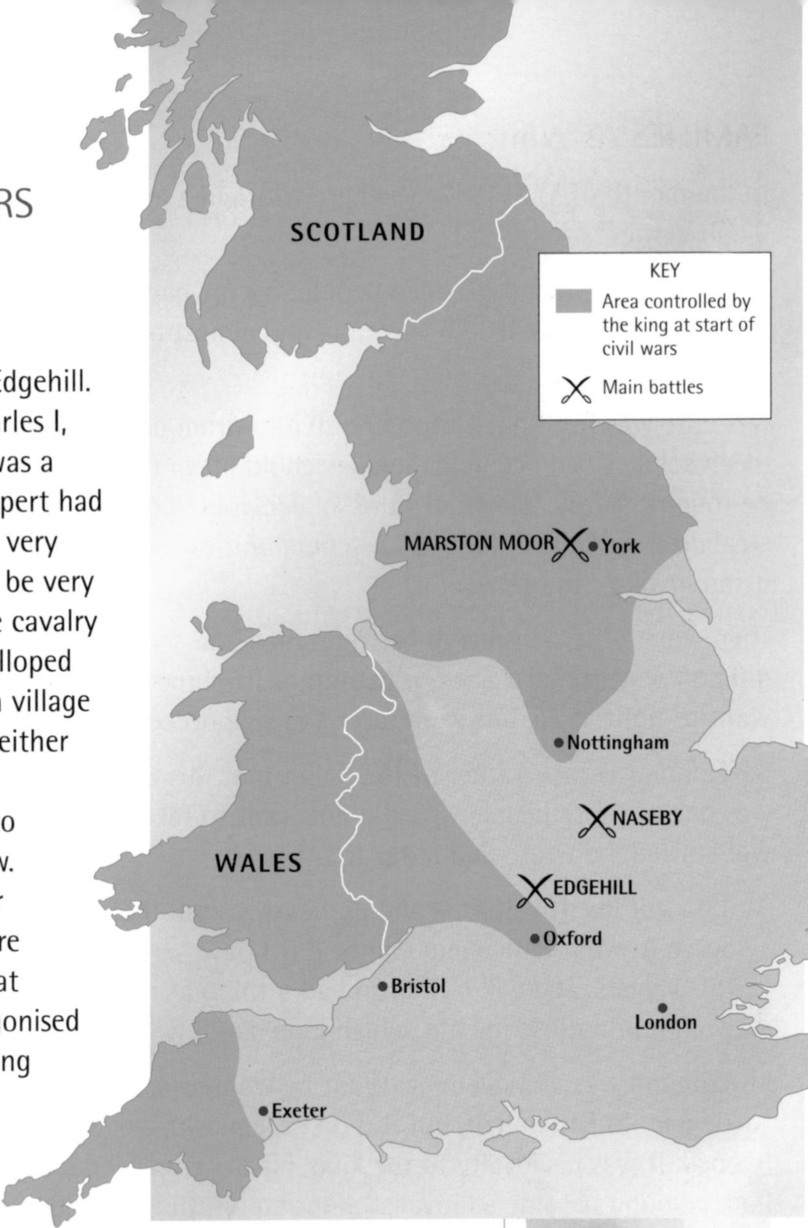

SCOTLAND
KEY
Area controlled by the king at start of civil wars
Main battles
MARSTON MOOR
York
Nottingham
NASEBY
WALES
EDGEHILL
Oxford
Bristol
London
Exeter

England and Wales in the civil wars.

THE BATTLES CONTINUE

When the war started, Parliament had control of London. This was an important advantage for the Parliamentarians. As the capital of England, London was the wealthiest and most powerful city. It was a good place from which to organise the war effort.

After Edgehill, Charles I marched towards London, but he was stopped from reaching it by an army supporting Parliament. Instead he marched on Bristol and was able to capture it. Bristol was also a good spot to control. As it was a port, Charles I could use it to land much-needed supplies for his army. Supplying his army had become very difficult for him, since Parliament had control of the navy as well as London. The navy sank Royalist ships and protected ships carrying supplies for Parliament.

Then Parliament gained another advantage. The Scots decided to join in the war on their side. They sent an experienced and well-trained army to attack King Charles I.

The Royalist army marched north to meet them and a bloody battle was fought at Marston Moor. This time Rupert's cavalry were badly beaten and he had to flee from the battlefield and hide from Parliament's army. The loss at Marston Moor meant that Parliament now controlled the whole of the north of England, as well as London and the surrounding counties. But King Charles I was not going to give up. He controlled Oxford, an important city, and from Oxford he controlled the southwest of England and Wales. Many of his supporters were the richest landowners in England. Most were in the Church of England, but a few were Catholics.

THE BIRTH OF THE NEW MODEL ARMY

While these battles had been going on, an MP called Oliver Cromwell was busy training a new army to fight on Parliament's side. Like many Parliamentarians, Cromwell was a Puritan and a small landowner. Other Puritans tended to be merchants and tradesmen. They were on Parliament's side, too. Cromwell had been a Member of Parliament and became very angry about the refusal of Charles I to give in to Parliament.

Although Cromwell was not a soldier, he turned out to have a great talent for warfare. His army was different from those that had come before and was called the New Model Army. He picked only men who were really committed to Parliament's cause. They were also religious men, believing that they were doing God's will. Cromwell said, 'If you choose a group of honest, Godly men to be captains, honest men will follow them'. Cromwell took great care of his soldiers and paid them well for their commitment. He was very strict about behaviour and would punish soldiers who got drunk or swore. He trained them rigorously. Unlike Rupert's cavalry, the New Model Army charged at a trot - much slower than a gallop – but this meant they were never out of control.

The New Model Army won a great victory over the Royalists at Naseby and were able to go on and capture Oxford from the king. Charles was desperate now! He gave himself up to the Scots, hoping that he could persuade them to change sides. Instead they handed him over to Parliament and received a cash reward for doing so. The first Civil War was over.

But Charles was determined not to give up. In secret, he arranged for another army from Scotland to march into England on his side. When the army came south, the second Civil War started. Cromwell was furious! He demanded that Charles I be put on trial. For the first and only time in English history, a king was tried by MPs on the charge of treason.

The Civil Wars 1642–9.

- **1642** — 1st CIVIL WAR STARTS
  - Battle of Edgehill.
  - Sir Edmund is killed.
- **1643** — Royalist army fails to reach London.
  - Royalist army captures Bristol.
  - Cromwell trains his New Model Army. (NMA)
  - Parliament loses two of its best leaders: Hampden and Pym.
- **1644** — Scots join in.
  - Battle of Marston Moor
- **1645** — NMA fight on Parliament's side.
  - Battle of Naseby.
- **1646** — Parliament captures Oxford from King.
  - King hands himself over to the Scots. Scots hand him over to Parliament.
- **1648** — 2nd CIVIL WAR STARTS
  - Cromwell defeats Charles.
- **1649** — Charles arrested and put on trial.

Question Time

1. What is the meaning of 'civil war'? How is a 'civil war' different from other wars?
2. In the account given, there are no dates. The civil wars lasted nearly seven years. Look at the timeline on the side of this page. It gives you the dates of the main events. Civil wars often last longer than wars between different countries. Why do you think this might be the case? Can you think of other reasons why this war lasted nearly seven years?
3. Find out the names of countries and areas where civil wars are being fought today or have ended recently. Approximately how long have these wars lasted?
4. As you have found out, Edmund Verney was killed at Edgehill. One of his sons, Mun, was killed at the end of the war. Another son, Ralph, had to flee abroad. Sir Edmund's daughters were also hurt by the war. Two of them lost husbands and the other five found it difficult to find suitable husbands. Explain how a civil war could affect a family.
5. Make a sketch of the map on page 34. Using the account of the wars on pages 34–5 and the timeline on this page, illustrate your map. Show:
   a land controlled by both sides
   b dates of the battles
   c the outcome of the two most significant battles.
6. Draw two columns. Write the heading 'King's Side' at the top of one column and 'Parliament's Side' at the top of the other. Use the account of the Civil Wars on pages 34–5 to work out who was on which side.

Activity Time

Think about why Parliament won the Civil Wars.

Using the account of the Civil Wars and your map:
Write a letter which Verney's eldest daughter might have written to her brother Ralph. He has gone into hiding abroad. Tell him about Parliament's victory and explain the reasons why Parliament won.

Plan your letter by making a list of the reasons first. For example, here is one reason:

- The New Model Army was more disciplined than the Royalist army. They were always under Cromwell's control – not like Rupert's cavalry!

Now think about the advantages the Royalists had. Make a list of reasons why it took Parliament so long to overcome these advantages.

IN WHAT WAYS WAS 1649 A YEAR OF GREAT VIOLENCE?

At the end of the Civil Wars, there were winners and losers. These winners and losers had very different ideas about how power should be shared. As you read the three stories below, try to work out who were the winners and who were the losers in 1649, and how the winners treated the losers.

Question Time

1. Find out what 'Republic' means.
2. Find out what 'Commonwealth' means.
3. What do you think foreign rulers might have felt when they heard about the execution?

THREE BLOODY STORIES FROM 1649

Execution of the king, January 1649

In January 1649, having been found guilty of treason, King Charles was beheaded by a Parliament that had been purged of all MPs who might support the king. It was called the 'Rump'. Right up to the very end, Charles refused to 'give in' to Parliament. Just before the axe fell and severed his head from his body, Charles said, 'All the world knows that I never did begin a war with Parliament ... I believe it is evil men who have been the cause of all this bloodshed ... I die a Christian of the Church of England ...' His last word was 'Remember...' . Many people came to watch the execution. Some fainted with shock. Some had come from the continent to report back the events in England to their rulers. As a result of this bloody event, England was a republic for the only time in its history!

Burford, May 1649

Many of the soldiers in Cromwell's New Model Army were Levellers. Levellers had very different ideas from Cromwell about how power should be shared out. Levellers thought all men were equal and should share power. Cromwell did not agree! These ideas were too extreme for him.

There were other tensions. Like all of the New Model Army, the Leveller soldiers were owed pay. In May 1649 some of them mutinied. Cromwell was falling out with his own men! On the instructions of the Rump, Cromwell chased the Levellers across two counties to Burford, Oxfordshire. At Burford Cromwell captured about 300 Levellers in a night attack. He locked them up in a church and forced them to watch as their leaders were shot dead by firing squad.

SOURCE 1

Women and children drowning at Wexford.

Drogheda and Wexford

Even though the king was dead, Parliament did not feel safe. There was always a chance that the Royalists would fight back. They were still rich and powerful landowners. Many of them wanted to bring over one of Charles I's sons from France and make him king. Parliament was worried that the Royalists might use Ireland as a base. Most Irish people were Catholic and opposed Parliament. Ireland was also a good strategic place from which to attack England. There were other problems to do with Ireland. In 1641 many Irish Catholics had rebelled against English policies in Ireland. They wanted Home Rule and they wanted to protect the Catholic religion.

In 1649 Cromwell went to Ireland to crush the Catholics. He destroyed the Drogheda garrison and massacred 3500 people. His treatment of the defeated Irish was very severe and part of a policy of terror. He hoped that it would put off any more Irish rebellions. All the Irish soldiers were killed or transported to Barbados. He treated Irish Catholics at Wexford in the same way. At Wexford, women and children also died. Source 1 shows Irish women and children drowning at Wexford. Some people think Cromwell deliberately drowned them and others think they drowned trying to escape from his troops.

Question Time

1. What impression of Cromwell do you get from the three bloody stories?
2. Write the title 'Winners and Losers in 1649'. Use the three bloody stories to decide:
   - **a** who were the 'winners' in 1649?
   - **b** who were the 'losers' in 1649?

WHY DID THE CIVIL WARS HAPPEN?

On page 39 is information about England before 1625 when Charles I became king. In the sixteenth century there were some very important changes that affected all of society. We need to go back to the sixteenth century in order to understand why Charles I and Parliament had problems with each other.

RELIGIOUS CHANGES

Religion is about faith and belief. It is also about power and money! Henry VIII wanted to be more powerful in England than the Pope, and this was one of the reasons why he changed the religion of England. Eventually, England became a Protestant country. But Ireland and France stayed Catholic. English people started to fear and hate Catholics. By 1625, Catholics were seen as foreigners and possible invaders of England.

There were problems between Protestant groups as well as between Catholics and Protestants! There were different kinds of Protestants. Some called themselves 'Puritans'. They wanted religion to be as simple and as close to the Bible as possible. They hated statues, candles, music and stained glass windows in churches. They also hated the power of the bishops and priests, many of whom were corrupt. Many Puritans were small landowners and merchants. By 1625 there were many Puritans in Parliament. They were becoming very powerful.

SOCIAL AND ECONOMIC CHANGES

Social changes affect people, their attitude, beliefs and ways of life, whereas economic changes are to do with money, who has it and how they make it. Since the Middle Ages there had been important changes in how the people of England lived. There were more 'middle-class' people who made money by buying and selling things. They wanted more of a say in how the country was run. Many of them were also Puritans and had become members of Parliament (MPs).

WHAT HAPPENED DURING THE REIGN OF JAMES I?

James I believed that kings got their power from God. He called this 'Divine Right'. Therefore kings must be obeyed! Parliament didn't agree with him. In 1610, he asked Parliament for more money and was offended when Parliament would not provide it. James I always wanted more money from Parliament. He spent large sums of money on himself and on his friends. He also had a reputation for being lazy and drinking too much. This was to create difficulties for his son, Charles.

Question Time

Below is a list of good advice for Charles I when he becomes king in 1625.

- Don't spend too much money on yourself or your friends.
- Don't have anything to do with Catholics.
- Work really hard.
- Be nice to the Puritans - they are powerful and rich.
- Give up this idea that kings are like gods – it upsets Parliament.
- Listen to Parliament - you need them to get money.
- Don't drink alcohol.

1. Choose the four most important pieces of advice.
2. Explain why the four you chose are the most important.

SO WHAT *DID* CHARLES I DO?

In the boxes below are pieces of information about Charles' reign. Read them carefully. As you read, think about these questions:

- Could this really upset some people? How?
- Could this be a cause of the Civil Wars?

1625–49

Like James I, Charles I believes that kings get their power from God and must be obeyed.

1625–49

Charles I is married to Henrietta Maria. She is Catholic. There are rumours that Catholics will take over.

1629–40

Charles I spends large sums of money on himself. He likes paintings and expensive clothes.

1635

Charles needs a lot of money. He makes people pay a special tax called 'Ship money'. Those who refuse are put in prison.

1633

Charles I makes William Laud the Archbishop of Canterbury. Laud does not like Puritans.

1633–40

Laud changes Church of England services. He introduces the statues, music and candles that Puritans hate.

1639

The Scots attack England because they do not like the religious changes. Charles has no army or money to fight.

1640

Charles I has to call Parliament to ask for money to fight Scots.

1640-50

The Long Parliament sits. The MPs are very angry with Charles for ruling without them for eleven years.

1640

Strafford is executed by order of the Long Parliament and Laud is put in prison.

1641

Catholic Irish rebel and kill many Protestants in revenge for loss of land in the sixteenth century.

1641

Charles needs army to put down Irish rebellion.

1641

Pym tries to pass a law giving control of army to Parliament, not the king.

1642 January

Charles tries to arrest Pym and four other MPs. He marches on Parliament with soldiers. This is not allowed!

1642 January

Charles fails to arrest the MPs and is forced to run away from London.

1629–40

Charles I rules without Parliament. But he needs money.

1637

Laud's changes are forced on the Scottish church. Many Scots are Puritans.

1630s

Earl of Strafford rules Ireland for Charles. He is very unpopular with the Irish and with the Long Parliament.

1641

John Pym, MP fears that Charles will use the army against Parliament.

Activity Time

A

Each piece of information in the boxes on pages 40–1 could be a cause of the Civil Wars.

Historians organise causes into different categories to help them make sense of the past. They try to see patterns and links. This can help them to understand other power struggles and civil wars, even ones being fought today.

1. Take four blank cards and using the information on page 39 write four causes from before 1625.
2. Sort *all* the causes into categories. There are many different ways that you can do this! Compare your categories with others.
3. Make a list of all the different ways that the causes can be sorted.
4. Do you think that some of the categories are 'better' than others for explaining the Civil Wars? Which category do you think is most important?

IN WHAT WAYS DO HISTORIANS DISAGREE ABOUT THE CAUSES OF THE CIVIL WARS?

Historians use different categories. These are some of them:

- Long term – happened a long time before 1642
- Short term – happened just before 1642
- Economic – to do with money and how it is made
- Political – to do with power, who has it and how they use it
- Religious – to do with faith and worship
- Social – to do with people, their attitudes, beliefs and ways of life
- Conflicts between Parliament and royalty
- Conflicts between England, Scotland and Ireland
- Charles' personality and behaviour.

How many of the different categories do you think can be used to explain the causes of the Civil Wars?

DIFFERENT OPINIONS

At the time of the Civil Wars, some Englishmen wrote about why they had happened. They did not all agree with each other!

The Earl of Clarendon (Lord Chancellor for Charles II, who came to the throne in 1660) blamed the conflict on mistakes made by Charles I after 1625; James Harrington, a philosopher, blamed it on changes that went right back to the reign of Henry VIII. Sir William Dugdale, a Royalist, blamed the war on Puritan plotting and scheming. Benjamin Rudyerd, a Parliamentarian, blamed the war on the king's failure to call Parliament regularly.

Even today historians have different views on the reasons for the Civil Wars. Below are two different interpretations of the Civil Wars. Read them carefully.

Historian's Interpretation 1

The Civil Wars happened because of a relentless struggle between Parliament and the king. Parliament was the defender of the people. It protected their freedom. It protected the people against the king. The king was the enemy of Parliament. He did not listen to them. The king tried to take away the freedom of the people and so he had to be stopped. Charles I was not the only king to ignore Parliament. Many kings before him had behaved in this way, too. That is why the Civil Wars happened. They were an important step towards the democracy we have today.

Historian's Interpretation 2

The Civil Wars happened because of changes that had been going on for a very long time. The most important change was not between Parliament and the king, but in the people. A new group of people came into being. They made their money by buying and selling things. They were mostly merchants and lived in the towns and cities. They were rich, confident and cultured.

Question Time

1. Who blamed the war on *short-term* causes: Clarendon *or* Harrington?
2. Who blamed the war on *long-term* causes: Clarendon *or* Harrington?
3. Why might Dugdale blame the war on Puritans?
4. Why might Rudyerd blame the war on mistakes made by the king?
5. When we read what Dugdale and Rudyerd wrote, we learn about them as well as about the Civil Wars. Think about what we can learn about Dugdale from what he said about the causes of the war:
   a Which 'side' was he on?
   b Whom did he dislike?
6. What do we learn about Rudyerd from what he said:
   a Which 'side' was he on?
   b Whom did he dislike?

They knew they were important. They wanted to have a say in how the country was run. They were not prepared to accept that kings had 'Divine Right'. The Civil Wars were therefore a class struggle between the 'new middle class' and the traditional landowning rulers.

POLITICAL THEORIES

Marxists believe that money and how money is made is always one of the most important reasons for change. They say that history is about struggles between those who have money and power and those who want it. When a new group gets money, they want other things, too. They want power. They want to have a say in how the country is run.

Whigs believe that English history is all about the development of democracy. This is also about people becoming more free, free to move around, free to speak their mind, free to own property, free to make money. Kings and queens have tried to stop people being free. Parliament has tried to help them be free. So history is about a struggle between royalty and Parliament. These struggles lead to changes which make life better than it was before.

WHAT DO HISTORIANS THINK TODAY?

Today there are still different interpretations of why the Civil Wars happened.

Historians such as Conrad Russell and Derek Hirst think that they happened because Charles I made lots of mistakes. He was stubborn. He would not change the way he did things. Before 1625 there was no reason for trouble, and England was peaceful and rich. The worst mistakes were made after 1640. These mistakes 'triggered' the war.

Question Time

1. One of the interpretations on page 42 is by a historian who is a Marxist and the other is by a historian who is a Whig.
   a Which group wrote Interpretation 1: Marxists *or* Whigs?
   b Which group wrote Interpretation 2: Marxists *or* Whigs? Explain your answer.
2. Look back at the cause boxes on pages 40–1. What event after 1640 might have been the 'trigger' for the Civil Wars?
3. Why did you choose that event?
4. Which explanation by a historian is most similar to your explanation of why the Civil Wars happened?
5. At this very moment, historians are writing new interpretations of why the Civil Wars happened. Why do you think the Civil Wars are so important to historians today? Compare your ideas with the others in your class.

WHAT DO SUCCESSFUL MONARCHS DO?

Look at pages 40–1 to find out what Charles I did.

As we have found out, some historians today say the Civil Wars happened because of mistakes made by Charles I. Use all you have learned so far to make a list of mistakes made by Charles I.

For example:
- Charles spent large amounts of money on himself.
- Charles had a Catholic wife, even though most English people hated and feared Catholics.

Activity Time

Do's and Don'ts for ruling countries!

It is 1649. The King of Sweden is worried about what has happened in England. He doesn't want to lose his head as well! How might an adviser have prepared a list of 'Do's and Don'ts' for him?

Start by turning all the mistakes into do's and don'ts.
For example:
- Don't spend a lot of money on yourself.
- Choose your wife very carefully!
- Be tactful: if you must spend money, do it quietly!

WHY DID THE 'WINNERS' OF THE CIVIL WARS ARGUE AMONGST THEMSELVES?

In January 1649 the king was dead and the Commonwealth was born, but in some ways the problems were just beginning...

The most important problem in 1649 was knowing how Britain should be ruled. Many different groups of people thought they had the answer. But they all had different ideas about power and how it should be shared. Some thought all men should have a share. Some thought only rich men should have a share. These ideas were bound to clash!

WHAT WAS THE CLASH OF IDEAS?

Look at the cartoon and read the information.

Each description matches one of the people in the cartoon. Work out which match using the information on page 45.

Republicans

This group was led by Oliver Cromwell. Before the Civil Wars, Cromwell had believed that the king should share power with Parliament. If the king wouldn't share, he had to go! By 1649 Cromwell and the Republicans believed that Parliament should rule. But they did not believe that all people were fit to rule in Parliament. They said only religious men who had some property should rule. They did not think everyone was equal. Most Republicans were small landowners and merchants. Many of them were also Puritans.

Levellers

The Levellers believed that all men were equal. They wanted all men to have the vote, even poor men. Their leader, John Lilburne, said, 'No man is marked by God as more important than another. Therefore the poorest has a right to vote as the richest and the greatest.' This would mean that Parliament would truly represent the views and interests of all men. The Levellers also wanted the justice system to be fair. This included the right of everyone to trial by jury. Cromwell was frightened by the ideas of the Levellers. Although he wanted a change from royal rule, the Levellers were going too far for him.

Diggers

The Diggers wanted all men in society to be equal. They believed this could happen only if everybody owned the land together. That is, all land would become common land, shared by everyone. They made a start by squatting on common land, but they were chased off by mercenaries hired by large landowners.

The clash of ideas, 1649.

Royalists

The royalists were horrified at living in a Commonwealth. They wanted to have a king or queen again. They did not want life to change.

Question Time

1. The Levellers' ideas were very radical at the time, but they were excluding (keeping out) a large section of the population. Which group did the Levellers not think about giving the vote to?
2. Why do you think the Diggers were given that name?
3. Read the information about Republicans again. Why would they not support the Diggers?
4. Make a copy of the diagram below.

Very radical		Moderate		Very conservative
Wanted major changes		Wanted a few changes		Wanted no changes

Insert the following groups on the Radical/Moderate/Conservative scale:
Levellers Diggers Royalists Republicans

5. Find out the meanings of 'democracy' and 'democratic'.
   a Which side of the diagram is most 'democratic'?
   b Which side of the diagram is less 'democratic'?
   Give reasons for your choices.

BRITAIN AS THE COMMONWEALTH 1649–53

After the Burford church incident (see pages 37–8), the Levellers were no longer a serious threat to Cromwell. Their leader, John Lilburne, was charged with treason and imprisoned. He died in prison. The Diggers also stopped being a threat after being cleared from common land on which they had squatted.

So, the main question was still how Britain should be ruled. It was a very difficult question. Britain had never been a republic before. Only two countries in Europe were republics at this time and they were much smaller. How should Britain, the republic, be governed?

Two groups thought they might have the right answer:

- Parliament
- the conservative army generals (including Cromwell).

From 1649 to 1653 these groups were involved in a power struggle.

PARLIAMENT AND THE ARMY GENERALS: A POWER STRUGGLE 1649–53

The Rump Parliament

Most MPs were frightened by how things were turning out. They had not expected to live in a republic. It was too radical for most of them. They were worried that ideas about equality might spread. They could lose their land and wealth. Some wanted to ask Charles I's son to be king, but others accepted the Commonwealth. They thought there should be elections to elect a new Parliament now the king was dead.

MPs were also very divided about religion. They quarrelled amongst themselves about important religious questions. For example, should baptism happen to children or adults? Cromwell became increasingly annoyed with their quarrels.

Army generals

The army generals had risked their lives fighting against the king. They had seen soldiers die for greater freedom and democracy. They had many different feelings in 1649 - anger at the past seven years, pride in winning the struggle, sorrow at the loss of life.

Unlike the MPs, army generals were not used to power. They were not used to ruling England in Parliament. But they did have the power of the sword. They had weapons and knew how to fight. They would not agree to new elections.

Question Time

1. Who do you think won the power struggle of 1649–53? Give reasons for your choice.
2. a What disadvantage did the army generals have when it came to power?
   b What advantage did the army generals have when it came to power?

WHO WON THE POWER STRUGGLE OF 1649–53?

By 1653 Cromwell was very fed up with all the quarrels in Parliament. He wanted to get on with the business of ruling. He used his soldiers to close down Parliament saying, 'You have sat here too long for the good you do. In the name of God, go!' He took on the title of Protector and ruled until his death in 1658. The army generals had won!

BRITAIN AS THE PROTECTORATE 1653–8

For the next five years, Cromwell was in charge. Although he did call some Parliaments, none of them pleased him, so he kept power to himself. But he could not do everything. The local areas needed ruling. Cromwell could not ask the rich Royalist landowners to rule them.

WHO HELPED HIM?

Cromwell used relatives, including his two sons, and old friends from the army to help him rule. In 1655 he divided the country into eleven districts. Each district was ruled by a Major General from the army. They invited Cromwell to be king, but he refused. He carried on being Protector and was paid a huge amount of money for doing the job.

WHY DO PEOPLE INTERPRET CROMWELL IN VERY DIFFERENT WAYS?

Historians still argue today about Cromwell, what he did and his motives. His actions do seem contradictory. For example, he hunted down and killed the king for not listening to the people. But he also hunted down and killed the Levellers for wanting democracy and equality between men!

As you read the information below, look for other ways in which Cromwell's behaviour seems contradictory or surprising.

WHAT WAS LIFE LIKE IN THE PROTECTORATE?

Cromwell saw himself as Protector of the Puritans. So people had to live a Puritan lifestyle. No swearing, gambling or drunkenness was allowed. Sport was banned, including football. Anyone caught playing could be whipped. Theatres were closed and Christmas was abolished. Some army officers closed down pubs too.

Although everyone had to live by Puritan ideas, they did not have to become Puritans. People in England and Wales were not persecuted for their religion. Jews were tolerated for the first time since 1290.

Under Cromwell's rule, England was at peace – there were no wars. He made friends with France, which made England a more powerful country within Europe. Other European countries left Cromwell and the Protectorate alone. They did not try to help put Charles I's son back on the throne.

The press was censored. This means that newspapers could only print what Cromwell wanted them to print. Instead of newspapers, the government put out its own 'journals'.

DID LIFE GET BETTER FOR THE POOR UNDER CROMWELL?

Taxes on the rich increased under Cromwell and the money was given to the poor. Historians have done two studies on the treatment of the poor at this time. Both of the studies, of Cheshire and Warwickshire, found that the poor were better treated under Cromwell.

DID LIFE GET BETTER FOR WOMEN UNDER CROMWELL?

You may have noticed that no group, not even the radical Levellers, asked for women to have the vote. Women continued to be excluded from power in other ways. Married women lost all their property to their husbands. Girls were less well educated than boys. Both of these facts made women less powerful than men.

SOURCE 1

A picture of a 'She Soldier' in the Civil Wars.

This does not mean that women were invisible or unimportant at this time. In 1642 women enabled parliamentary troops to enter Bristol and in 1649 thousands of women protested against the treatment of the Levellers. Many women went to war with the men. Elizabeth Alkin looked after wounded soldiers. She became a spy on the side of Parliament and wrote pamphlets supporting Parliament. Some women disguised themselves as men and joined the fighting. They were called 'She Soldiers'.

One She Soldier, called 'Mr Clarke', joined the army on Parliament's side with her husband. She fired muskets, wrestled, drank and smoked with the men. She even gave birth while fighting in the civil war!

Some minority religious groups did make women equal within their church. Among the Quakers, for example, women could become priests. This was a very radical way of looking at the role of women.

SOURCE 2

The statue of Oliver Cromwell outside the House of Commons in London.

THE VERDICT ON CROMWELL

In 1660 the monarch was restored in England (see page 54). This meant that many people came to see Cromwell's rule as an embarrassing mistake. Until the early nineteenth century, historians viewed Cromwell in a critical way as well.

However, during the nineteenth century steps were taken to increase democracy in Britain. More and more men were given the right to vote (though women didn't receive the vote until 1928) and Parliament became more important in helping rule the country. This change in attitude to the role of the monarch also led to a change in attitude towards Oliver Cromwell and historians are now much more sympathetic to him. In Ireland, however, it has proved very difficult for Cromwell's reputation to be restored.

Question Time

1. Historians have debated about whether Cromwell was a protector or a dictator.
   A protector is someone who looks after the people and their freedom.
   A dictator is someone who tells the people what to do. He/she does not let them have any freedom, or severely limits their freedom.
   In pairs, decide who will make the case that 'Cromwell was a protector' and who will make the case that 'Cromwell was a dictator'.
   Prepare your cases by reading all the information about Cromwell in this Unit.
2. Select the information that supports your case.
   Prepare a five-minute speech in favour of your case.
   In your pairs, read your speeches to each other.
   You may want to challenge or ask questions after you have listened to the speech.
3. What is your conclusion: was Cromwell a protector or a dictator?
4. Some historians think that the explanation for the strange contradictions in Cromwell's behaviour lies in his background. He had become a Puritan. Puritans wanted greater democracy and equality. He was also brought up in a landowning gentry family. The gentry believed that only those with property should have political power. Do you think his background helps us to understand his behaviour? Why/why not?
5. Look at the photograph in Source 2. It shows the statue of Cromwell outside the Houses of Parliament. Why do you think there is a statue of Cromwell outside Parliament?
6. How do changes in the roles of Parliament and the monarchy help to explain why people admired Cromwell in the nineteenth century?

IRELAND: A DIFFERENT STORY!

WAS CROMWELL A HARSH DICTATOR IN IRELAND?

Cromwell behaved differently in Ireland from how he behaved in England. In groups, write out all the pieces of evidence on the jigsaw pieces onto separate cards and share them out among the group. Take it in turns to say whether your piece(s) of evidence are:

- very relevant
- quite relevant
- not relevant

to the question 'Was Cromwell a harsh dictator in Ireland?' and why you reached that decision. You may want to argue with each other!

Use all the ideas of your group to write one or two paragraphs answering the question 'Was Cromwell a harsh dictator in Ireland?'

Cromwell has been accused of being a 'war criminal' because of what he did in Ireland. A war criminal is someone who breaks the rules of war. Today war criminals can be taken to court and imprisoned.

The rules of war in the seventeenth century were:

- Do not kill people, even soldiers, except in battle.
- Never kill women and children.
- Take only enough food for your army.

Using the pieces of evidence, say why some historians might think Cromwell was a war criminal.

The land was given to Protestants from England and to soldiers. They drew lots for the land!

Transplanting means their land was taken away and English plantations were set up instead.

Between 1654 and 1655, thousands of Irish Catholics had their land taken away from them.

In England, soldiers were not massacred in this way.

Cromwell ordered all soldiers to be killed at Wexford and Drogheda, including English soldiers fighting on the Irish side.

Question Time

1. Write a letter to a newspaper *either* supporting a trial for Cromwell as a war criminal *or* opposing it.
2. Suggest some reasons why Cromwell behaved differently in Ireland than in England.

Some Irish writers call the years 1641–53 'an cogadh do chriochnaigh Eire' which means 'the war that finished Ireland'.

In 1575 the English naval 'hero', Sir Francis Drake, killed all the men, women and children on Rathlin island.

Cromwell carried on the sixteenth century practice of transplanting Irish Catholics.

In England, Cromwell's soldiers did not burn and destroy crops and houses

After 1658 the proportion of Irish land owned by Irish Catholics fell from 59 per cent to 20 per cent.

In 1988 an Irish Tourist Board video described the destruction of the Drogheda garrison as a 'black day'.

During the campaigns of Cromwell's armies in Ireland, soldiers deliberately destroyed houses and crops in order to starve the Irish people. Historians believe that up to half the population died as a result.

Cromwell closed down Gaelic schools.

Cromwell transported 12,000 Irish to the West Indies.

Women and children drowned either trying to escape from Cromwell's troops at Wexford or were drowned on Cromwell's orders.

WHAT HAPPENED AT THE RESTORATION?

CHARLES II AND THE DECLARATION OF BREDA: READING BETWEEN THE LINES

Cromwell died on 3 September 1658 and his son, Richard, succeeded him as Lord Protector. Richard was not popular with the army officers, who plotted to overthrow him and bring back the Parliament. He tried to organise troops loyal to him to prevent this, but was unsuccessful and was forced to retire as Protector.

Now that the Protectorate was over, Parliament was restored, but it also fell out with the army. The army disbanded it and set up its own Committee of Safety to rule the country. This faced so many problems that eventually the commander of the army in Scotland, General Monck, marched on London and restored the Parliament. It proved to be so unpopular that eventually King Charles I's son was invited to return to England to rule as Charles II. This was known as the Restoration.

SOURCE 1

Charles II returning to London as king in 1660.

Charles II was given a great welcome on his return to England. John Evelyn, an eyewitness of Charles' return and coronation, wrote,

> 'The way was strewn with flowers, the bells ringing, the streets hung with tapestry, the fountains running wine'

Before his return Charles II made some promises in the Declaration of Breda about how England would be ruled.

The Rules in the Declaration of Breda

1. The army will be disbanded.
2. The Church of England will be restored.
3. There will be religious tolerance.
4. Parliament is to control the king's finances.
5. Charles II can decide when to call Parliament.

Question Time

1. Why do you think many people were tired of being ruled by Puritans?
2. Why do you think Charles agreed to the Declaration of Breda?
3. Why do you think Charles II was able to break some of the promises made in the Declaration of Breda?

WAS THE WORLD TURNED UPSIDE DOWN?

You must decide how far the world was turned upside down in the seventeenth century.

Charles also promised to pardon those who had been involved in the Civil War, Commonwealth and Protectorate. This did not include the MPs who had signed his father's death warrant. Those still alive were executed. The body of Oliver Cromwell was dug up and hanged.

Once he was in power, Charles II and this Parliament did not keep all the promises made at Breda. For example, in 1664 it was made an offence to worship outside the Church of England. This made life difficult for Puritans and for Catholics.

Activity Time

1. Design your own poster called 'The World Turned Upside Down'. Put on it the main ideas that people had for change. You should use words and images.
2. **a** Draw a timeline from 1642 to 1660. Put on it all the changes that happened in that period. Think about:
   - in which years were there changes in who ruled the country?
   - in which years were there changes from peace to war and vice versa?
   - in which years were there changes in Ireland?
   - in which years were there changes in religious policy?
   - in which years were there changes in laws about how people should behave?
   - in which years was there a conflict in ideas about power and political rights? Between which groups? Who 'won' and when?

   b Use your timeline to answer these questions:
   - What were the times of greatest change?
   - How different was England in 1660 from how it had been in 1642?

   You may want to use the headings from **a** to organise your ideas.

Unit 9: From the 'Glorious Revolution' to the '45 – how united was the kingdom?

WHY DID THE BIRTH OF THE 'WARMING PAN' BABY CAUSE SO MUCH CONTROVERSY?

Before you read the 'Warming Pan' story, you'll need to know who the people involved were, and what their relationship was to each other.

Look at the family tree carefully. The people we're concentrating on are James II, who began his reign in 1685 when his brother Charles II died; James' two daughters, Mary and Anne; and James' second wife, Mary of Modena.

The Stuart Family Tree.

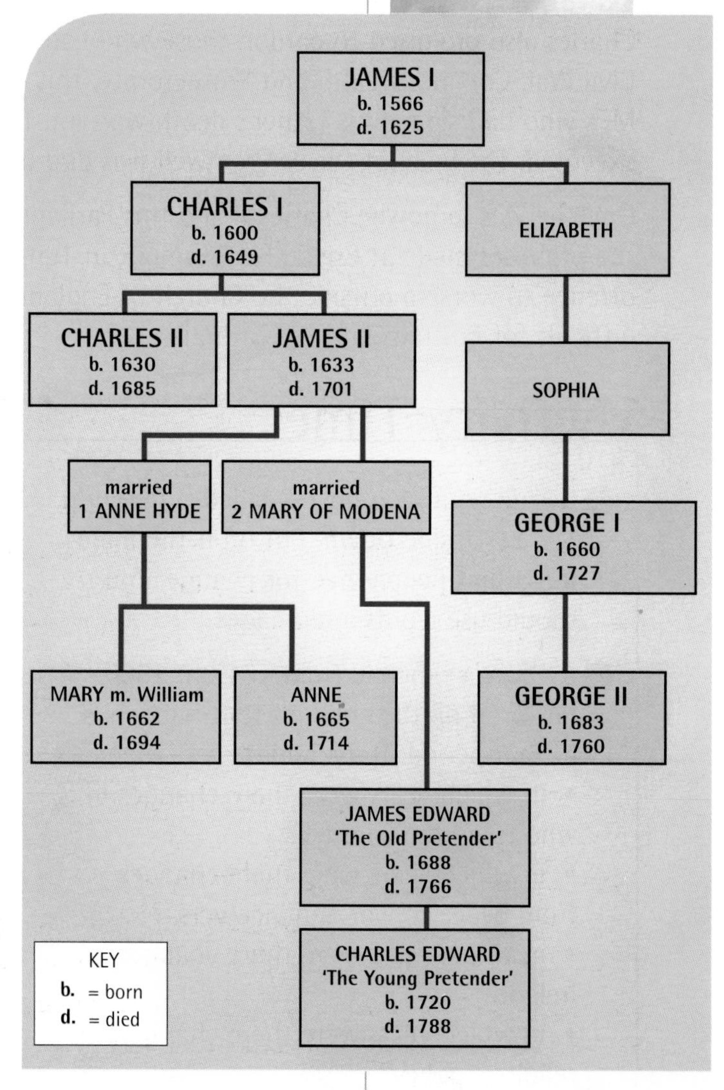

THE 'WARMING PAN' BABY

It is 10 June 1688. In London it is very hot, and the River Thames is stinking. The king, James II, is fifty-five years old. He has two daughters. Mary is twenty-six years old and married to her Dutch cousin, Prince William. She is living in the Netherlands. James' second daughter, Anne, is twenty-three years old. She is married to Prince George of Denmark and they are both living in England. Mary and Anne's mother, James' first wife, died from cancer seventeen years earlier.

But James married again. And now his second wife, Mary of Modena, is in labour and will shortly give birth. Will it be a boy this time, a male heir for whom James longs? Mary has had several miscarriages and five babies who were alive when they were born, but who died soon afterwards. James paces up and down, occasionally glancing at his wife's bed. This time it has to be different!

James doesn't just need a son. He needs a Catholic son. James' first wife was a Protestant and so, supposedly, was James. Their daughters Mary and Anne were brought up as Protestants. But in 1672, James openly became a Catholic and his second wife is a Catholic, too. So any children of theirs will be brought up as Catholics. If this baby turns out to be a boy, he will inherit the throne of England before his half-sisters Mary and Anne. James hopes against hope that this will happen and, when the boy becomes king, he will turn England back to Catholicism. But in June 1688, these are nothing more than daydreams. For the moment, the noises of childbirth and the quiet comings and goings of doctors and courtiers are all that fills James' head.

Suddenly it is all over. A baby splutters, cries and then yells lustily. Seconds later, two physicians and a trusted courtier bow low in front of James. 'Her Majesty is safely delivered of a son.' The baby is taken into another room and James hurries over to his wife, who lies back, pale and tired, on silk pillows. His dream has begun! Soon it will turn into a nightmare.

Well, that is how it may have happened. What is certain is that on 10 June 1688 James' second wife, Mary of Modena, gave birth to a son and nothing was ever the same again.

SOURCE 1

Imagine a troop of Catholics ravishing your wives and daughters, dashing your little children's brains out against the walls, plundering your houses and cutting your throats. Cast your eye towards Smithfield, imagine you see your father or mother tied to the stake in the midst of the flames. With heads and eyes lifted up to heaven they scream and cry out to God, for whose cause they die. This was a frequent spectacle last time the Catholics ruled amongst us.

This is an extract from a pamphlet printed in London in 1679.

SO, WHERE DOES THE WARMING PAN COME IN?

That's just the point. No one knew whether it did or it didn't. Soon after the birth of this baby – called James Edward – rumours started circulating. And these rumours weren't particularly kind. They said that Mary of Modena had not been pregnant and that there was no royal birth. They said that a miller's son (later it was said to be a bricklayer's son) had been smuggled into the palace and secretly put into the royal bed in a warming pan. The royal physicians, who were part of the plot, then proclaimed a royal birth.

It is true that warming pans were often used to warm people's beds. Warming pans were like large, shallow saucepans with long handles. When filled with hot coals, they were pushed into beds to warm them. A warming pan would have been large enough to hold a newborn baby. But no one knows whether or not a warming pan was put into the royal bed and, if it was, no one knows whether it contained hot coals or someone else's baby.

Question Time

Think about the warming pan story and read Source 1 on page 57.

1. How does Source 1 help you to understand why people were frightened of having a Catholic king?
2. Who would probably have started the warming pan story: Catholics or Protestants? Why?
3. How likely is it that the warming pan story was true? Remember to give reasons for your answer.

'WHAT WAS THE 'GLORIOUS REVOLUTION'?

In order to understand what the 'Glorious Revolution' was all about, and why it happened, you have to start with this 'warming pan' baby.

WEREN'T PEOPLE HAPPY AT THE BIRTH OF A PRINCE?

No, not really. The problem was that the child would be brought up as a Catholic and that he would one day be a Catholic king of England. People were afraid that he would try to turn England back into a Catholic country again.

HOW LIKELY WAS IT THAT ENGLAND WOULD BE TURNED BACK TO CATHOLICISM?

James II, the baby's father, had already had a go at relaxing some of the laws and customs that kept Catholics out of public affairs:

- He began appointing Catholics as government ministers and sacking Protestant ministers who opposed him.
- He appointed Catholics as army officers and to positions in local government. This was against the law. The courts complained that the king couldn't do this. He couldn't just ignore the laws he didn't like.
- James sacked judges he didn't trust and stopped all the gentry who were against these changes from becoming Justices of the Peace (JPs).

- In 1685, the Duke of Monmouth led a Protestant rebellion against James II. This was cruelly put down: about 250 men and women were hanged, drawn and quartered, and about 1000 transported to the West Indies and sold as slaves. In England, pamphlets were circulated that said these rebels were martyrs.
- From April 1687 James allowed all Christians to worship as they wished. This, of course, included Catholics.

SOURCE 1

To my grief, I saw the new pulpit set up in the popish Oratory at Whitehall for the Lent preaching. Mass being publicly said, and the Romanists swarming at Court with greater confidence than had ever been seen in England since the Reformation, so that everybody was worried what this might lead to.

This is an extract from John Evelyn's diary, 5 March 1685.

WHO SHALL BE KING?

People were afraid that James II's son would carry on his father's work when he, in his turn, became king. When the Archbishop of Canterbury and six other bishops protested against these changes, James had them arrested and put on trial.

In August 1688, a jury found the Archbishop of Canterbury and his bishops 'not guilty' and they were set free. Londoners went wild with delight and lit bonfires in the streets. James II was shattered. This was the first time an English monarch had lost an important law case. He believed, like his father, that kings could do what they liked and that they were answerable only to God.

Enough was enough. Leading politicians moved quickly. They wrote to the Protestant Prince William of Orange, who was married to James' daughter Mary. They invited him to come to England and restore England's 'true liberties'.

Question Time

1. James II became king in 1685. Look at the things he did to help Catholics in the first three years of his reign. Was he:
   a trying to be fair to all religions by treating them equally?
   b starting to turn England back to being a Catholic country?
   c making stupid mistakes?
2. Read Source 1 above. Was John Evelyn a Catholic or a Protestant? How do you know?
3. Read Source 1 again. Find out what these are: the popish Oratory, Lent, Mass and Romanists.
4. Where and what, in the seventeenth century, was Whitehall? What happened there to James II's father?

THE 'GLORIOUS REVOLUTION'

This was revolution indeed! Powerful people inviting someone to invade their country and make himself king! William didn't take long to make up his mind. He wasn't too bothered about English liberties or even England's Protestant religion. But he was interested in power and in politics. The one thing he didn't want to happen was for Catholic France to ally with a Catholic England. One way of stopping this happening was to prevent England from becoming Catholic. James and his baby son had to go!

William set sail from the Netherlands with an army of around 15,000 Dutch and English soldiers. By 4 November, William was ready to land, but his English supporters suggested he wait for another day. Later, English Protestants were to make much of the fact that England had twice been 'saved' from the Catholics on 5 November. So, on 5 November 1688 William and his troops landed at Brixham, in Devon. Steadily they marched toward London, through the mud and the pouring rain. As they went, local gentry joined them and poor people cheered their 'Protestant saviours'. Men pinned orange colours on their coats and women wore orange petticoats.

WASN'T THERE A GREAT BATTLE?

No – nothing of the kind. When James became king in 1685, he inherited a loyal Royalist army. But he had been busy appointing Catholic officers, and the mainly Protestant troops frequently disobeyed them in small matters. Furthermore, most soldiers approved of the acquittal of the Protestant Archbishop of Canterbury and his six bishops. The loyal army had become

SOURCE 2

This picture shows William and his troops landing in Brixham, Devon in 1688.

rebellious. Too late, James realised he could not trust them to fight for him, their Catholic king, against Prince William, the Protestant invader. Indeed, his best general, John Churchill, deserted and took his men over to William's side.

DID JAMES AND HIS SON-IN-LAW WILLIAM MEET TO SORT THINGS OUT?

No. James ran away. In fact, he ran away twice. This is what happened. On 20 December 1688, James secretly sent his wife and his baby son to France. At three o'clock the next morning, James himself, heavily disguised, crept out of his palace and made for a boat at Sheerness in Kent to go on to France. As luck would have it, some suspicious fishermen boarded the ship as it waited for the tide. They found the king and he was taken back to his palace at Whitehall under military protection.

No one wanted him there. He could do no good by staying and couldn't be seen to leave again in secret in case people thought William had forced him out. William, meanwhile, was waiting patiently at Windsor, about 25 kilometres (15 miles) away, for things to sort themselves out. And they did. There were careful negotiations between the two sides. Then William sent his troops to London. The king ordered the Coldstream Guards, who were guarding his palace at Whitehall, to give way. The Dutch guards took over and so for one night James was guarded by William's soldiers. Then he left openly, sailing down the Thames for Rochester, where he took a boat for France, to join his wife and baby son, James Edward Stuart.

Question Time

1. Look back at the Stuart family tree on page 56. William was invited to become king. But do you think there was anyone with a better claim? Could this cause a problem later on? Remember that it was the eldest son who inherited. If there was no son, then the eldest daughter had the strongest claim, and then her children, with sons coming before daughters.
2. Now look at both William and James in the family tree. Make a list of the claims James had to be king. Make another list of the claims William had to be king. Which man had the better claim? Why did William become king?
3. What did James do wrong? Was there any way in which he could have kept his throne? If you had been advising him, what would you have said?

WHY DID WILLIAM AND MARY BECOME JOINT MONARCHS?

The simple answer is that Parliament asked them. But it was a bit more complicated than that, as Source 3 shows.

WERE WILLIAM AND MARY DIFFERENT FROM JAMES AS MONARCHS?

Yes and no. They were Protestants where James had been a Catholic, and this made a great deal of difference to the readiness with which people and Parliament accepted them. In some ways, things went on much as before. The monarchs appointed their own cabinet, negotiated with foreign governments and saw to the running of the country. But in other ways, things were very different and would never be the same again. William and Mary had been chosen by Parliament; they were not there because of their birth or because they believed God had chosen them. These monarchs were 'constitutional monarchs'. This meant that they had to obey the laws of the country and if they wanted to change them at all, Parliament had to agree. The Bill of Rights (1689) set this out very clearly. It said that Parliament alone had the right to raise taxes, pass laws and control the army. Parliament could debate what it liked without fear of prosecution. And no Catholic could ever become king or queen of England. Nothing would ever be the same again.

SOURCE 3

William did not say anything on the matter for several weeks. Then he called for the Marquis of Halifax, the Earls of Shrewsbury and Danby and some others to explain himself clearly. He said no man could hold a woman in higher regard than he did the Princess Mary. But he was so made that he could not think of holding anything by apron strings; nor did he think it reasonable for him to have a share in government unless he was king and king for life. If they were going to settle things differently, then he would go back to Holland and have nothing more to do with English affairs.

Shortly after these events, G. Burnet wrote six books called *A History of My Time*. This is part of what he wrote about William's attitude to the Crown passing to his wife alone.

Question Time

1. Re-read page 39 to make sure you understand the term 'Divine Right of Kings'. Explain the term in your own words.
2. What was the Bill of Rights? What did this mean for the ways in which monarchs ruled?
3. What made a monarch more secure – to rule by the Divine Right of Kings or to rule by the Bill of Rights?
4. William and Mary became joint monarchs in January 1689. Why didn't the Stuart crown simply pass to James' daughter Mary? (Look again at the family tree on page 56 and at Source 3.)
5. What, or whom, in January 1689, was the greatest threat to their throne?

WHAT IMPACT DID THE GLORIOUS REVOLUTION HAVE ON IRELAND?

This all depends on knowing how the Irish had been treated by James II when he was king.

HOW DID JAMES TREAT THE IRISH CATHOLICS?

Remember that James was a Catholic himself, and under the three years of his rule, Irish Catholics had more freedom than they had had for over a hundred years. James appointed an Irish Catholic, the Earl of Tyrconnel, as Lord Lieutenant of Ireland. Catholics could worship freely, they could become judges and sheriffs and they could sit in the London Parliament as MPs. By 1688, James had a large Catholic army in Ireland, led by a Catholic general.

WHAT ABOUT THE PROTESTANTS?

In the north of Ireland, the Protestant settlers in Ulster had all these freedoms already. But they had plenty to be worried about. In 1649, Oliver Cromwell had defeated the Catholic Irish at Drogheda and at Wexford. His 'settlement' of Ireland meant that the large Catholic estates had been split up and divided amongst Protestants. Now, forty years on, Irish Protestants became more and more uneasy as they watched the Catholic majority become equal to them under the law and have equal freedoms granted. They were particularly worried by the large Catholic army. Would James ever use it against them? They decided to fortify the city of Londonderry, so that they would have somewhere safe to retreat to if things started looking dangerous.

DID JAMES GO TO IRELAND WHEN HE FLED FROM ENGLAND IN 1688?

Yes, but he went first to France. There the Catholic king, Louis XIV, helped him raise an army. Early in 1689, James landed at Kinsale with a large French army and joined up with his Irish Catholic supporters. He called a Parliament in Dublin and it quickly passed laws that reversed the settlement imposed on Ireland by Oliver Cromwell. Land was to be taken back from the Protestant English and Scottish settlers. The Protestants were angry and terrified.

THE SIEGE OF LONDONDERRY, 1689

James was determined that the Protestants would not hold out against him. With his Irish-French army, he marched on the fortified Protestant city of Londonderry. As his army approached, the citizens slammed the doors in the city walls and refused to let the Catholic James and his Catholic army inside. James was determined to take the city, but he knew it was well fortified. He simply camped outside and his troops stopped all supplies getting in. He was going to starve the city into submission.

The Protestant English tried to help. King William sent a fleet laden with food and other supplies. But it couldn't get into the harbour because James' soldiers had blocked it off with a great barrier. Then the supply ship *Mountjoy* sailed at the barrier and, on the second attempt, smashed through. The siege was over. It had lasted for 105 days. Fifteen thousand Protestants died from starvation, even though they had tried to keep alive by eating dogs and rats and by drinking the blood of horses. Nearly all the city's children were dead.

This map of Ireland shows the places where the events described in this section happened.

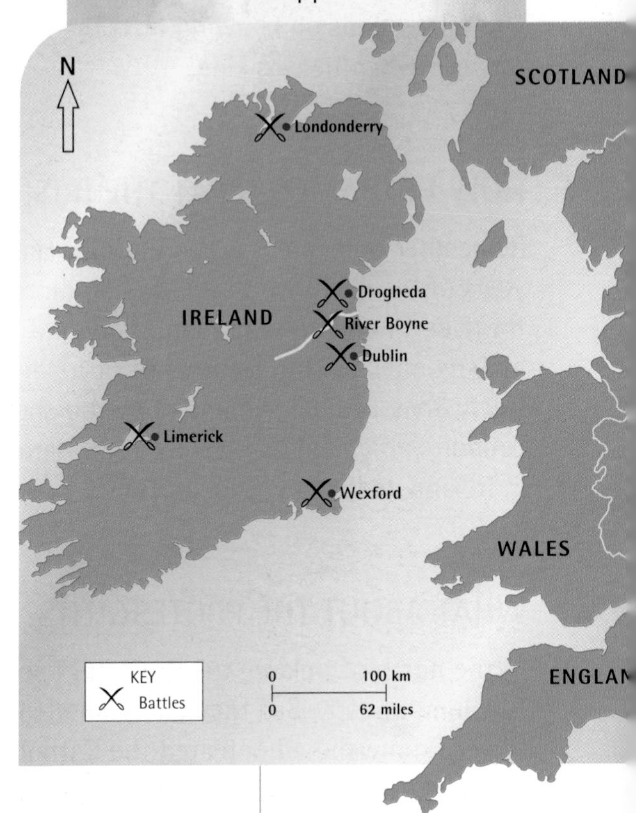

THE BATTLE OF THE BOYNE, 1690

Part of the problem was that King William wasn't particularly interested in Irish affairs at this time. He was much more concerned with organising a war against King Louis XIV of France. However, Parliament was extremely concerned and ordered William to send an army to sort things out. At first, he sent a rather feeble army. The supply officer was secretly loyal to James and pocketed money intended for the soldiers. One 'regiment' consisted of two clerks and a flag, and where regiments did contain soldiers, they were in no condition to fight. That winter, 7000 troops died of disease in Dundalk.

William had to try again. Parliament made him. He took command of a new army. On 14 June 1690, he landed in Ireland with a very different army that contained a crack regiment of Dutch troops – the best in Europe. This Protestant army confronted James' Catholic army for the first and only time on 1 July 1690 at the River Boyne, north of Dublin. The battle raged all day until, around five o'clock, James turned and fled. The Irish Catholic rebellion was nearly over.

SOURCE 1

This modern wall painting shows William at the Battle of the Boyne in June 1690.

Left without a leader, the Irish Catholics struggled on and were finally defeated at Aughrim in 1691. The Catholic city of Limerick surrendered soon afterwards, and the Protestant conquest of Ireland was complete. But worse was to come for the Irish Catholics. William offered a generous deal to Limerick's defenders. The 'Articles of Limerick' promised that all Catholic soldiers and all those Catholics they were protecting, would keep their lands and liberties and would be able to worship as they wished. Rebel soldiers were allowed to slip away and join Louis XIV's troops in France. But the English Parliament thought differently. Four thousand Catholic landowners lost their land and Catholics were not allowed to be soldiers or school teachers, sailors or town councillors. Limerick was called 'The town of the broken Treaty' and Irish Catholics lost everything they had gained under King James II.

Question Time

1. When the Protestant William became king, what would the hopes and fears of Protestants and Catholics in Ireland have been?
2. James seems to have made a habit of running away! Each time, if he had stayed, do you think the outcome would have been different?
3. In what ways were the siege of Londonderry and the Battle of the Boyne similar? How were they different?
4. Very few soldiers were killed at the Battle of the Boyne, so why is it thought to be such an important battle?
5. Make spider diagrams of the outcomes of the 'Glorious Revolution' for Irish Catholics and Protestants. Which group had most reason to fear the future?
6. Look at Source 1. Why should people, four hundred years later, remember this battle?

WHAT WAS THE IMPACT OF THE 'GLORIOUS REVOLUTION' ON SCOTLAND?

In 1689 the Scottish Parliament did just what the English Parliament had done, and accepted the Protestant William as king. This suited the Scottish lowlanders, who were mainly Protestants, especially when the Presbyterian Church (Kirk) was allowed again to become a strong force in the land. It certainly did not please the Highlanders, most of whom were Catholics and bitterly resented both the new King William and the Presbyterian Church.

WHAT DID THE HIGHLANDERS DO ABOUT IT?

In July 1689 they rebelled. John Graham of Claverhouse (sometimes called 'Bonnie' Dundee because he was brave and romantic – and Viscount Dundee) gathered together a force of about 2000 Highlanders who were going to fight for the return of King James II and the Stuarts. They were not trained fighters, but they were brave and they were angry. They tracked about 4000 government troops, led by Hugh Mackay of Scourie, to the pass of Killiecrankie, about 6 kilometres (4 miles) from Blair, in Perthshire. John Graham's men positioned themselves high on the slopes above the pass. As the government soldiers filed out of the pass, Graham's men charged, straight down the hillside at breakneck speed, screaming their clan battle cries. They must have been a terrifying sight. The Highlanders fell on the soldiers, massacring them with their broadswords in hand-to-hand fighting. By the end, 2000 government soldiers were dead and 500 had been taken prisoner. The rest fled. Far fewer Highlanders were killed and wounded, but 'Bonnie' Dundee was dead. With his death, the Highlanders' rebellion faltered. A month later, all Scottish resistance to William was crushed at the Battle of Dunkeld. Defeated and depressed, the Highlanders began the long trek back home. The Stuart cause seemed doomed.

DID WILLIAM PUNISH THE HIGHLANDERS?

No, not really. He and his government decided to be merciful. The government was anxious to make sure that the Highlanders did not rebel again. Few Highlanders were punished. Instead, a kind of bargain was made. Royal agents made it known that they had £12,000 to distribute amongst the Highland clans, provided the clan chiefs took an oath of loyalty to King William. If any clan chief failed to take the oath, this would be regarded as treason. The clan members would be outlaws and their lands would belong to the Crown.

TAKING THE OATH

The date set for the oath to be taken was 1 January 1692. By that date, only Alexander MacDonald of Glencoe had failed to take the oath. But he had tried. Held up by bad weather and deep snows, he had finally got through to Fort William, only to find that there was no magistrate there to take the oath. The Governor told him that the oath had to be taken in front of the sheriff at Inveraray. So Alexander MacDonald set off to walk the 80 snow-covered kilometres (50 miles) to Inveraray. He got there on 2 January, only to find that the sheriff was away celebrating Hogmanay (New Year). It wasn't until 6 January 1692 that Alexander MacDonald of Glencoe took the oath of loyalty to King William on behalf of his clan. But he was a week too late. What would happen?

King William was a Dutchman and he didn't know a lot about Scottish politics. He relied on his Scottish adviser, Sir John Dalrymple. What William didn't know was that Dalrymple was a member of the Campbell clan, sworn enemies of the MacDonalds. So, when Dalrymple advised punishing the entire MacDonald clan, William thought Dalrymple was simply offering good advice. He agreed to an attack on the MacDonald clan, provided it could be proved that they had not taken the oath of loyalty. Dalrymple saw to it that the written evidence of the oath was destroyed.

SOURCE 1

You are ordered to attack the rebels, the MacDonalds of Glencoe, and put all to the sword who are under seventy years old. You are to have a special care that the old fox and his sons do upon no account escape your hands. You are to secure all exits so that no man escapes. You are to do this at exactly 5 o'clock. By that time, I will try to be with you along with a stronger army. Don't wait for me. This is by the King's special command, for the good and safety of the country, that these rebels be cut off root and branch.

See that this is done without fear or favour. Or else, you may expect to be dealt with as a traitor.

This is part of a letter written by Major Robert Duncanson to Captain Robert Campbell of Glenlyon, in 1692.

THE MASSACRE OF GLENCOE

The letter (Source 1) from Major Robert Duncanson explains what Captain Robert Campbell was expected to do. Everything went according to plan. On government orders, about 120 soldiers from the Campbell clan were stationed in the MacDonalds' houses in Glencoe.

Although the Campbells and the MacDonalds were sworn enemies, Highland custom said that all feuding had to stop when hospitality was offered and accepted. For about a week everything seemed well. Then suddenly and without warning, at five o'clock on 13 February 1692, the killing began. Men, women and children were butchered in their beds. Alexander MacDonald was shot dead as he struggled out of bed in a vain attempt to defend his people. No one knows how many were killed that day. Thirty-eight bodies were found. Men, women and children escaped the massacre by fleeing up the glen and over the frozen, treacherous wastes of Rannoch Moor, only to die there of exposure.

WHY WAS THE MASSACRE AT GLENCOE SO SIGNIFICANT?

There were many feuds and massacres in the Scottish Highlands. The Campbell clan and the MacDonald clan had a long history of violent raids against each other. What made this one different?

It was probably partly the enormous betrayal of trust. The clan was massacred even though the clan chief had taken the oath of allegiance to King William; the MacDonalds of Glencoe trusted their guests, the Campbells, to abide by the unwritten rules of Highland hospitality; the king's minister had been involved in planning the massacre and the king's forces had carried it out. What, the Highlanders wondered, had been William's own involvement?

Certainly, those who carried out the massacre were known to all, but they were never punished. Old feuds carried on festering and mistrust of the English was kept alive in the Highlands. The Stuart cause was gaining supporters.

Question Time

1. Why did John Graham of Claverhouse's rebellion fail?
2. How did King William try to keep the Highlanders peaceful after the Battle of Dunkeld?
3. How would **a** a Campbell and **b** a MacDonald have explained to their grandchildren what happened at Glencoe in 1692?
4. What part did Sir John Dalrymple play in the massacre?
5. How likely was it that King William knew exactly what he was doing when he agreed to the massacre going ahead?
6. How could King William's enemies use the massacre to turn people against him?

WHAT WAS THE REACTION IN SCOTLAND TO THE ACT OF UNION 1707?

In order to understand why people and politicians reacted as they did, you have to go back to why most politicians in both countries finally decided to unite.

WHY DID THE SCOTS WANT TO UNITE WITH THE ENGLISH?

Most Scots were Protestant lowlanders. They hated the Catholic Highlanders more than they hated the English. They would be quite glad of the protection of English troops in their country.

England was a powerful and rich trading country. Scottish merchants wanted a share in this wealth by being allowed to trade on equal terms with England's growing empire.

WHY DID THE ENGLISH WANT TO UNITE WITH THE SCOTS?

Most English people wanted to make sure that they would always be ruled by Protestant kings and queens. William and Mary had no children. The Princess Anne, who succeeded them in 1702, had many children but they kept dying as babies. Parliament said that, if she died without any children living, the throne should pass to the German Protestant, Princess Sophia of Hanover. She was a granddaughter of James I. But what if Scotland chose differently? What if Scotland chose the 'warming pan' baby? He was now grown up and some people were calling him 'King James III' or were talking about 'the king over the water'. This could end in war between the two countries. It seemed best to unite them quickly under a Protestant monarch.

England was fighting a war against France and wanted all the help possible. Scotland and France had often become allies in the past. Indeed, the friendship between the two countries was called 'the auld (old) alliance'. It would be disastrous for England if the 'auld alliance' between Scotland and France was to start up again.

BUT THERE WERE PROBLEMS

- Many Scottish people said they wanted to choose their own monarch, regardless of what the English Parliament decided.
- Many English merchants didn't want to share their trading privileges with Scottish merchants.
- Many lowland Scots were Presbyterians and many English people didn't want to support that kind of Christianity.

THE ACT OF UNION 1707

The Act of Union was finally agreed between the two Parliaments. On 16 January 1707, the Scottish and English Parliaments voted themselves out of existence. A new, joint Parliament in England was elected in its place, with 513 MPs from England and Wales and 45 from Scotland. Sixteen Scottish lords joined the House of Lords in London.

What else was agreed?

- Scotland kept its Presbyterian Church.
- Scotland kept its own, different, laws and system of law courts.
- Scottish merchants traded on the same terms as English ones.
- The same customs duties applied throughout the United Kingdom.
- The same weights and measures were to be used throughout the United Kingdom.
- English coinage was to be used in Scotland.

HOW DID THE SCOTTISH PEOPLE REACT?

There were angry demonstrations and bloody riots on the streets of Edinburgh and Glasgow. In the Highlands, men and women brooded and plotted rebellion.

Angus Gilles
A Catholic Highlander, aged 36, living on the island of Barra. Owns a small croft on which he runs black cattle, pigs and some sheep.

Isobel McLennan
A Protestant, aged 25. The wife of a young, ambitious wine merchant, James. They have three young children and live in the town of Leith, Edinburgh's port.

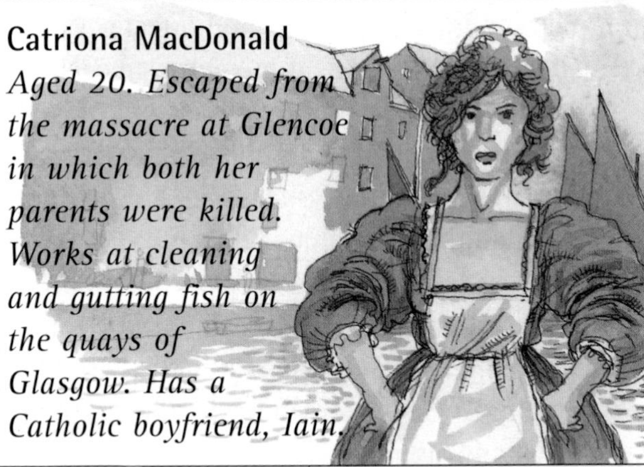

Catriona MacDonald
Aged 20. Escaped from the massacre at Glencoe in which both her parents were killed. Works at cleaning and gutting fish on the quays of Glasgow. Has a Catholic boyfriend, Iain.

James McPhinn
Aged 57. A lawyer living in Inverness, with a thriving practice. His wife, a Presbyterian, is anxious and worries about everything. Their two sons have joined the army.

Question Time

1. Make a large poster that is *either* trying to persuade English people that they will benefit from union with Scotland *or* trying to persuade Scottish people that they will benefit from union with England.
2. Which country do you think gained most from the Union? Why?
3. Read the four character cards on page 70 carefully. For each one, work out whether the person would be likely or unlikely to support the Act of Union.
4. What, or who, threatened the union of the two countries?

WHY DID THE REBELLION OF 1715 FAIL?

In order to understand why there was a rebellion in the first place, you have to go back to the Stuart family tree.

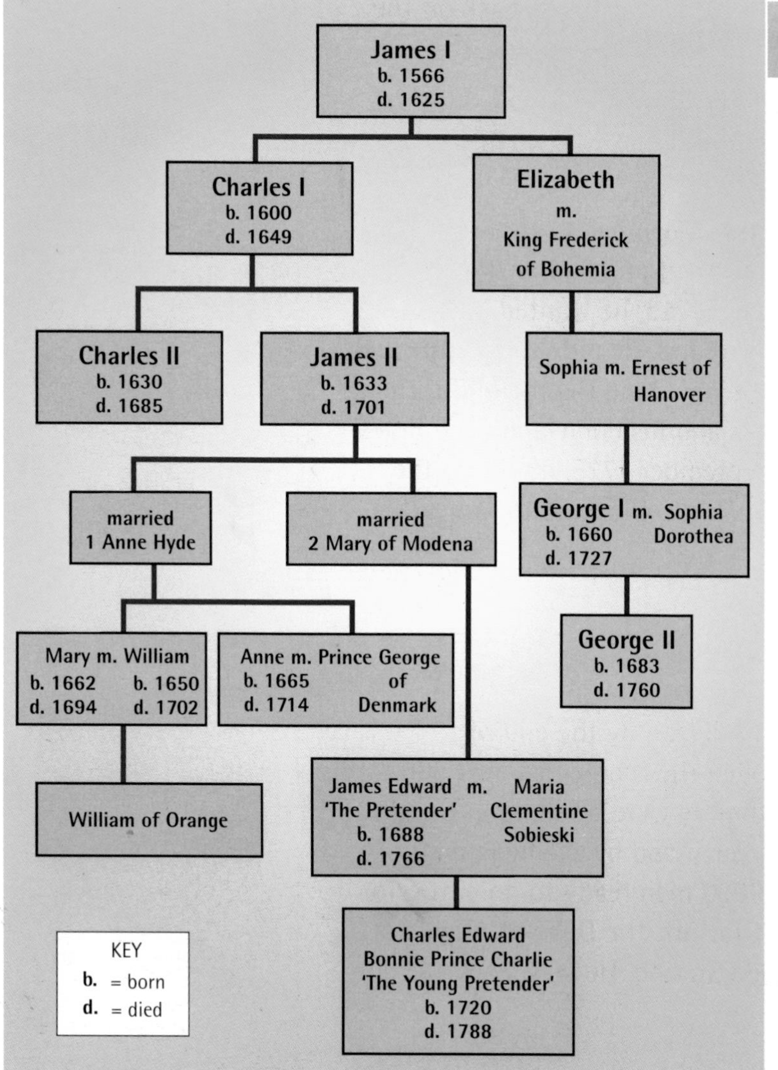

The Stuart Family Tree.

Activity Time

Queen Anne died in 1714. All her children were dead. Who would be monarch? Look carefully at the family tree. You are going to work out who had the best claim to the throne of Great Britain.

1. Make a list of the people who were alive in 1714 and who might think they had a right to the throne. Beside each person, write down why they had a claim.
2. Now make a decision. Which person's claim was, in your judgement, the best?

WHAT STARTED A JACOBITE REBELLION IN 1715?

When Queen Anne died, many Jacobites thought their time had come. She had no children. There was no obvious heir, waiting in England, to inherit the throne. Maybe now the Catholic children of King James II would claim what the Jacobites believed was rightfully theirs.

Parliament thought differently. Back at the time of the Act of Union, Parliament said that, if Queen Anne died without any children, the throne should pass to Princess Sophia of Hanover. By the time Queen Anne died, Princess Sophia was dead as well. So, Parliament offered the Crown to her son, Prince George, and he accepted.

King George I was not popular in England and there were riots when he arrived in London. He was German and didn't speak any English. This meant he had to leave most of the running of the country to his chief minister, Robert Walpole. The supporters of the deposed king, James II, and his son James Edward Stuart, were delighted. Was this the moment to put the Stuarts back on the throne?

ENTER THE EARL OF MAR

The Earl of Mar took matters into his own hands. He was one of the Scottish lords in the new Parliament and had, in 1707, supported the Act of Union. But, by 1713, he wanted the Act repealed and independence for Scotland. He didn't have any luck finding favours at the court of the new King George and turned to rebellion. He sailed for Scotland and his homelands, the Braes of Mar. There, at Braemar on 6 September 1715, he set up the Jacobite standard and called upon all people loyal to James Edward Stuart to join him.

REBELLION!

The Highlanders' response was spectacular. By the end of September, the Earl of Mar controlled the Highlands: over 5000 clansmen men had joined him and more were flooding in every day. The Earl made his headquarters at Perth and by the beginning of November he had a force of over 9000 men ready to do battle for James Edward Stuart. Battle wasn't far off. The Duke of Argyll was waiting, with a smaller force, outside Stirling. He was ready to fight for King George. The two sides met on 13 November 1715 at Sheriffmuir. No one seemed quite sure who won, or, indeed, if anyone did. Argyll's soldiers retreated to Stirling in an orderly way. The Earl of Mar's forces retreated as well, first to Perth and then to Inverness. They never did battle again.

Question Time

1. Find out why the supporters of King James were called 'Jacobites'.
2. On a map of Scotland, plot a timeline of the 1715 Jacobite rebellion.
3. A London newspaper has sent a journalist to France to interview James Edward Stuart about the failure of the 1715 rebellion. What questions do you think the journalist should ask? Make a list. How do you think James Edward Stuart would have answered them?
4. Write a piece for *either* a Scottish Catholic journal *or* an English Protestant newspaper explaining why the 1715 rebellion failed. Remember to write in a way that gives the sort of interpretation of events that the paper you have chosen would find acceptable.

WHERE WAS JAMES EDWARD STUART?

Where was the man the Jacobites believed was their rightful king? Where was the 'king' for whom they had been fighting and dying? James Edward Stuart's advisers persuaded him to go to Scotland. Reluctantly, he boarded a boat at Dunkirk, in France, and sailed for Scotland. The journey took six days. On 22 December, he landed at Peterhead. It was wet and cold and he was miserable. Altogether, James Edward Stuart, the dream king of the Catholic Jacobites, spent six depressing weeks in Scotland. He made no great rallying speeches and fought no battles. The Earl of Mar, frightened that the Duke of Argyll would capture him, persuaded James Edward, the Old Pretender, to return to France. The so-called rebellion was over – at least for the moment.

WAS THE RISING OF 1745 A REAL THREAT TO KING GEORGE II AND THE HANOVERIAN SUCCESSION?

By the time the Jacobites staged another rebellion, King George I was dead and his son, George II, was reigning in his place. By 1745, the Hanoverians (remember they were rulers of Hanover as well, and so were called Hanoverians) had been reigning in Britain for 31 years. Indeed, George II had been on the throne since 1727 and it didn't look as though he was going to be dislodged easily. On the other hand, the 1745 Jacobite rebellion was a much more serious affair than the one of 1715.

WHY DID THE JACOBITES BELIEVE THAT 1745 WAS A GOOD YEAR FOR A REBELLION?

There were many different reasons for the rebellion starting in 1745. Some of the reasons were long-term and some were short-term. They all came together in 1745:

- Many Catholics and nearly all Scottish Catholics believed that James Edward Stuart (the 'warming pan' baby and the Old Pretender) was the rightful king of Scotland and of England.
- Charles Edward Stuart was James Edward Stuart's son. He believed his father was the rightful king.
- Charles Edward Stuart believed he could put his father on the throne.
- After the Act of Union in 1707, there were several attempts to put the Stuarts back on the throne, so rebellion in Scotland was not unusual.
- France usually supported Jacobite plots.
- Scottish people did not like having to pay taxes – and, after 1707, they particularly didn't like paying them to a government in London.
- After 1715, the British army recruited Highlanders, but it did not allow them to form separate Highland regiments.
- After 1715, some of the defeated Scots joined the Old Pretender and travelled round the courts of Europe, stirring up trouble against the Hanoverians.
- In 1744, France planned to invade England. The French king, Louis XV, invited Charles Edward Stuart to join the invasion fleet. The fleet was smashed in a violent storm, but France still declared war on England.
- A Scot called Aeneas MacDonald, who owned a banking house in Paris, was willing to give a lot of money to fund a rebellion led by Charles Edward Stuart.
- Highlanders began calling Charles Edward Stuart 'the Young Pretender' and 'Bonnie Prince Charlie'.

So, it was not really a surprise when, in July 1745, Charles Edward Stuart landed at Eriskay, a small island off the west coast of Scotland. He had seven men with him, his political, financial and military advisers, and he was determined to put his father on the throne.

Question Time

1. 1745 seemed, to many Jacobites, a good year to stage another rebellion. Look at the list of reasons for this, and sort them into long-term reasons and short-term reasons.
2. Now sort them again, but this time into political, economic, religious and personal reasons. Which, in your judgement, were the most important reasons for the rebellion?
3. How likely, at this point in 1745, was it that Charles Edward Stuart would be able to put his father on the throne of Great Britain? If you were one of his advisers, what three things would you tell him he *had* to be sure of before he was likely to be successful?

THE 1745 JACOBITE REBELLION

Bonnie Prince Charlie and his small group of advisers quickly made their way to Glenfinnan, on the mainland of Scotland. There, on 19 August, he raised the Stuart flag and proclaimed his father, James Edward Stuart, king. By now, he had 200 men with him. Quickly, Bonnie Prince Charlie set about gaining support. He was joined by hundreds of men from some of the large clans - the Camerons, Frasers and Mackintoshes - as well as men from the smaller ones. Soon, over 4000 men were ready and willing to march with him and fight for the Jacobite cause.

In September 1745, the Jacobites marched on Edinburgh, Scotland's capital city. Many of Edinburgh's citizens were sympathetic to the Jacobite cause and Bonnie Prince Charlie's men soon controlled the whole city, except the castle. They rested and gathered their forces together, ready to face the battle with government forces they knew must come. On 21 September, Charles led 5000 Highland clansmen against General Cope's troops at Prestonpans, east of Edinburgh.

SOURCE 1

We began to march an hour before day and found no opposition, so we had time to form before the enemy saw us. Our dark clothes helped. Once I saw we were in a strong position, I ordered the MacDonalds to fire. The enemy tried to return our fire but were disorganised. They ran away and the MacDonalds went after them. The rest of the enemy soldiers began to panic. We rushed in with such fury upon the enemy that they did not have time to reload. Arms and legs were cut off and heads split to the shoulders, never such wounds were seen. The enemy was chased so closely that they threw away their standards and colours and abandoned their horses. Eighty four officers and fourteen hundred others were taken prisoner. The Prince said he would never forget what had been done for him that day. He said he would not rest until the wounded had been cared for.

John William O'Sullivan fought on the side of Charles Edward Stuart at Prestonpans. This is part of his account of the battle. It wasn't published until 1938.

CHARLES' CHOICES

What was Charles to do now? Scotland was, more or less, under his control. Should he stay in Scotland and build up his power there, or push on into England, and challenge George II directly? His advisers said he should stay in Scotland. Charles disagreed.

He thought, if he pushed on down into England, English Catholics would flock to join him. They would bring with them money and soldiers. He would, or so he believed, stand an even better chance of putting his father, James Edward Stuart, on the throne. He was dreadfully, awfully, wrong.

INTO ENGLAND!

Charles and his Highlanders set off, marching south into England. They marched through Carlisle and through Preston. Only about 300 English supporters joined his army. None of them were important or wealthy Catholics.

SOURCE 2

This cartoon was published in London in 1745. It was called 'The Highland visitors'.

RETREAT

Charles and his men stopped when they got to Derby. They were 220 kilometres (138 miles) from London. Should they push on and try to capture the capital city? Should they give up now? Charles' advisers said 'Turn back'. Charles wanted to carry on and grasp London and the Crown. But many of the Highlanders were uneasy at being so far south. They had been away from their homes for far too long. Crops had to be sown and livestock killed. They knew the English Catholics hadn't really rallied to their cause. How could they be sure of being successful? How could they be sure they could put James Edward Stuart on the throne? What they didn't know, of course, was that King George II had packed his bags and was ready to leave his capital city.

Bonnie Prince Charlie and his army had hoped for massive support from Catholics in Cumbria, Lancashire and Cheshire. Whilst some English Catholics had joined them, and others had given money, it was not nearly enough to support what would have amounted to a full scale revolution.

Depressed and demoralised, the Highlanders turned and trudged back to Scotland. They were freezing and they were starving. To make matters worse, they were pursued by English soldiers.

On 19 December, Charles and his men reached the Scottish border. There they split up in order to confuse their pursuers. The main part went to Glasgow and on 3 January they headed for Stirling.

At Falkirk, the Jacobites turned and made a stand. They defeated a small government force that had been recruited in Scotland, but were not strong enough to take Stirling. All the time, individuals and small groups of men were slipping away, back to their families who depended on them. Charles headed for the Highlands and safety.

SOURCE 3

As the Highlanders came nearer, our people became more alarmed and a great many of them left town taking with them food and belongings. About noon, there came a sergeant and a drummer in Highland dress, with a woman on horseback carrying a drum, which they beat and asked for volunteers. The Prince came in to Manchester about noon, walking in Highland dress in the middle of a large group and went to Mr Dickenson's house. The next day he proclaimed his father (James Edward Stuart) to be King James III. About thirty of our neighbours volunteered to join him.

John Byrom sympathised with the Jacobites, though he never joined Bonnie Prince Charlie's march south. This is part of what he wrote, on 1 March 1746, about what happened when the Jacobite army came to Manchester the previous autumn.

SOURCE 4

The Prince was advised that it would be better to retreat. He was astonished at this suggestion. The Chiefs and others were sent for. They all advised that this was the only course of action. The young Prince, who saw himself within three days of the capital where he would restore the true king, hated the word retreat. But as everyone else was in favour, he had no alternative but to agree. I never saw anyone so disappointed.

John William O'Sullivan explains how the decision to retreat was made.

CULLODEN

The Duke of Cumberland, George II's son, at the head of a well-trained and disciplined English army, was in hot pursuit of the Jacobites. He was determined to wipe them out so that never again would the Stuarts threaten the throne of Great Britain.

Cumberland caught up with Bonnie Prince Charlie and his remaining Jacobite army at Culloden Moor, a few miles from Inverness. But he didn't fight them immediately. Cumberland's men delayed for a few days at Nairn, where they celebrated his birthday. Meanwhile, the Jacobites, waiting a few kilometres away on Culloden Moor, made disastrous mistakes.

SOURCE 5

This picture of the Battle of Culloden was painted in 1746. Captured Highlanders posed for the artist.

Lord George Murray, one of Charles' best commanders, advised that the Jacobites should cross to the mossy, soft ground over Nairn Water. There, the ground was ideal for the Highlanders' fighting techniques and hopeless for cavalry horses. Charles took no notice. He ordered his men to stand and wait for battle on the flat, springy ground of Culloden Moor, ideal for Cumberland's well-trained and disciplined cavalry. But Cumberland's men were relaxing, drinking brandy and eating cheese in Nairn, forcing the Jacobites to wait for about three days. The Jacobites' food was in Inverness and no one had thought to arrange for carts to bring the supplies to the men, waiting at Culloden, 10 kilometres (6 miles) away.

When Cumberland's men finally arrived to do battle, the Jacobites didn't stand a chance. They were half-starved and exhausted, badly equipped and outnumbered two to one. Charles ordered his tired army to charge and Cumberland's men shot them to pieces. At the end of the day, 1200 Jacobites and 76 English soldiers lay dead.

Cumberland's men showed no mercy. They chased the fleeing Jacobites, hunting them down and slaughtering them without mercy. After Culloden, the Duke of Cumberland was given the nickname 'Butcher'.

AFTERMATH

Culloden was the last battle to be fought on British soil. But even though the battle was over, the fighting did not stop. 'Butcher' Cumberland's men rampaged through the Highlands, raping, killing, capturing and plundering as they chose. Above all, they were looking for Bonnie Prince Charlie. They never found him. A hunted man, always on the move and often in disguise, loyal Highlanders hid him and protected him from discovery by the hated red-coated soldiers. For five months, poor crofters in the Highlands and Islands hid their Prince and never betrayed him. Eventually, Flora MacDonald, the step-daughter of the commander of the militia on Uist, rowed him across the treacherous waters of The Minch to the island of Skye. There, a boat was waiting to take him from Portree to France and safety.

The government did its best to smash the Highland clan system. Parliament passed laws which took away the power of the clan chiefs and forced the clansmen to give up their kilts and their weapons.

Question Time

1. On an outline map of Scotland and the north of England, plot the course of the 1745 rebellion. Remember to mark places and dates accurately.
2. Bonnie Prince Charlie made two important decisions early on in the rebellion. One was to invade England and the second one was to turn back when he reached Derby. Were these decisions wrong? How could this part of the rebellion have been managed better? Or were all choices bound to end in disaster?
3. Look back over the whole section about the 1745 rebellion, including the sources. What sort of a leader was Bonnie Prince Charlie? Back up what you say with hard evidence.
4. Did the Jacobites ever really stand a chance of winning?
5. Look at Source 2 and read Source 3. What different impressions do they give of the ways the Jacobites behaved when they were in England? Why do they give such different impressions of what happened? Must one of them be wrong?
6. Look at Source 5 and read the caption carefully. How accurate a picture of Culloden is this likely to be?

JUST A MEMORY?

The Scottish Highlanders, their clans and their loyalty, their hopeless fight for the Stuarts and, above all, Bonnie Prince Charlie, became a romantic and treasured memory.

Speed bonnie boat, like a bird on the wing
Onward, the sailors cry
Carry the lad that's born to be king
Over the sea to Skye.

Loud the winds howl, loud the waves roar
Thunderclaps rend the air
Baffled our foes stand by the shore
Follow they will not dare.

Though the waves leap, soft shall ye sleep
Ocean's a royal bed
Rocked in the deep, Flora will keep
Watch by your weary head.

Many's the lad fought on that day
Well the claymore could wield
When the night came, silently lay
Dead on Culloden's field.

Burned are our homes, exile and death
Scatter the loyal men
Yet ere the sword cool in the sheath
Charlie will come again.

SOURCE 6

A film poster showing David Niven and Margaret Leighton in *Bonnie Prince Charlie*. The film was made in 1948. Alongside it are the lyrics from the *Skye Boat Song*, a song inspired by the life of Bonnie Prince Charlie, who escaped to Skye after the Battle of Culloden in 1745.

SOURCE 7

A shortbread tin showing a painting called 'Fiona MacDonald's farewell to Bonnie Prince Charlie, Isle of Skye, 1 July 1746', painted by S. Joy.

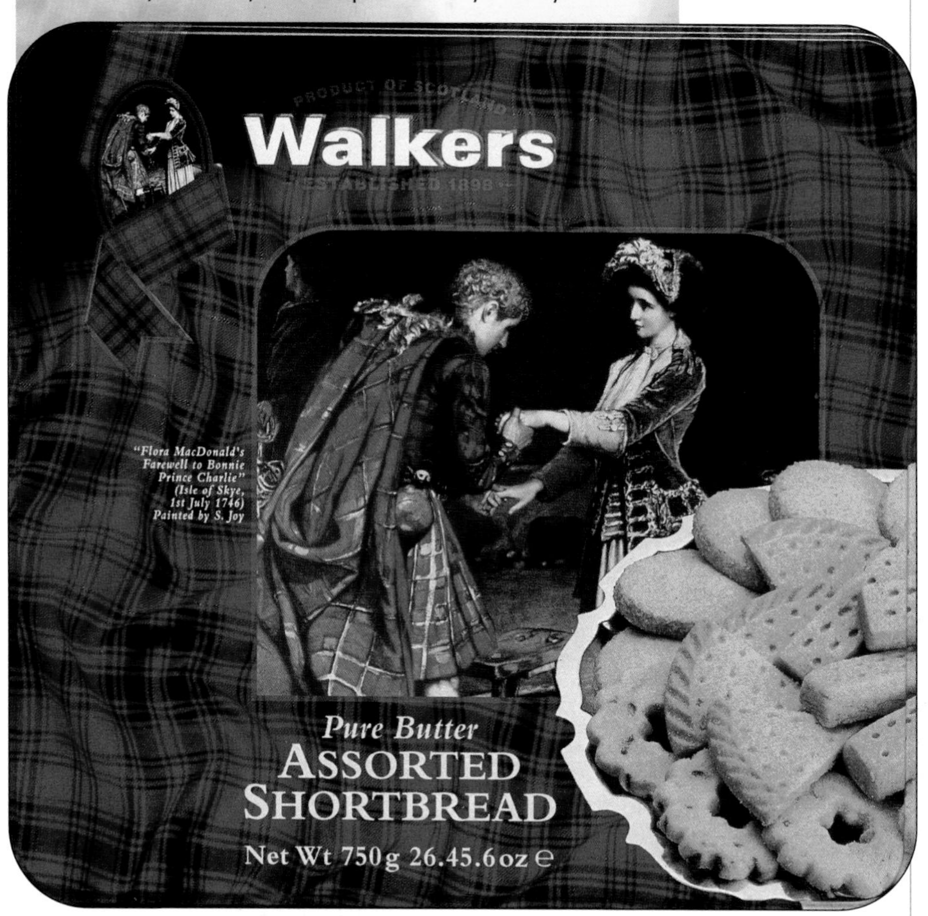

Question Time

1. Look at and read Sources 6-7 very carefully. For each source, work out how reliable it is as an interpretation of Bonnie Prince Charlie.
2. Why do you think Bonnie Prince Charlie became such a romantic folk hero?

UNITING THE KINGDOM?

By now, you will have found out a lot about the ways in which Scotland and Ireland united with England and Wales, and will have understood some of the problems involved.

King George II died in 1760. What advice might he have passed on to his son before he died about the state of the *United* Kingdom? How united was it in law and reality? What should the new king, George III, do to keep his kingdom together?

Unit 10: France 1789–94 – why was there a revolution?

BEFORE AND AFTER: WHY ARE THE EVENTS IN FRANCE KNOWN AS A REVOLUTION?

We often use the word 'revolution' to describe a time of dramatic and sudden change in history. However, as well as referring to events that happened over a short space of time, 'revolution' is also used to describe changes in other aspects of life, such as transport, agriculture and industry, which take place over many years. Between 1789 and 1794 a revolution took place in France and the ideas of the revolution spread to other countries in Europe. But why was there a revolution in France?

Are you surprised at what is happening in Source 1? It is unusual to see a monarch, a respected leader of a country, beheaded in front of an angry crowd. This is one of the most famous events of the French Revolution, but does this event alone justify it being called a revolution?

After all, England executed its king in 1649, but few people nowadays refer to this as a revolution. King Louis XVI and his wife lost their lives and the throne, but there were other groups whose position in society was turned upside down. These are what make the events in France a revolution.

SOURCE 1

A contemporary painting of the execution of King Louis XVI on 21 January 1793, by an unknown artist.

We have seen that the execution of the king was one of the most dramatic events of this period, but he was not the only person affected and he was not the first to have his power removed. Three groups were affected dramatically by the French Revolution:

- the monarchy
- the clergy (priests, monks and nuns)
- the nobility (powerful wealthy families).

They were all privileged groups, which means they had a lot of things that were not available to most of the population, such as wealth and power. These three events show how their lives changed.

Read all about it...

Massacre of prisoners, including priests, monks and nuns – panic sweeps through Paris

September 1792

Crowds in Paris have heard rumours that Austria has successfully invaded France in support of the King. They have panicked and killed over 1000 people – anyone whom they suspected of being in support of the Austrians and against the Revolution. Many of the victims are religious men and women, held prisoner by the revolutionaries.

Down with favouritism – no more special titles for the nobles!

June 1790

The wealthy nobles have been cut down by law. Their titles such as duc, baron and prince have been got rid of. This leads the way to equality. They are not even allowed to have a family coat of arms.

Louis XVI executed – hope or crisis for the future of France?

January 1793

The trial of King Louis resulted in the death sentence. He was found guilty of plotting against France. The executioners would not let the King speak to the crowd on the scaffold. A huge crowd gathered to see the event, screaming and rushing to steal a souvenir. One man even dipped his finger in the King's blood and tasted it.

LOSING ALL PRIVILEGES – BEFORE AND AFTER

We can see how the three privileged groups seemed to lose a great deal, but how can we tell if these events were really significant? We need to find out more about the groups and their lives before 1790. Then we can work out what really made these actions revolutionary. The period before the French Revolution is called the *ancien régime*, which means old or royal rule. Traditionally there were three 'Estates' or groups in society. In reality only the First and Second Estates had any power. They made up the ruling body called the Estates General.

The Three Estates in France before the Revolution

THE REAL POWER HOLDERS

The monarchy

The monarchy believed in the Divine Right of Kings – that they were chosen by God to act in any way they wished. It was the responsibility of the monarch to make decisions about war, taxes, laws and choosing a government. The monarchy had traditionally given the First and Second Estates privileges and estates to run. This dates back to the Middle Ages when the king relied on the nobles and the clergy to run the country.

The clergy: the First Estate

The clergy were often the only educated people, apart from the nobility, so they held a lot of power in political, as well as religious matters. The clergy and religious institutions owned over 10 per cent of the land, but they had been exempt from paying taxes. In fact, they were actually paid taxes, called tithes, by the people, and had their own law courts.

The nobility: the Second Estate

The nobles often inherited their positions or received titles in return for working for the monarchy in some way. In return for their loyalty, they were let off most taxes. They owned and managed over one-third of all the land in France. They exercised their power as landlords, and peasants had to pay them taxes in the form of money or labour. The nobles also got special treatment in the law courts.

Changes of the Revolution

The government of Louis XVI became known as corrupt and inefficient. France's revolution brought the Third Estate to take over the government. Major changes took place in French society, including the execution of Louis and the removal of the monarchy. The key reforms were:

- Monasteries and convents were closed down.
- All church lands were confiscated.
- Priests had to be elected by the people and swear an oath of loyalty to France.
- A tax on land was introduced.
- New law courts were introduced.
- Several taxes were abolished.
- Local councils were elected by local people.
- All men over twenty-five were given the right to vote.

Question Time

1. Why might priests, nuns and monks be seen as enemies of the Revolution?
2. Research the *ancien régime*, to find out about the privileges that the monarchy and the First and Second Estates had before the Revolution. Key words to search for are: wealth, power, laws, taxes, tithes.
3. Sum up the power changes of the revolution by writing 'before' and 'after' sentences for each of the Three Estates.
   For example, 'Before the Revolution, the monarchy made all the decisions about wars, taxes and laws.'

WHAT DIFFERENT CAUSES LED TO THE REVOLUTION?

The French Revolution is an important and dramatic event. It affected not only the whole history of France but also that of several other countries, so we need to understand why it happened.

We have found that there were three groups who held all the power. Is the existence of these groups enough to explain the Revolution to us? Let's look at the problem like a mathematical equation. Does this make sense?

Rich and privileged people = French Revolution

Think about these two pieces of information:

- The clergy in France had enjoyed their privileges for centuries without a revolution.
- In countries in Eastern Europe, such as Russia, the wealth and privileges of these groups was even greater, but there was no revolution there.

It does not seem that the existence of privileged groups is enough for a revolution to take place. We need to investigate what else was happening in France to make such a difference and make its people want to take action against the *ancien régime*. There are several more factors on the next few pages which will help us to complete the equation below.

Rich and privileged people + X = French Revolution

What we need to know is what 'X' is.

NEW IDEAS OF THE ENLIGHTENMENT

In Europe

New ideas were becoming fashionable during this period. Thinkers called philosophers and scientists began to question old ideas. They believed in reason and using scientific methods to test new ideas. All over Europe people were talking about the different ways of ruling, and questioning the power of groups like the monarchy and the Catholic Church. Some people were beginning to criticise the way that society worked and rethink long-held beliefs.

In America

The American Revolution took place in 1776. Britain's North American colonies wanted their freedom and were prepared to fight for it. When they won, they declared their independence from

Britain. The American revolutionaries organised a constitution (list of rules) that their government had to follow. France supported America in the war and these ideas quickly spread through France.

In France

People in France soon began to challenge the *ancien régime*. A philosopher and poet called Voltaire criticised the way that the king ruled, although he still agreed with having a monarchy. He also argued that the Catholic Church had too much power over ordinary people. Most people in France did not think about any violent changes, but they had begun to think that their lives could be different.

FINANCIAL PROBLEMS

In the early eighteenth century, France had been a very wealthy country. It made great profits from trade and industry, and merchants spent money on luxurious homes and fine living. However, the government was becoming bankrupt. The king had been borrowing money to fund the expensive lifestyle of his family and court, and was paying back increasing amounts in interest. In 1788, 41 per cent of Louis' expenses was spent on interest payments. This was nearly double what he spent on the army and navy put together. However, this did not stop Louis spending 150,000 livres on a new palace for his extravagant wife, Marie Antoinette.

Another factor led to France's bankruptcy. The expense of supporting North America against Britain in the American Revolution was huge and the government borrowed all of the money necessary. Interest payments rose further. Something had to change.

SOURCE 1

The Cellar Café in Paris where people in late eighteenth century France would come to read and discuss new ideas. It was drawn by an anonymous artist at the time.

NOT ENOUGH TAXES

The potential amount of wealth received from taxes was quite great and the taxes were not just paid on income. The gabelle was a tax on salt; the corvée was a tax on labour, where men had to work to mend the royal roads; and the octroi was a special tax paid by merchants.

So why didn't Louis simply increase the taxes to repay France's debts, especially as there were so many wealthy merchants? The tax system itself was Louis' biggest problem. Traditionally, it was the Third Estate who paid most of the taxes – but they were the ones without any money. Members of the Second Estate were exempt from paying several taxes, as it was one of their traditional privileges. Added to this was the problem of the corrupt officials, who kept some of the taxes they collected for themselves.

Why couldn't the poor just pay up? After all, they had always paid taxes on their goods. Well, the gap between rich and poor was growing larger. Bad harvests in 1788 and 1789 had ruined wheat crops, raising the price of bread even further. Peasants could barely afford to feed their families. So they struggled to meet the present tax demands. There was no way that they could afford to pay more.

SOURCE 2

This is a French cartoon from about 1789. The peasant is being crushed by a stone supporting the clergy and nobility. 'Impots' means taxes and 'corvées' are forced labour.

Why didn't Louis just increase the taxes on the richer members of society or change the tax system? Well, he tried again and again – but the French parliament was made up of the Second Estate, and they were not going to raise their own taxes if they could help it. The situation was reaching crisis point.

PROBLEM PEOPLE

Louis XVI was seen as a weak ruler. His wife, Marie Antoinette, was considered vain and interfering, and was hated for spending money unnecessarily. Her brand-new palace was thought to be an expensive and unnecessary toy. Also, the couple were mourning the death of their son from tuberculosis in June 1789 and refused to go out in public.

The French people also resented the government's method of using sealed letters with the king's signature to banish people from the country or imprison them. Anyone who criticised the *ancien régime*, could receive one of these letters and had no power against it. During Louis' reign, 140,000 sealed letters were sent out. The reputation of the monarchy and government was rapidly getting worse.

There were several new men arriving on the political scene in Paris. After the Tennis Court Oath (see page 91), the power of the Third Estate increased. They were represented not by poor peasants, but by lawyers like Robespierre, and officials who said that they spoke for the rights of the ordinary person in France. These people were rapidly gaining support.

Question Time

1. Why would the factors relating to new ideas, economic crisis and the king's way of life encourage people to want dramatic change? Draw a flow diagram of ideas for each factor to show step by step how it could lead to a revolution. One example has been started for you:

   New ideas about freedom are printed and spread around Europe ➔

   People begin to think about how they could be free ➔

   They join up with others with similar ideas...

2. Do you think that any one factor is stronger than the others? In making your decision, think about how many people were affected by each factor and how big a problem each one was.

3. Rewrite the equation on page 86 so that it fits our new information.

WHY DID THE REVOLUTIONARIES THINK THAT THE TENNIS COURT OATH WAS SO IMPORTANT?

What is often the subject of paintings and portraits: rich families, a dramatic battle, a noble leader, beautiful scenery? Below is a painting of a meeting held by the Third Estate in June 1789. Now, such a meeting would not normally be considered to be an exciting subject for a painting, so what was so special about this one?

SOURCE 1

The Swearing of the Tennis Court Oath by Jacques-Louis David. He was a supporter of the Revolution and painted this picture in 1791. Notice that some clergymen have joined the Third Estate in their meeting.

Fact File: The Tennis Court Oath

What was it?

- An oath sworn by the Third Estate in an indoor tennis court on 20 June 1789.
- The group swore not to leave until the king agreed to a constitution, which everyone including the king had to follow, that would change the way that France was ruled.

Who swore the oath?

- A group of lawyers and officials representing the poorer people of France.
- One of the three groups (Estates) that made up the Estates General.

Why were they in an indoor tennis court?

- Louis XVI had been forced to call a meeting of the Estates General to try to sort out the financial crisis in France. He needed their agreement to increase taxes and change the tax system.
- The Third Estate had been locked out of the hall that they were supposed to be using for a meeting. They were furious but determined to meet, so they used a nearby indoor tennis court instead.

WHY WERE THE THIRD ESTATE SO DETERMINED TO MEET?

The situation in France was getting tense. These are the key events during the early days of the Revolution:

- There is a desperate financial situation. The king needs support from the Paris parlement (law courts) to bring in a land tax. Talks with the parlement fail; people protest in the streets; there are riots in Paris.
- In 1787 Louis finally agrees to call a meeting of the Estates General to try to change the tax system.
- The Third Estate make some demands on the king. They want double the number of men as representatives in the Estates General and for all three Estates to meet at the same time. They do not trust the other Estates.
- May 1789 sees the first meeting of the Estates General since 1614. The demands of the Third Estate are not met. The king is desperate but does not want to give in to the people.
- The Tennis Court Oath is sworn. Now the Third Estate are joined by some clergy and a few important nobles. They have clear aims.

Question Time

1. How much does the painting on page 90 tell us about the revolutionaries in 1789? Does it tell us what they did/said/thought/wore/wanted/what mood they were in?

2. The artist who drew the painting was a strong supporter of the Revolution.
   a How could this affect what he chose to paint?
   b Can we still trust it as evidence?

3. Explain how members of the Third Estate might have felt in each of the situations listed below. You could write their ideas as thought bubbles.
   a finally asked to meet by Louis XVI
   b locked out of the meeting room
   c holding a meeting anyway and swearing an oath
   d joined by supporters

4. Explain why the Tennis Court Oath was so important to the revolutionaries, giving the background and short-term reasons in your answer.

5. The Third Estate were actually locked out of the meeting hall accidentally, but they preferred to believe that it was a deliberate plot by the king to cut off their rights. Do you think that the Revolution would still have taken place if the doors to the original meeting hall had not been locked?

WHY WAS THE BASTILLE ATTACKED AND DESTROYED?

Each year the French celebrate 14 July and have a national holiday. The event which they remember is the attack by some revolutionaries on the Bastille prison in Paris in 1789. They released some prisoners, killing anyone who stood in their way. News of the event soon spread all over France and abroad, appearing in newspapers, pictures and stories. We need to find out why the Bastille was attacked, what people thought about it and also why an attack on a prison is so important that it is still celebrated today.

WHEN DID IT TAKE PLACE?

The Tennis Court Oath meant that Louis' attempts to make changes and consult the Estates General had failed. People were encouraged by the actions of the Third Estate, now joined by members of the Second Estate, in the forming of the new National Assembly. This would replace the Estates General and make decisions about ruling France from now on. There were riots in Paris and across France. Troops were sent out to quash the trouble makers. The attack on the Bastille was a turning point – the Revolution had started.

SOURCE 1

In this engraving by James Gillray called *The Triumph of Liberty in the Opening of the Bastille*, published in 1790, revolutionaries are releasing prisoners. Gillray was British.

SOURCE 2

The attackers were astonished to find so few prisoners. Many believed there were others, hidden in some secret cave or dungeon ... On 18 July four gaolers were questioned separately. They confirmed that the Bastille contained on 14 July only seven prisoners: four forgers, a Count whose family had wanted him locked up and two men (one was an Englishman).

A historian, Jacques Godechot, writes about the Bastille in 1965.

Activity Time

A

1. Write some labels to go around Source 1 above to explain what is going on to someone who has not studied the period before. Try to use some key words and point out everything that you can see.
2. Write a caption to go with Source 1 for a pamphlet that is sympathetic to the revolutionaries. Use adjectives that make them look brave and explain how important their aims were.

Fact File: The Bastille

- The Bastille prison was famous for holding prisoners who had criticised the monarchy or the government. Often these people were imprisoned without trial, so the building represented the power of the *ancien régime*.
- People thought the prison was an armoury (a store for weapons and ammunition) that was being used against the people rioting in Paris.
- The governor of the Bastille was killed along with several guards.
- There is evidence that prisoners there were treated very well indeed, having good food and conditions, and some freedom.
- There were only seven prisoners in the prison at the time of the attack and none of them had been imprisoned for political reasons (disagreeing with the government).
- The attack started off a chain reaction in the Revolution. It led to more rioting across France and was a focus for revolutionary feeling. Its was an achievement that gave the revolutionaries courage to carry on protesting. They also became more violent.
- The event has come to represent the fight for freedom and equal rights for people in France – even today.

Question Time

1. What do you notice when you compare Sources 1 and 2 on page 93 and the fact file? Mention the number of prisoners and the conditions they were kept in.
2. Why do you think that Sources 1 and 2 are so different? Think about why they were made and by whom, when they were done and what information they might have been based on.
3. We know that the revolutionaries only released seven prisoners from the Bastille, so why was it such an important event? Explain as many reasons as you can: **a** why they attacked it in the first place; **b** why it was important in the long term.
4. Which is more important to historians – what actually happened at the Bastille or what it represented?

WHY DID THEY KILL THE KING?

At the start of the Revolution very few people wanted the king's death. What were the events that caused the mood of the country to become more violent, leading to a demand for the execution of the monarch and his wife in 1793? At first, the protesters only wanted to have more members in the Estates General and more say in decisions that influenced the country. Then the National Assembly published the 'Declaration of the Rights of Man', which took away the power of the church and the nobility, but kept the monarchy.

FLIGHT TO VARENNES

King Louis, Marie Antoinette and their children quickly put on their disguises and bundled into the carriage that waited outside. They had to hurry before the guards returned. The family were dressed as Russians with Louis as their servant. They left the luxury of their life in Paris and nervously travelled towards Austria, to be helped by the queen's brother, the emperor of Austria. Here they could plan an invasion and overthrow these trouble makers. Stopping at an inn in a small village 50 kilometres (30 miles) from the border, their disguise was revealed. The local postmaster recognised Louis from a 50 livre banknote (livre was the currency at the time). Their hopes were dashed. At the nearby village of Varennes, Louis was stopped and forced to admit his disguise. On the journey back to Paris, guarded and under arrest, the royal family did not know what to expect. Would the people trust Louis? Already he could hear crowds shouting 'Louis the False' and see them spitting at the carriage as it passed by. Strangely, when Louis' carriage reached Paris, the crowd looked on in silence.

SOURCE 1

This contemporary cartoon of the royal family shows them being returned to Paris on a cart like animals going to the market. The caption read 'The family of pigs is brought back to the pigsty'.

Fact File: What happened 1789–92?

- In 1789 the National Assembly produce the 'Declaration of the Rights of Man', removing the power of the nobles and the church. Any opponents of their ideas are imprisoned.
- In June 1791 the king and queen try to escape to Austria, but are arrested and brought back to Paris. The new Constitution says that Louis XVI is king of the French but not king of France. He cannot make decisions alone.
- In April 1792, France declares war on Austria as rumours of invasion spread. Austrian and Prussian armies invade and crowds riot in Paris. Anyone opposed to the Constitution or in favour of the monarchy is killed. This includes priests who are thought to be traitors.
- In August 1792 angry crowds attack the Tuileries Palace in Paris, searching for Louis and calling him a traitor. Over 600 guards are killed. There are massacres all over France as law and order is lost.
- The king and queen are imprisoned as tension increases – their power is removed and France is declared a republic (a country ruled without a monarchy). In September 1792 a group called the National Convention is set up, replacing the National Assembly. From now on the balance of power is in the hands of the Third Estate.
- The king, seen as a threat to the republic, is put on trial and found guilty of thirty charges of high treason. Out of 693 members, 374 vote for his execution. He is executed by guillotine. His last words are believed to be, 'I die innocent'.

SOURCE 2

The nation can never feel safe with a man who organises a secret escape and gets a false passport. He then travels to a border area, full of traitors and deserters, and plans to return to our country with an army to bring back his strict laws. What kind of job must this be ... where you do not have to have experience nor ability. You can get the job by chance of your birth and be an idiot or a madman. The 30 million livres that it costs to keep a king in luxury gives us a very easy way of reducing taxes.

This is an extract from an article written in July 1791 by Tom Paine, a British sympathiser of the Revolution. After being charged with treason in Britain, he fled to France to give the Revolution his support.

WAR WITH AUSTRIA

Marie Antoinette's brother, Leopold, had threatened to get together an army from several countries to help restore Louis' control over France. Leopold was powerful as emperor of Austria, but he had not really intended to fight. However, when Louis and Marie Antoinette were arrested, he became worried about them.

Then events in France forced his hand. Rumours of an Austrian invasion became so strong that the revolutionaries actually declared war on Austria. As a result, the Austrians had to attack.

Louis disagreed with the war and was declared a traitor who did not protect his own country from invasion. As the Austrian army, along with troops from Prussia, got nearer to Paris, the crowds went wild with panic. In September 1792 revolutionaries rioted in Paris and killed over 1400 prisoners, thinking they might be supporters of the Austrian invasion and enemies of the revolution. These murders became known as the 'September massacres'.

SOURCE 3

Like everybody else, I was shaking with terror for fear that Royalists would escape from prison to murder us. While shuddering with horror, we thought of the killings as more or less justified.

A thirteen-year-old seamstress describes the September massacres.

Many people hoped that war with Austria would return the monarchy and normality to France. Others hoped that it do away with the royal family altogether. Either way it seems to have been a nail in the coffin of Louis XVI, who was executed in 1792.

Question Time

1. What is the difference between being 'king of the French' and 'king of France'?
2. Read Source 2 carefully. Find and explain three different criticisms of Louis XVI.
3. Why do you think that the cartoonist of Source 1 has drawn the royal family as animals?
4. Why do you think that war with Austria made people more violent in their protests?
5. What were the effects of each of the events that we have looked at? Copy and fill in the chart below to find out. In the last column, label each event to show whether the cause is due to:
   a external factors – other people or countries
   b the king's actions
   c the actions of the revolutionaries
   d a combination of all three.

Event	What did people think of Louis?	How likely was his execution?	Type of cause?
The failed flight to Varennes			
War with Austria			
Declaration of the Republic			

WINNING SUPPORT

Revolutionaries were also fighting a war of words and pictures. Newspapers across France spread propaganda against Louis. Cartoons and pictures of the problems of the *ancien régime* were published. One such newspaper was the *Père Duchesne*, which was popular with the more extreme revolutionaries. It was written by Jacques Rene Hébert. He often wrote as if he was a worker and he encouraged the revolutionaries with rude jokes, stories and lots of swearing and slang.

The Convention was demanding freedom of the press so there would be no courts who could challenge what was said as untrue or exaggerated.

SOURCE 4

This cartoon shows a revolutionary wiping his bottom on a papal brief (a message from the Pope). The Pope had criticised the revolutionary government for its treatment of the clergy.

Activity Time

1. Produce a front page edition for the *Père Duchesne* for December 1792, demanding the death penalty for Louis XVI. Remember that you will need to exaggerate and shock your readers. Include a cartoon or some pictures of the king if you can.
2. Sum up all the different reasons for the king's execution in a flow diagram. One example has been started here. Show the impact of each event or factor by writing along your arrows.

Flight to Varennes ➔ *Republic* ➔ *Execution*

DID ALL THE REVOLUTIONARIES WANT THE SAME THINGS?

Make a quick list of what you would expect a revolutionary to be like – think about what jobs they would do or what clothes they would wear, for example. How do your ideas compare with the rest of the class? We have the impression that the French revolutionaries were all male workers from Paris, troublemakers dressed in scruffy clothes. These impressions are actually stereotypes. In fact, there were many different groups of revolutionaries, often with different backgrounds, aims and motives.

THE *SANS CULOTTES*

This is the name given to a group of revolutionaries who hated the idea of a monarchy and equally hated the nobles and the church. They fought against any kind of inequality. They got their name by refusing to wear the breeches or *culottes* worn by the nobility. *Sans* in French means 'without'. They wore baggy trousers and woollen jackets, often in red, white and blue – the revolutionary colours. They wanted all adult men to be given the vote, and wealth and land to be shared out by law. They also wanted to limit food prices, stop wage cuts and improve conditions. They believed that a republic was the future for France. They were prepared to take violent action to get their way. Nobles and anti-revolutionaries had to be killed.

SOURCE 1

This popular Parisian singer shows his support for the *sans culottes* by wearing typical *sans culottes* clothes. The picture was painted by a French artist in 1792.

PROVINCIAL WORKERS AND PEASANTS

Provincial workers and peasants are so called because they lived in the provinces – in towns and villages other than in Paris. They thought that the *sans culottes* were too radical (extreme). Instead, they wanted to remove many of the traditional taxes that were crippling the peasants so badly. They also wanted a fairer legal system and were unhappy with the government's order to join the army. In the Vendée area, peasants were so angry that in 1793 they carried out an armed protest. Peasants also resented the privileges of the nobles as they noticed the gap between the rich and poor getting wider.

MODERATES

Moderates were often deputies in the new Confederation – the new government in Paris. They disagreed with the *sans culottes* and thought that they were too radical. Moderates wanted to keep law and order and protect people's private property. They disagreed with the use of extreme violence.

SOURCE 2

We can be reborn only through bloodshed.

Written by Manon Roland.

SOURCE 3

The Revolution is devouring its own children.

Written by Pierre-Victurnien Vernigand.

SOURCE 4

It will be, it will be, it will be
We'll hang noblemen from the street lights...
Freedom will be ours for ever
We'll put an end to cruel tyrants...

This song was sung on the streets of Paris in 1789.

WHO WERE THE REVOLUTIONARY LEADERS?

Who were the actual leaders of the Revolution? Do they fit the stereotype of desperate Parisian workers? Meet Monsieurs Talleyrand, Danton and Robespierre, Lafayette and Mirabeau, leaders of the Revolution. What jobs do you think they had – factory worker, trader, shopkeeper? Actually, they were all educated and middle class men.

Talleyrand was Bishop of Autun; Danton and Robespierre were both lawyers; Lafayette and Mirabeau were actually noblemen. None of them would be desperate for better wages or working conditions for themselves. We need to find out what their motives were in working for the Revolution in order to answer the question at the beginning of this section. 'Motives' means the reasons that people have for doing something. Just like the different groups of revolutionaries, the leaders themselves had varied motives.

SOURCE 5

The revolutionary leader, Danton. This cartoon from the time suggests that he was master of the guillotine.

SOURCE 6

France needs a war to get rid of the wickedness of tyranny. It needs a war to drive out those who might poison liberty.

Revolutionary propaganda written by Jacques-Pierre Brissot, a leading journalist.

SOURCE 7

He is first tied to a plank of wood ... with cords about the arms, body and legs ... the executioner inserts his [the prisoner's] head ... the axe falls down, and the head, which is off in an instant, is received in a basket ready for that purpose, as is the body in another basket.

A description of execution by guillotine, published in 1793. The guillotine was invented by Dr Joseph Guillotin, to be a quick and painless method of execution (see pages 104–5).

SOURCE 8

Men are born equal and remain free and equal in rights which are liberty, property, security and resistance to oppression.

'Declaration of the Rights of Man' – the focus of the Revolution.

SOURCE 9

Layafette returned home to his native land full of ideas about liberty and republics. He, and others like him, believed in the right of the people to throw out any government that was unfair. Little did he know what would happen as a result of this.

Written in 1805 by Joseph Weber, a relative of Marie Antoinette.

Question Time

1. Sources 1–4 each concern revolutionaries, but which type? See if you can match each source up against one of the three types on page 99. Explain your ideas fully.
2. Write two speech bubbles or phrases for each type of revolutionary. For example, a *sans culottes* might say 'Fight for Freedom'.
3. In groups, look at Sources 5–9. Which sources suggest that **a** revenge for wickedness or **b** the attraction of freedom was the main motive of the revolutionary leaders?
4. Choose one of Sources 5–9 and make up two slogans to match what it says about the purpose of the Revolution.
5. Your slogans were probably quite different from those of some of the other groups in your class. Why do you think that is? Try to give more than one reason why there was more than one version of the leader's motives in your class (try to think about different people, but also different sources).
6. Are the revolutionary leaders the type of people you expected them to be? Discuss this in your groups.

WHY DID ROBESPIERRE LEAD A REIGN OF TERROR?

WHO WAS ROBESPIERRE?

What sort of man does the person in Source 2 seem to be? Is he clever, gentle, friendly? Or murderous, violent and brutal?

This is Maximilien Robespierre, who had trained as a lawyer and had been involved in the Revolution as a member of the National Assembly. He became leader of the National Convention in 1793, and he led the 'Terror' that took place in France between 1793 and 1795.

SOURCE 2

Maximilien Robespierre, leader of the National Convention, painted in the eighteenth century.

WHAT WAS THE TERROR?

All over France, everybody suspected of being an enemy of the Revolution was imprisoned, deported or executed. During Robespierre's time in power, over 14,000 opponents of the Revolution were executed. The fashionable method of death was the guillotine, which came to represent the tremendous power of the revolutionary leaders.

WHY DID THE TERROR HAPPEN?

The leaders of the Revolution felt threatened by royalists and enemies abroad who could overthrow them. France was in a state of chaos. The National Convention could not control the people and peasants were rioting in Paris and in the provinces. The Committee of Public Safety was set up to bring in emergency measures to cope with the crisis. It decided to enforce strict laws and punishments to bring order back to the country.

WHAT ELSE DID ROBESPIERRE DO?

The government led by Robespierre passed laws to fix maximum prices for food and gave possessions of any anti-revolutionaries to the poor. It also changed the calendar as an act of rebellion against the traditional power of the Catholic Church. Year One was 1792 and there were twelve months with new names, each made up of thirty days. Sundays were banned.

SOURCE 3

Jean Baptiste Henry, aged eighteen, a tailor, convicted of sawing down a tree of liberty, executed September, 1793.

Jean Julien, wagoner, sentenced to twelve years' hard labour, took it into his head to cry, 'long live the King', brought back to the tribunal and condemned to death.

François Betrand, aged thirty-seven, convicted of having provided the defenders of the country with sour wine, condemned to death and executed the same day.

Some victims of the Terror, listed in the execution record of 1793.

SOURCE 4

What is our aim? The enjoyment of liberty and equality. Terror is used to achieve that. In a republic there are no citizens other than republicans. The royalists, the traitors, are all enemies.

From a speech by Robespierre.

SOURCE 5

A revolutionary guillotine.

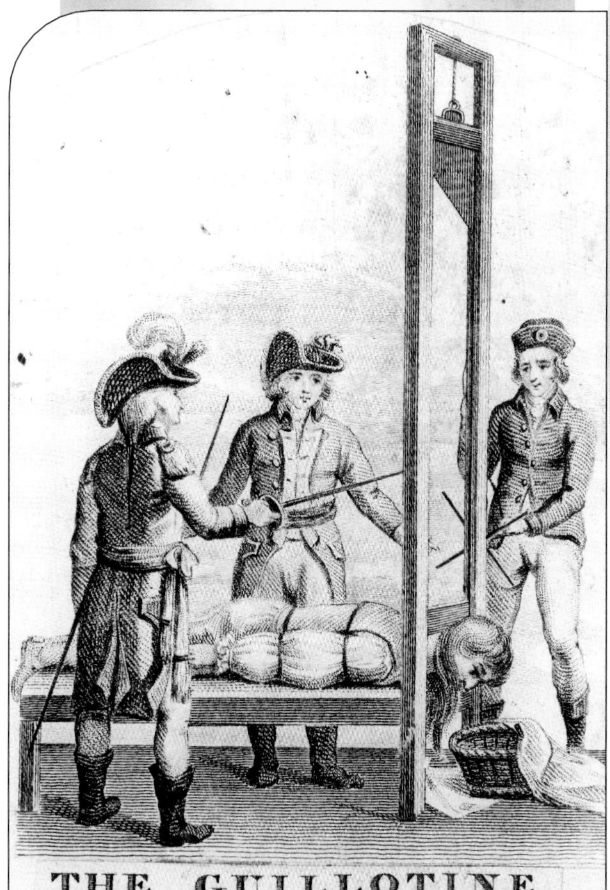

DID ROBESPIERRE DESERVE HIS DEATH?

Robespierre had been known as 'the Incorruptible' (meaning someone who would not take bribes or be unfair). He ended his life being blamed for the Terror. He survived an assassination attempt, then turned a gun towards himself to commit suicide. He survived, only to be executed later by those who plotted against him. The public had turned against the violence of the new government, but some people say that Robespierre was a scapegoat for the Terror. He had actually ordered the deaths of only seventy-two of the thousands of victims of the execution campaign. Many of the other murders were ordered by the Committee of Public Safety, which included over 100 representatives who had power to take any actions necessary to restore order to France.

Question Time

1. Look at Source 2 carefully. What is it that makes Robespierre seem a nice person?
2. Do you think that Robespierre would have approved of the image of him in Source 2?
3. What does the term 'scapegoat' mean?
4. Research into the Jacobins and the Girondins (rival revolutionary groups). Who were they and what did they do?
5. What does the execution list in Source 3 tell us about the Terror?
6. Why do you think Robespierre got so involved in the Revolution and the Terror that followed? Historians disagree about this. Try to think of two different arguments: one which gives a sympathetic reason for his actions and one which is suspicious of his motives.

MAKING LINKS – WAS ROBESPIERRE UNIQUE?

In order to understand fully the impact of Robespierre on France we shall compare him to another revolutionary – in another country, England. Historians disagree about both of them. Can we compare these events and their leaders?

THE ENGLISH REVOLUTION – A REMINDER OF WHAT HAPPENED

Oliver Cromwell led the Parliamentarian forces against King Charles I of England in the Civil Wars between 1642 and 1649. You will have learned about him in Unit 8. He was the son of a landowner and became an MP before the outbreak of the war. He was a talented military leader, respected for his victories at the battles of Marston Moor and Naseby. Cromwell became Lord Protector after the execution of Charles I for treason and made England a republic. He was a strict Puritan but did not let the extremists take over in Parliament. However, he did bring in laws banning festivals, plays and certain sports. He was offered the position of king of England but refused. He died in 1658.

Oliver Cromwell and Maximilien Robespierre – ruthless dictators or dedicated revolutionaries?

Question Time

1. Research Robespierre and Cromwell in more detail.
2. Draw up a chart to compare the two revolutionaries. Use the topics below as headings. Have one column for Robespierre and another for Cromwell.
   - Background
   - Leadership qualities
   - Time in power
   - Aims for the country
   - Popularity with the people
   - Motives
   - Death
   - Reputation

   Are there more similarities than differences? Explain your answer.
3. Why do you think that historians disagree about the role of both of these men?

WHY WAS THERE A REVOLUTION?

Now it is time to answer the 'big' question that we have been investigating. We know that there are few straightforward answers in history, so we have carried out a lot of research to investigate what was happening in France at this time.

Write an entry for a brand new young person's *Internet Encyclopaedia* answering the question, 'Why was there a Revolution in France between 1789 and 1794?' The aim of this encyclopaedia is to help students aged 11–13 understand key events in the past.

- You will need to use words and phrases that students will understand – but don't make them too easy. Include some new key words, too.
- You will also want to include pictures, but these will need captions explaining what they tell us about the 'big' question. Use pictures from this book or from your own research.
- Split up your ideas into different paragraphs and try to argue point by point inside a paragraph. Each point needs a fact or an example as back-up. Use the Key Words box for some ideas, but look up others in your book.
- You may want to make a plan of your ideas first or use a word processor to help you move different ideas around. You could make a list or a spider diagram of each section and include the key words that you want to use.
- Your writing should answer the 'big' question by explaining the answers to several smaller questions! On page 109 there are some paragraph headings and openings to help you. You do not have to use them all.

KEY WORDS

Bastille	The Terror	Three Estates
Louis XVI	Estates General	Marie Antoinette
nobility	clergy	propaganda
Versailles	Tuileries	Varennes
privilege	ancien régime	American Revolution
financial crisis	Liberty, equality, brotherhood	
monarchy	'Declaration of the Rights of Man'	
royalists	moderates	sans culottes

Why was there a Revolution?

Introduction: The French Revolution was…

Causes of the Revolution

There were many different factors behind the French Revolution. One reason was to do with…

Some of the reasons had been present in France for many years…

Other factors were more short term – for example…

There are several different reasons why the Revolution happened. Many of these factors led to others – for example…

What did the revolutionaries want?

Not everybody wanted the same from the Revolution. Some people wanted freedom – for example … Others wanted to improve their lives by…

How the aims of the Revolution changed through time

The point of the Revolution was not actually straightforward. The aims of the revolutionaries changed as they got more and more confident and were swept along by events. For example…

My conclusion about the Revolution is…

Question Time

1. Would you agree that the events of the French Revolution became more and more violent as time went on?
2. Look back through this Unit to see what happened *after* or *during* the Revolution and compare it with events *before* the Revolution. Make a chart like the one below to show what each group lost. Think about how much power, wealth and freedom they had.
3. For the events in France to be called a revolution, they had to be dramatic and result in enormous change. Explain what made the actions in France between 1789 and 1794 revolutionary.
4. Which group do you think lost the most during the Revolution?

	Monarch/royal family	*Clergy*	*Nobles*
What did they lose?			

Unit 11: Industrial changes – action and reaction?

Between 1750 and 1900 Britain changed from being a rural country, where most people earned their living from the land, to being an urban country, where most people lived in towns and earned their living from industry. In 1750, there were about seven million people living in Britain; by 1900, there were thirty-seven million. In 1750, 13 per cent of the population lived in towns; by 1900 this had risen to 87 per cent.

THE GREAT CHANGES

People living in Britain saw huge changes. Factories were built in towns to make production more efficient. Roads were improved, canals were dug and, later, railways were built. People, raw materials and finished goods could be moved easily between ports and factories. Towns grew and grew as people moved from the countryside to the towns to live and work. Fields and meadows were drained and fenced in, the land was fertilised, better crops were grown and animals were bred for their meat, milk or wool. All of these changes were inter-related. They depended on each other. For example, towns couldn't grow unless the countryside could produce more food than was needed for the people living there and could supply the towns, where people weren't producing food. The factories couldn't produce goods unless there was a transport system to get raw materials to them and take the finished goods away.

Sometimes, in some parts of Britain, these changes happened slowly. Sometimes they seemed to be happening very quickly indeed. Everyone in Britain was affected in some way by the great and dramatic changes that were happening in town and country.

WHAT INDUSTRIAL CHANGES HAPPENED LOCALLY?

WHAT HAPPENED WHERE YOU LIVE?

You'll need a starting point, and the best starting point for this kind of investigation is a map. Find a modern map of where you live. Find your school and your home. Find all the features that you know about around your home and school. When were they built? When did your place get to look the way it does? One way of finding out, very roughly, is to get another map, but this time an older map. Try to get hold of a map that is about fifty years old. What changes happened between the two maps? Then go back in time again to an even older map and work out what the changes were. You'll build up a pattern of change over time and this can be the starting point for digging deeper.

LOOKING AT MAPS

Look at this modern map of Settle. Settle is a small market town in North Yorkshire.

SOURCE 1

What can you find on this map that makes Settle the town it is? The market square? Shops? Houses? Schools? A railway? A canal? Factories? A lighthouse? Public parks? Make a list of all the features you can find.

Now look carefully at this map of Settle. It was drawn in 1851.

SOURCE 2

Do exactly the same with this map as you did with the modern one. Make a list of all the features you can find. Now compare the two lists. What changes happened to Settle between 1851 and 2000?

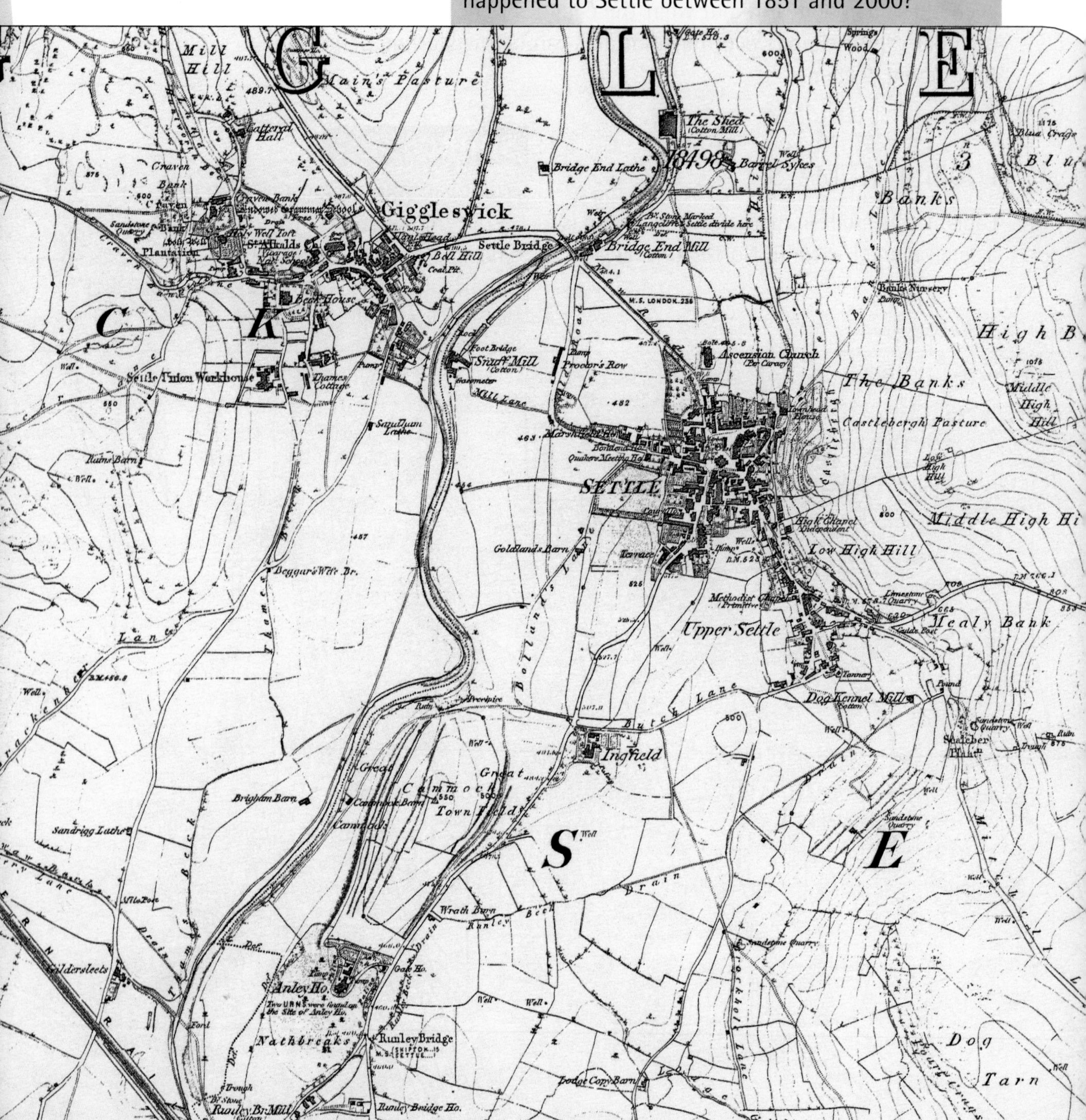

Reproduced from the 1851 1:10,560 Ordnance Survey® map

BRADFORD, WEST YORKSHIRE

Bradford is about 70 kilometres (45 miles) from Settle. They are now two very different places. Settle is a small market town, whereas Bradford is a busy industrial city. But 200 years ago, they weren't so very different.

Look at this map of Bradford. It was drawn in about 1802 by John Johnson.

SOURCE 3

John Johnson's map of Bradford, West Yorkshire, drawn in about 1802.

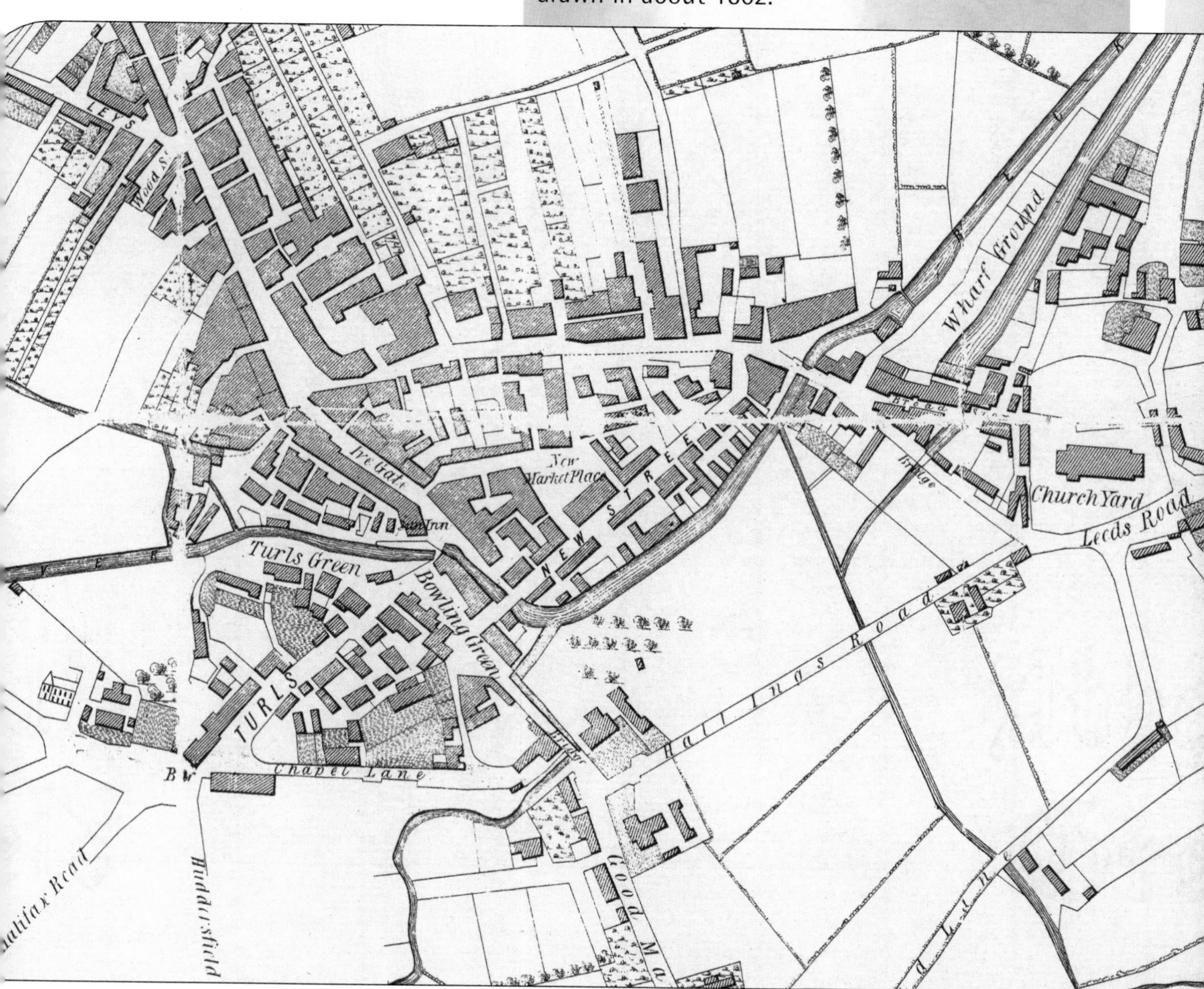

Now look at this map of Bradford, which was drawn just over fifty years later by J. Rapkin. It was drawn to a smaller scale than the map in Source 3.

SOURCE 4

J. Rapkin's map of Bradford, West Yorkshire, drawn in about 1854.

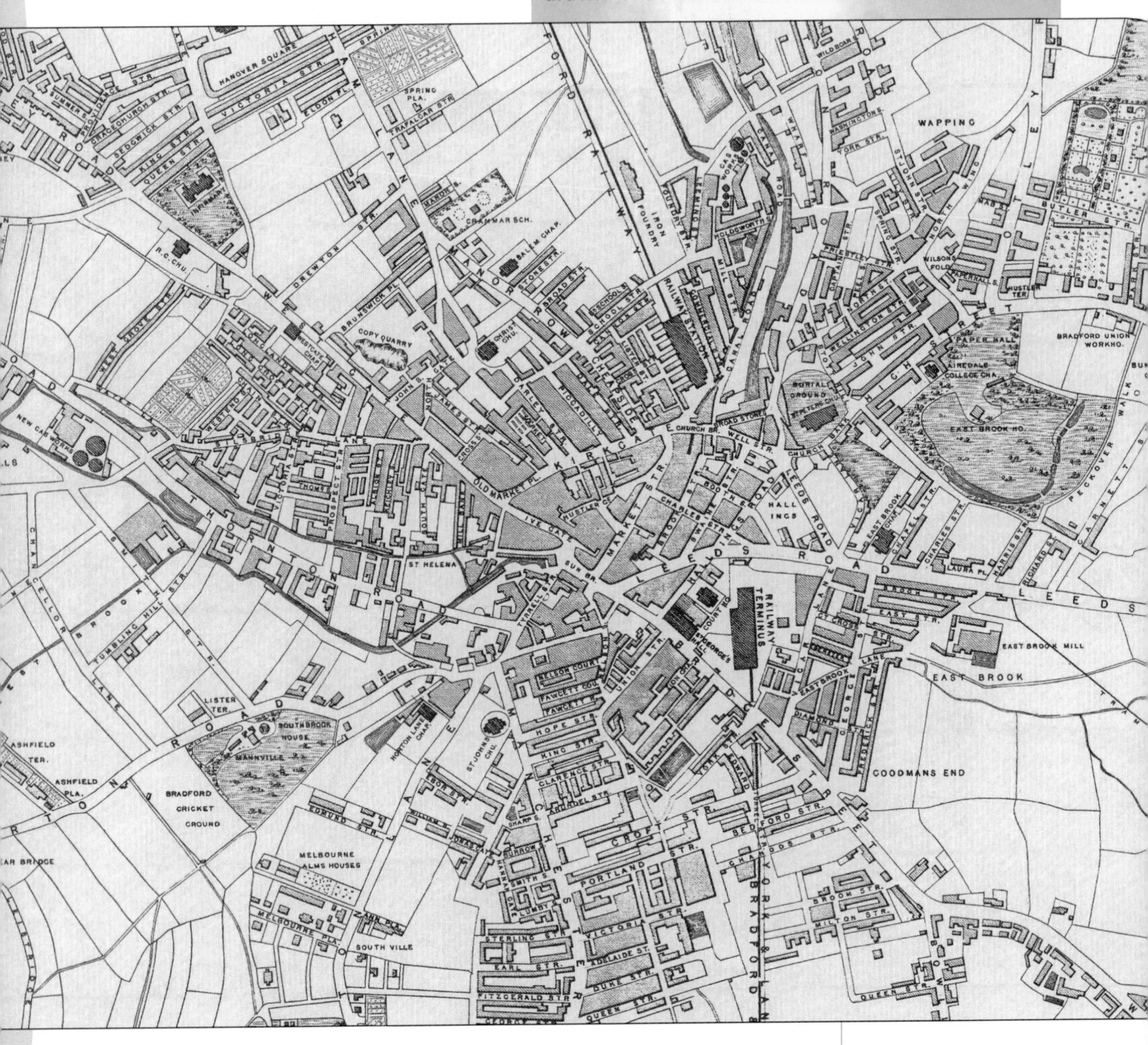

Question Time

1. Look carefully at both maps of Bradford.
For *each* map, make a list of the things that are connected with transport, religion, industry and education.
Now compare your lists.
Which features appear on both lists? Which on the 1802 list only? Which on the 1854 list only?
What sorts of reasons might there be for features being on one list and not the other?
How could you check out whether these reasons are right or not?

2. Find nineteenth century maps of your area and ask the same questions. Have you got the same answers? Did your area change in the nineteenth century as much as Bradford did? Make a flow chart to show the ways in which changes in your local transport, agriculture and industry were linked.

3. Now go back to the 1802 and the 1854 maps of Bradford.
Look at both maps and find the street which was called Kirkgate in 1854. Look at the area north of this street.
What differences are there in the ways in which the land was used in 1802 and 1854?
Can you suggest reasons for this?
Are there any clear changes of land use between the times the maps of your area were drawn?
Why do you think this was?

4. Find Bridge Street on the 1854 map of Bradford. One of the textile mills in this street was owned by John Wood. He would have been a child when the 1802 map was drawn and could have been a grandfather in 1854. Using only the two maps, write down what he might have said to his grandchild about the changes he had seen happen to the centre of Bradford since the time he was a boy.
OR
Write the same sort of account, but relating to the maps of your local area.

LOCAL INDUSTRY: WHAT HAPPENED?

It would be sensible, if you are going to find out about the development of industry in your locality, to focus on just one industry. It may be connected with the transport industry, like the building of a railway or a canal; it may be focused on the production industry, like cotton or pottery; or it may be focused on the agricultural industry, like enclosure or steam-powered farm machinery. You will need to work out the 'big' question you want to ask. This could be something like 'What was it like to be a child worker in a woollen mill?' or 'What happened to the farm workers when the land was enclosed?' Then you will have to find source material and ask 'little' questions that will build up to helping you answer the 'big' one.

THE TEXTILE INDUSTRY

If you were going to look more deeply into the textile industry (usually wool or cotton), you might find one of your local factory owners giving evidence to a Parliamentary Commission. In 1830, Parliament set up a Commission to inquire into children's working conditions in factories. The findings of this inquiry influenced the people who drew up an Act of Parliament that reduced the hours children worked in textile mills.

SOURCE 1

Q *When does your regular day's work begin?*

A *The mills start at six in the morning and end at seven in the evening.*

Q *How many holidays do your workpeople have?*

A *Eight days' holiday throughout the year, at the fairs, Lent, Easter, Whitsuntide and Christmas.*

Q *Explain your rules about charging fines for absence or bad behaviour or to make your workers obedient.*

A *There are no fines. The children under eighteen years of age are allowed one hour per day, during working hours, for attending school, where they are taught reading, writing, arithmetic, sewing or needlework. To make the children obedient, they are sometimes punished by being kept away from school.*

Q *Is corporal punishment allowed?*

A *No.*

Q *Do you have to employ children under twelve years old?*

A *Some work can only be done by children under that age. Their main work is joining the threads as they break in the process of weaving. This requires children with small hands.*

Q *Do you want to say anything about regulating the number of hours that can be worked in a factory?*

A *Ten hours a day working is sufficient for all who are employed in mills; more than this cannot be done without permanent injury to health.*

This extract is taken from the evidence given to the Commission by John Wood, who owned a woollen mill in Bradford.

This sort of evidence tells us what John Wood thought was happening in his woollen mill. Or, perhaps more importantly, it tells us what he wanted the Commission to believe about conditions in his woollen mill. It would be useful if we had some other evidence from someone else connected to the same mill. By good chance, we do.

SOURCE 2

Q *What happens if any children are ill?*
A *We have authority from Mr Wood to send them to Dr Sharp ourselves and Mr Wood pays for it himself.*

Q *Have you any baths in the works?*
A *We have cold and warm baths now on the premises, for use of the workpeople.*

Q *For the children?*
A *For the children and for the men, too, I have used them myself many a time.*

Q *When new workers have been employed for some time, do you notice a change in them?*
A *Yes. They come in rosy-faced and plump and fat. They are generally lively and spirited. After a month or five weeks I can see a falling in their faces and a paleness. They become spiritless and languid.*

Q *Do you use rewards or punishments?*
A *Mr Wood has always allowed a penny a week to every child as a reward if the child does his work well and is obedient. The way I punish the children is this: I have a card and write the crime on it. I make the child stand up in the room, holding the card. If a child has done something worse, I make him walk up and down the room and make every child read his card. If the crime is greater, I make him tell every child in the room what he has done. If the crime is even greater, I make the child pass into the next room and do the same thing there.*

Q *Does this method of punishment keep the children attentive to their work?*
A *In ordinary cases, yes. But in obstinate cases they are beaten.*

Q *Why are children not employed to join broken threads together after the age of fourteen?*
A *They get too big for that sort of work.*

Q *Could people aged more than fourteen do the work if the frames were made higher?*
A *Yes.*

Q *Would there be much difficulty in altering the height of the frame?*
A *The only difficulty would be that we could not afford to pay older children more wages than the younger ones for doing this work.*

Q *What do you think is the most time that a child could work without becoming ill?*
A *I think if they are ever so well treated, they should not work for more than ten hours.*

This is the evidence given to the same Commission about the same mill. This time it is given by John Hall, a man employed as an overseer by John Wood.

Comparing two pieces of evidence like this is very useful as it can point up differences and lead to other avenues of inquiry. As you work through the questions in the 'Question Time' box, think of what other sources you would want to find to help you explore further what working conditions for children were really like in textile mills before 1833.

Question Time

1. According to the evidence, how many hours do children work in John Wood's mill? How could you check to see whether or not this was typical of all textile mills?
2. On which points do John Wood and his overseer, John Hall, agree?
3. Is there anything that John Wood tells us that John Hall doesn't? Is there anything that John Hall tells us that John Wood doesn't?
4. On which points do John Wood and his overseer disagree?
   Why do you think this is?
   Whose account do you believe, and why?
5. Using the evidence of John Wood and John Hall, what were working conditions like in John Wood's woollen mill?
6. How could you check that working conditions for children were like this in all woollen mills?

Now work out how you would present your findings to your class. Would you get together with some other pupils and act out a scene in which John Hall and John Wood show their differences? Or would you mock up an interview of one or both men? Can you think of a better way?

HEAVY INDUSTRY

It may be that in your area there is heavy industry like iron and steel manufacturing, coal mining or ship building. There will probably be a lot of source material to do with specific companies and organisations. Your problem will be sorting it out and using only that which is relevant to your study. Remember always to ask yourself 'Will this help me answer the question I have asked about this industry?' If it won't, discard it. If it will, or you think it will, keep it and work out the sort of questions you would want to ask of the source to turn it into evidence.

SOURCE 3

This picture was published in 1861. It shows part of the Bowling Iron Company in Bradford, West Yorkshire.

Question Time

1. Look carefully at the questions around the picture of the Bowling Iron Works. For each question, work out what kind of sources might give you the answer.
2. The Bowling Iron Works were in Bradford, West Yorkshire. So was John Wood's woollen mill. Which gives you a better idea of industry in Bradford: the picture or the evidence given to the Commission? Which source gives you the most reliable evidence? Why?
3. How would you use the maps of Bradford to tell you more about John Wood's woollen mill and the Bowling Iron Works?
4. If you are asking questions like these about a picture of an industry local to you, try to find the sources and work out the answers.

TRANSPORT

If you live in an area where there is a railway or a canal, you might find records of the canal or railway company. You might find plans made by the railway or the canal engineers. You might find working diaries or photographs. You might find letters from people who wanted to make long and complicated journeys. You might find timetables.

But you might not live anywhere near a canal or a railway. Wherever you live, there will be roads, and you might be lucky enough to come across a document like this:

SOURCE 4

To the worthy Gentlemen, the Commissioners of the Turnpike Road leading from Sparrows Herne to Aylesbury

Thomas Saunders, a poor parishioner of Berkhamsted, having a sickly wife and five children for whom he is scarce able to procure Bread by his utmost Endeavours, humbly prays to be appointed a Gate Keeper to the Turnpike. If he is so happy as to succeed, he will discharge the trust reposed in him with the utmost Diligence and Integrity.

We, whose names are here unto subscribed, do believe Thomas Saunders of Berkhamsted to be a poor, industrious, honest Man with a large family. He has always tried to look after them. We do also believe him to be a proper person to keep the Turnpike Gate for which he now applys to the Commissioners.

Thos Herbert Noyes
John Jeffreys (Rector)
Thos Bland
Thos Egerton
Thos Smart
William Timbrell
John Deene

Robert Potter
Wm Franklin
James Springall
John Stevens
W Johnson
Thomas Cook
Guy Abraham
Thos Wilkinson

This is an application from Thomas Saunders. He wants the Sparrows Herne Turnpike Trust to give him the job of gatekeeper on the turnpike road which ran between Sparrows Hearne, on the Hertfordshire/Middlesex border, and Aylesbury, in Buckinghamshire. It became a turnpike in 1762.

TURNPIKE TRUSTS

Before you can deal with this source, you will need to know something about Turnpike Trusts. Originally, parishes were responsible for looking after their own local roads, but very little was done about main roads. As towns grew and industry developed, the main roads were used more and more, and their surfaces deteriorated. The first real efforts to improve these important roads were made by Turnpike Trusts. A Turnpike Trust was really just a group of important local people, with money to invest, who took over a certain road or length of road. They set up toll-gates, where a gatekeeper collected money from travellers before they could use the road. The money was used to keep the road in good repair, pay a wage to the toll-gatekeeper, provide for the upkeep of the toll-gatekeeper's house, and pay the investors interest on their investment. Thousands of Acts of Parliament were passed in the eighteenth century to allow these Turnpike Trusts (usually the local gentry and businessmen) to collect tolls from road users. Sometimes, as you will see later, these Trusts caused a lot of local resentment.

Question Time

1. Read Thomas Saunders' application (Source 4) carefully. Why did he want the job? How is he trying to convince the Turnpike Trust that he is the right man for the job?
2. The 15 men who signed Thomas' application were probably well-respected local people. How could you find out more about them?
3. Why would it probably be more difficult to find out more about Thomas Saunders? Would there be any way of checking whether what he said about himself was true?
4. Do you think Thomas Saunders would have written this application himself? Could you find out?
5. Why would it be helpful to the members of the Turnpike Trust to have applications for jobs made out like this?

AGRICULTURE

Maybe you live in an agricultural area. Perhaps you can find farming records, maps and plans of farms and field use, lists of animals taken to market and the prices they fetched, nineteenth century invoices for steam reaping and threshing machines and lists of farm hands taken on and the wages paid to them. Here, too, when dealing with a lot of different records, you must be very strict with yourself and only use those sources that will help you answer directly the question you set yourself.

WHAT WAS 'ENCLOSURE'?

Some of the most commonly found agricultural records are to do with enclosure. Landowners needed to make their land more productive in order to supply the growing towns with food and to increase their own profits. They had to make their farming methods more efficient.

They started to buy up the smaller parcels of land worked by villagers. In this way they could join up their land holdings and introduce new farming methods and techniques. If people could not agree about what should be done, the larger landowners could get Parliament to pass an Enclosure Act for them which would force the redistribution of land. Between 1750 and 1820, there were around 4000 Enclosure Acts.

WHAT HAPPENED ON ENCLOSED LAND?

The landowner put hedges and fences round his enclosed fields. He could now try out new methods and increase his productivity. He might try out the Norfolk four course rotation of crops, pioneered by Viscount Townshend, to enrich his land and improve his yield of barley or oats; he might try selective breeding to produce high quality sheep meat or cows that would yield a lot of milk; he could drain his land using the new earthenware drains or invest in mechanical seed drills and horse-drawn hoes.

DID THIS SORT OF ENCLOSURE HAPPEN EVERYWHERE?

No! Not everywhere was enclosed at the same time and in the same way. These eighteenth and nineteenth century enclosures happened mainly in the Midlands, East Anglia and the counties north of the River Thames. Most of the farming land in the south of England was enclosed in Tudor times or earlier. In the north of England, enclosure often involved only the enclosure of common land and waste land. Common land was often enclosed in the Midlands and south, too, but along with the great open fields.

If you live in an area where land was enclosed in the eighteenth or nineteenth century, you may be lucky enough to find an enclosure map like the one in Source 6.

SOURCE 5

The law is strict on man or woman
Who steals a goose from off a common,
But lets the greater felon loose
Who steals the common from the goose.

Enclosing common land really hit the poorer villagers. For hundreds of years, villagers had had the right to use this land in their parishes as they wished. Villagers who couldn't afford to have any land of their own to work, could use the common land to run a few hens and geese, a cow or two and some sheep. They collected firewood from the woodland and let their pigs root around in the coppices. Now this was all gone. Rhymes like this one were often heard.

SOURCE 6

Enclosure map of Aston Blank, Gloucestershire, in 1752 showing what it was like before and after enclosure.

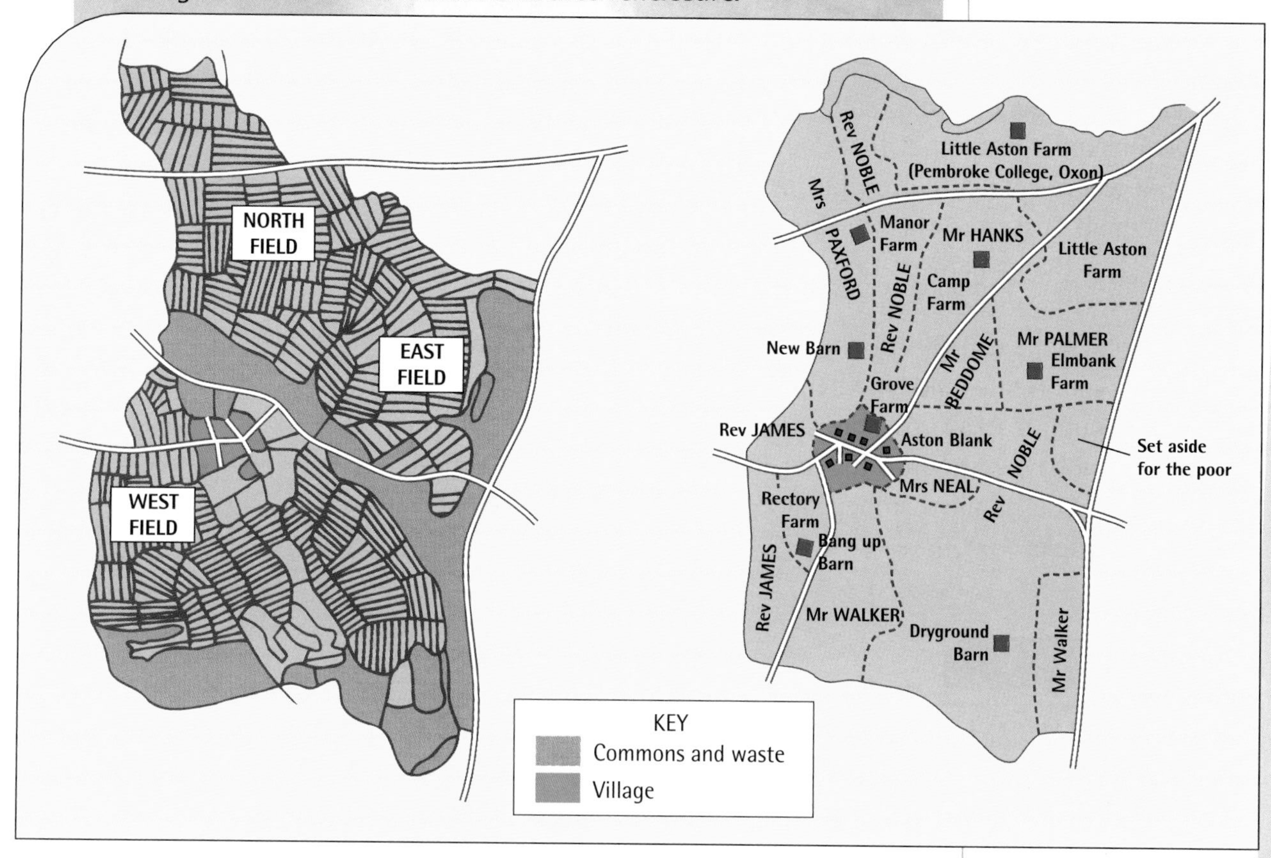

THE NATIONAL PICTURE: WHAT HAPPENED?

You have been looking at a tiny piece of the jigsaw that is the real story of the great changes in industry, agriculture and transport in the eighteenth and nineteenth centuries. Use your textbook, your school and local library and the Internet to find out what the national changes were.

Question Time

1. Look very carefully at Source 6, the enclosure map of Aston Blank. Who were the landowners? Who was the biggest landowner?
2. Now look at the map of Aston Blank before enclosure and compare it with that of Aston Blank after enclosure.
   How would a villager have described the differences between Aston Blank before and after enclosure?
3. How could you find out what changes the landowners introduced and whether or not they were successful?
4. Did your locality follow the national trend, or buck it?
   Can you suggest why?
5. Write an account explaining the differences between your local study and the national picture.

DID EVERYONE AGREE WITH THE INDUSTRIAL CHANGES?

A lot of people felt very threatened by the changes that were happening around them. Many people were frightened that the new machines would put them out of work. A mechanised loom could weave wool or cotton far faster than one person working a handloom. A steam-powered threshing machine could thresh corn far faster than a gang of farm labourers using wooden flails. There was no social security, redundancy pay or unemployment benefits in the eighteenth and nineteenth centuries. The parish in which you lived would give help (called relief), but this would be just enough to keep you and your family from starving and you might all have to go into the local workhouse. This meant that you and your family had become paupers, a horrific prospect for most people.

SOURCE 1

1797	*1800*	*1805*	*1810*	*1816*	*1820*	*1824*	*1830*
30s	*25s*	*25s*	*19s*	*12s*	*9s*	*8s 6d*	*5s 6d*

These statistics show what happened to the wages of one handloom weaver living in Bolton, Lancashire. A young man in 1797, he would certainly be facing old age as a pauper.

NED LUDD

Hundreds of workers took out their anger on the machines themselves. Organised gangs broke into mills and factories and simply smashed the machinery that was taking away their livelihoods. They attacked at night and in secret. They swore oaths of loyalty to each other, kept their weapons hidden, and drilled, unseen, in the hills and quiet valleys around the mill towns. Luddites were usually skilled workers who picked out specific targets. Often, gangs would leave a message in the wrecked machines and the message was always signed 'Ned Ludd'. This is why the machine-breakers were called 'Luddites'. No one knows whether there really was just one leader, or whether the different groups of Luddites were working more or less independently. But it was certainly enough to frighten the authorities into believing that there was a revolutionary movement afoot.

SOURCE 2

Which area of Britain?	*Which industry?*	*What did the Luddites do?*
Nottinghamshire and Derbyshire	*Hosiery and lace*	*Smashed weaving frames used to make stockings and lace*
Lancashire	*Cotton*	*Attacked spinning jennies, water frames and carding engines*
Somerset, Devon and Cornwall	*Wool*	*Destroyed gig mills and shearing frames*
Yorkshire	*Wool*	*Destroyed gig mills and shearing frames. Murdered William Horsfall, a manufacturer from Huddersfield.*

This table shows the main areas of Luddite activity.

WHAT DID THE AUTHORITIES DO?

Luddites had been breaking machinery since the 1770s. However, machine-breaking reached a peak in 1812. This was a crisis year in the wars with France: trade was at an all time low, many businesses had crashed and the price of bread was at an all time high. The government was frightened that a revolution would break out, similar to the one in France in 1789. There, the government had been overturned and the king beheaded. Quickly, Parliament agreed to a law which said that judges could pass the death penalty on anyone found guilty of machine-breaking.

SOURCE 3

This is a still from a modern film about the Luddites.

REBECCA

Farmers in Wales were in difficulties. Oats and barley, sheep and pigs were fetching low prices at market. Men were laid off and bread prices began to rise. Having to pay tolls at the gates on turnpike roads was, for many, the final straw.

Between 1839 and 1842, gangs of angry people attacked the toll gates. They pulled the gates down and burned them. Sometimes, just for good measure, they burned down the toll-gatekeeper's house as well.

What made these rioters different was that the leader was always dressed up as a woman. The woman was called 'Rebecca' and no one knows why. Some say it was because the first leader borrowed the clothes from a woman called Rebecca; others say it was because of a verse in the Bible (see Source 7).

Unlike 'Ned Ludd' and 'Captain Swing', it seems possible that 'Rebecca' was a real person. Many people think that 'Rebecca' was Hugh Williams, a respected Welsh lawyer, magistrate and landowner. He defended many Rebecca rioters when they came up before the magistrates and, in 1843, he agreed to draw up a petition to Queen Victoria explaining the causes of the riots. What is more, he is supposed to have told a friend that he was the 'undiscovered leader' of the Rebecca movement. But nobody really knows for sure!

SOURCE 7

And they blessed Rebecca and said unto her, 'Thou art our sister. Be thou the mother of thousands of millions, and let thy seed possess the gates of those that hate thee.'

This extract from the Bible comes from Genesis XXIV, verse 60.

a Norfolk farm labourer

a Lincolnshire gamekeeper

a Yorkshire woolcomber

WHAT DID THE AUTHORITIES DO?

It was difficult to catch the Rebecca rioters. Mothers and sisters, wives and husbands, fathers and sons, kept secret what they knew about the identity of the rioters. When men and women accused of rioting came up before the magistrates, they were often given light sentences or found 'not guilty' because some magistrates, like Hugh Williams, sympathised with them. However, 1842 was a particularly bad year for Rebecca rioting, and the authorities in Wales were forced to ask for help. Local soldiers quickly restored law and order. The two ringleaders, Dai'r Cantwr and Shoni Sgubor Fawr, were caught. At their trial they pleaded guilty and were sentenced to transportation.

Question Time

1. You are going to compare Ned Ludd, Captain Swing and Rebecca.
   Draw a grid for each 'person', but first work out the categories you are going to use to make the comparison. It might be sensible to use 'Where were the protests?' 'What were the protests about?' 'Who was protesting?' and 'What happened?'' You might want to think of more or different headings and you might want to put them in a different order.
   When you have drawn your grid, sort through the information on Ned Ludd, Captain Swing and Rebecca and fill in your grid.
2. What were the differences, and what were the similarities, between these three groups of rioters?
3. Do you think Ned Ludd, Captain Swing and Rebecca really did exist? If they did, why were these leaders never caught? If they didn't exist, why did the rioters invent them?
4. Look back to Source 4. Why do you think people sang protest songs in the eighteenth and nineteenth centuries? Do people sing protest songs nowadays? Make up your own Luddite, Swing or Rebecca protest song. (It might help you to listen to some late twentieth century protest songs by Bob Dylan, Joan Baez or Billy Bragg first.)

SHOULD THEY PROTEST?

Choose one of the seven 'person cards' on these two pages. Each one of them might have joined one of the protest movements you have been finding out about. Work out, for your 'person', what the advantages and disadvantages of protest would have been. Before you do this, you will have to look back through this section at the three different protest movements and you might need to do a little research into the 'plight' of the occupations below.

a Nottinghamshire framework knitter

a Lancashire handloom weaver

a Pembrokeshire farmer

a Sussex shepherd

HOW INDUSTRIALISED WAS BRITAIN BY 1850?

Look carefully at the images of Britain in Sources 1–5. As you do, begin to work out how industrialised Britain was by the middle of the nineteenth century.

SOURCE 1

More and more towns, throughout the nineteenth century, published street directories which listed all the shops and different trades that were carried out there. Here you can read a page from a Bradford, West Yorkshire, directory and a page from a Tring, Hertfordshire, directory.

234 *Bradford Directory* *Classification of Trades* 2.

Ramsden Thomas, High street, Great Horton
Thompson Thomas, High street, Great Horton
Thornton Benjamin, High street
Whittaker William, Dudley Hill, Bowling

Whitesmiths.
(See also Locksmiths and Bellhangers)

Campbell Richard, Reform street, Westgate
Cowman William, Mawson street, Thornton road
Dixon & Byrne, 77 Market street
Dove Thomas Pashley, 13 Ivegate
Fell James, 17 Nelson street
Hargreaves Charles & Michael, Cropper lane, Westgate
Hargreaves Peter, Ship Alley, Well street
Hill John & Co., 8 Cheapside
Holdsworth & Raistrick, Croft street, Manchester road
Martin Benjamin, Manchester road
Pearson John, Albion Yard, Ivegate
Rhodes William, 99 Westgate
Richardson Henry, 5 Bedford street, Bridge street
Smith Thomas, Bowergate, Tyrrel street
Woodhead Joseph, Keighley street, Silsbridge lane
Wyrill Frances, 8 Westgate (*see advertisement*)

Wine and Spirit Merchants.
Marked thus ‡ are British Wine Dealers Only.

‡ Bartle Timothy, 26 and 28 Market street
‡ Binns Eleanor, 25 Hustlergate
‡ Britton Robert, 10 Bridge street
Brumfit Charles, 27 Bermondsey (*see advertisement*)
‡ Carter John, 124 Manchester road
‡ Cockshott William, 32 Westgate
‡ Crowther John, 17 Market street
Greaves John, Tyrrel street
‡ Hargreaves Sarah, 30 Kirkgate
Laycock Peter (executors of), top of Ivegate
Lee Hannah, 11 Westgate
Popplewell Benjamin Briggs, 43 Market street
Richardson Francis, (late Wells), Westgate
‡ Smith Mary, 88 Westgate
Thompson Ann and Mary, 17 North Parade
‡ Walker Rachel, 69 Market street
Wright James, Hustlergate & Ivegate

Wire Drawers, and Window Blind, &c. Makers.

Bateman Daniel & Sons, Folly Hall, Wibsey
Rhodes Henry & Charles, Old Post Office Buildings, Bridge street
Rhodes William, 11 Northgate

Wool-Combers – (Machine)

Collier John, Duckitt's Mill, Nelson street, Bridge street
Collier William & Co., Duckitt's Mill, Nelson street
Donisthorpe & Co., Thornton road
Lister Samuel Cunliffe (and combing machine patentee), Mill street, Canal road
Todd David, Albion Works, Thornton road
Todd John & Son, Duckitt's Mill, Nelson street

Wool-Comb Makers.

Bates Miles, Silsbridge lane
Binns William, Bolton road
Clark James, Southgate
Crook William, Fawcett's Court, Nelson street
Day John, 3 Thomas street, Manchester road
Hammond Joseph, Ship Abbey, Well street
Smith & Speed, Westbrook terrace, Thornton road
Waddington William, Albion street, Silsbridge lane

Woollen Cloth Manufacturers.

Coates Henry, Bradford Moor
Coates James, Bradford Moor
Hudson George, Bradford Moor
Mirfield John, Bradford Moor
Roberts William, Bradford Moor
Wilcock Bradley & Co., Union Mill, Shipley
Wilcock George, Windhill, Idle
Wilcock Joseph (and wool dealer), Windhill, Idle

Woollen Drapers.

Bell & Prest, Tyrrel street
Brook, Gant & Co., 10 Westgate
Brown & Muff, 54 Market street
Chapman & Co., 26 Kirkgate
Dixon & Masser, 8 Bridge street
Farrar & Gillham, 20 Kirkgate
Hall Francis Stuart, 10 Manchester road
Hindle Thomas, 23 Darley street
Hunter John, 2 Market street
Hunter Thomas, 4 Westgate
Longfield William & Co., 30A Kirkgate
Milner Joshua, 3 Bridge street
Monies James & Co., 30 Kirkgate and 2 Exchange street
Moses & Son, 19 Bridge street
Ogden Michael & Co., 29 Kirkgate
Parkinson & Clark, 27 Kirkgate
Storey & Brook, 37 Kirkgate

Woollen Flock Dealers.
See Cabinet Makers, & also Upholster

Woolstaplers.
Marked thus * are also Foreign Wool Dealers
(See likewise Agents – Commission W and Top.)

*Adamson John & Son, Well street
Adcock John & Son, 60 Bridge stre
*Aked & Robertshaw, Cheapside
Aked Thomas, Brook street
Anderton John Ashworth, Hardcast lane, Well street
*Atkinson John, Cheapside
Aykroyd Jonathan & Son, Swaine street
Baines Thomas, Swaine street
Barker James, 38 Cheapside
Barrans James, Hustler's Buildings Market street
Bates Joshua, 23 Well street
Beanland Joseph, 16 Union street, Bridge street
Beaver William, 13 Cheapside
Bingham George, 20 Balm street a 9 Bolton road
*Booker Robert Alfred, Swaine str
Bottoms James, Back Tyrrel street
Brown Joseph, Hustler's Buildings Market street
Brown Matthew, Cheapside
Buck Bolland, 14 Cheapside
Buck & Holmes, 1 Exchange stree Duke street
Butterfield George, Swaine street
*Butterfield John & Son, Swaine st

CANVASS MANUFACTURERS

Cato William, Akeman st
Cutler George, Frogmore end
Olney Daniel, Dunsley
Olney William, Akeman st

CARPENTERS

Clark Thomas, Wilstone
Griffin William, Market st
Higgs William, Aylesbury road
Honour James, Aldbury
Honour Job, Frogmore end
Jones Garnett, Market st
Osborn John, Frogmore end
Stangroom Augustus, Long Marston
Williams Moses, Frogmore end

COAL DEALERS

Clark Thomas, Wilstone
Grover Wm. and Son, Gamnel wharf
Hanshaw James, Dunsley
Landon Thomas, Cow Roast wharf

COOPERS

Brinkman William, Market st
Rogers Joseph, Market st

CORN DEALER

Cato Sarah, Frogmore end
Grace Carter, Akeman st
Grover Thomas, New mill
Putnam Thomas, Frogmore end

FIRE, &c. OFFICE AGENTS

ALLIANCE, John Rolfe Glenister and Son, Market st
ATLAS, Henry Pattison, Market st
BRITANNIA, Geo. Lockton Faithful, Market st
COUNTY, Thos. Elliman, Market st
MEDICAL AND CLERICAL, Jno. Chapman, Market st
NORWICH UNION, Jno. Philbey, Market st
ROYAL EXCHANGE, Knight and Andrews, Market st
SUN, William Brown, Market st

GROCERS & TEA DEALERS

(See also Shopkeepers, &c.)

Butcher Thomas and Son, Market st
Norris James, Market st
Tompkins, Williams, Market st
Warcup Charles, Aylesbury rd
Wood Jas. (&oil&colourman), Market st

HAIR DRESSERS

Ludgate Thomas, Market st
Norris Thomas, Market st

HATTERS

Boyd Robert, Market st
Elliman Mary and Son, Market st
Elliman Thomas, Market st

HOP MERCHANTS

Butcher Thomas and Son, Market st
Norris James, Market st

INNS

Bell, Thos. Christmas, Market st
Green Man, Jane Tompkins, Market st
Harcourt Arms (and posting house), Samuel Brown, Tring station
Plough (and posting house), William Kingsley, Market st
Rose & Crown (& posting house and excise office), Timothy Northwood, Market st

IRONMONGERS

Clement Thos. and John (and watch makers), Market st
Limbrey John (and coppersmith and brazier), Market st
Rogers Joseph, Market st
Tompkins Wm. (& brazier), Market st

LINEN AND WOOLLEN DRAPERS

Elliman Mary and Son, Market st
Elliman Thomas, Market st

MALTSTERS

Brown John, Market st
Grace Carter, Akeman st

MILLERS

Grover James, Goldfield, nea. Tring
Grover Wm. and Son, Gamnel wharf

MILLINERS AND DRESS MAKERS

Clement Ann, Akeman st
Hanshaw Maria, Dunsley
Hinton Eliz. and Mary, Market st

PLUMBERS, PAINTERS AND GLAZIERS

Knight and Andrews, Market st
Philbey Charles, Akeman st
Philbey John, Market st

ROPE AND TWINE MAKERS

Ashby Robert, Market st
Bull James, Market st
Sutton Mary, Market st

SADDLERS AND HARNESS MAKERS

Ashby Robert, Market st
Bull James, Market st
Prouse William, Market st
Sutton Mary, Market st

SHOPKEEPERS & DEALERS IN GROCERIES & SUNDRIES

Adams John, Frogmore end
Atkins Thomas, Wigginton
Austin Beatrice, Akeman st
Austin Elizabeth, Akeman st
Bavin Thomas, Aldbury
Bransom James, Akeman st
Clark Thomas, Wilstone
Fleet Thomas, Akeman st
Foskett John, Frogmore end
Meade Elizabeth, Long Marston
Missenden Hannah (& seed dealer), Frogmore end
Page Jesse, Akeman st
Philbey Joseph, Wilstone
Read Richard, Long Marston
Rich Sarah, Market st
Rodwell James, Wilstone
Row Fanny, Akeman st
Short Humphrey, Aldbury
Springwell Thomas, Brook end
Tompkins Mary, Market st
Walter Thomas, Wilstone
Ware Jonathan, Akeman st

SILK THROWSTERS

Evans David & Co., Tring mills, Brook end, and 121 Cheapside, *London*

STRAW HAT MANUFACTURERS

Bailey Susan, Market st
Cheshire Jane, Akeman st
Clement Ann, Akeman st
Griffin Mary, Market st
Kindell Sarah, Market st
Moulder Elizabeth, Market st
Springhall Hannah, Market st

STRAW PLAT DEALERS

Amsden Thomas, Market st
Archer James, Market st
Fleet Thomas, Akeman st
Hall John, Aldbury
Rodwell James, Wilstone
Rodwell Thomas, Wilstone
Short Joseph, Akeman st
Smith George, Dunsley
West Samuel, Akeman st

SURGEONS

Dewsbury Peter Richard, Market st
Moody Robt. Jeninges, Frogmore hse
Pope Edward, Market st

SURVEYORS

Brown William, Market st
Glenister John Rolfe & Son, Market st

TAILORS

Brittain Jesse, Akeman st
Cosier John, Frogmore end
Dancer James, Wilstone
Elliman Mary and Son, Market st
Elliman Thomas, Market st
Hill George, Aylesbury road
Prentice Hy. (& clothes dealer), Aldbury
Smith Edward, Akeman st

TALLOW CHANDLERS

Butcher Thos. and Son, Market st

TAVERNS & PUBLIC HOUSES

Cow Roast, Thos. Landon, Cow Roast wharf
Crown, John Nash, Long Marston
George, Thomas Clarke, Fr
Greyhound, Mary Elliot, Aldbury
Half Moon, Jos. & Jas. Clark, Wilstone
Queen's Arms, John Price, near Gamnel wharf
Queen's Head, James Clark, Long Marston
Robin Hood, Ann Tompkins, Dunsley
Royal Oak, William Cato, Akeman st
Trooper, Ann Hall, Aldbury
White Hart, Jonathan Cox, Long Marston

TURNERS

Austin James, Akeman st
Page Jesse, Akeman st
Tompkins John, Aylesbury road

WHARFINGERS

Grover Wm. & Son, Gamnel wharf
Landon Thomas, Cow Roast wharf

WHEELWRIGHTS

Crawley William, Akeman st
Griffin Wm. (& gig maker), Market st
Montague Harley, Long Marston
Newman Thomas, Wilstone
Richardson Thomas, Aldbury

WINE & SPIRIT MERCHANT

Brown John, Market st

Miscellaneous

Beal William Henry, timber merchant, Aylesbury road
Brown John, dyer, Akeman st
Chapman John, chymist & druggist, Market st
Edwin Edmumd, confectioner, Market st
Gower William, fellmonger and parchment maker, Frogmore end
Holland Henry, engineer, Aylesbury road
Norris Thomas, fruiterer, Market st
Osborn Thomas, hay dealer, Aldbury
Warcap Charles, dealer in china curiosities, Aylesbury road
Webb Paul, basket maker, Frogmore end

SOURCE 2

This 1860s version of a threshing machine ran at eight horse-power and was used to separate seed-corn from straw.

SOURCE 3

As the railway network grew, people became much more mobile.

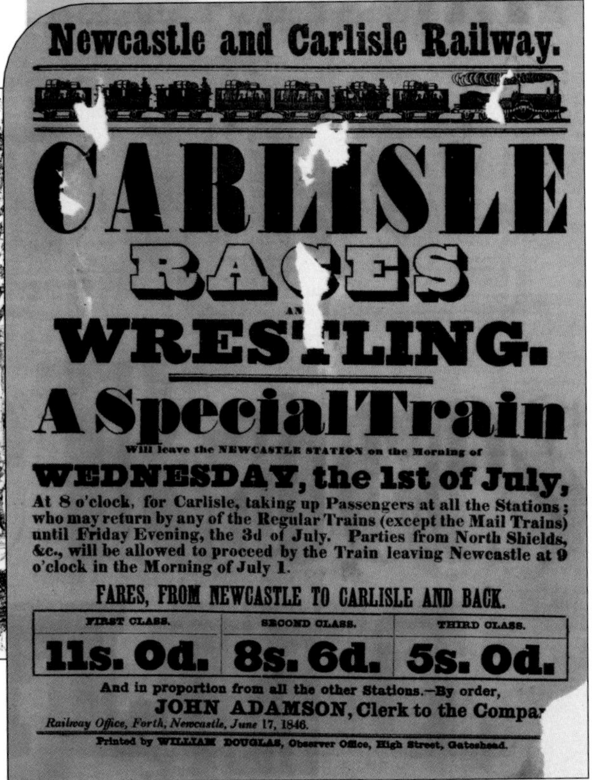

Newcastle and Carlisle Railway.

CARLISLE

RACES

AN

WRESTLING.

A Special Train

Will leave the NEWCASTLE STATION on the Morning of

WEDNESDAY, the 1st of July,

At 8 o'clock, for Carlisle, taking up Passengers at all the Stations; who may return by any of the Regular Trains (except the Mail Trains) until Friday Evening, the 3d of July. Parties from North Shields, &c., will be allowed to proceed by the Train leaving Newcastle at 9 o'clock in the Morning of July 1.

FARES, FROM NEWCASTLE TO CARLISLE AND BACK.

FIRST CLASS.	SECOND CLASS.	THIRD CLASS.
11s. 0d.	8s. 6d.	5s. 0d.

And in proportion from all the other Stations.—By order,

JOHN ADAMSON, Clerk to the Compa

Railway Office, Forth, Newcastle, June 17, 1846.

Printed by WILLIAM DOUGLAS, Observer Office, High Street, Gateshead.

SOURCE 4

In the mid-nineteenth century there were thousands of casual workers in Britain. This engraving is called *The Old Chair Mender* and you can see him weaving a new seat for the chair the woman has given him.

SOURCE 5

This engraving of workers in an iron foundry at Poplar, London, was printed in *The Illustrated London News* in 1863.

SOURCE 6

The youngest children are called trappers. The age of these children varies from five to ten years old. Their duty consists in sitting in a little hole, scooped out for them in the side of the gates behind each door where they sit with a string in their hands attached to the door, and pull it immediately they hear the wagons close by. The moment the wagons have passed, they let the door fall to, which it does of its own weight. They are in the pit the whole time it is worked, often about twelve hours a day. They sit in the dark. They are allowed no light but sometimes a good natured collier will give them a little bit of a candle as a treat.

In 1842, a Parliamentary Commission inquired into working conditions in British mines. This is part of their report.

SOURCE 7

It was a town of red brick, or brick that would have been red if the smoke and ashes had allowed it; but as matters stood it was a town of unnatural red and black like the painted face of a savage. It was a town of machinery and tall chimneys. It had a black canal in it and a river that ran purple with ill-smelling dye, and vast piles of building full of windows where there was a rattling and a trembling all day long, and where the piston of the steam engine worked monotonously up and down like the head of an elephant in a state of melancholy madness.

In 1854, Charles Dickens wrote a novel called *Hard Times*. In it, he described an imaginary town called 'Coketown'. This is part of what he wrote.

Remember that you began this Unit by looking at three main areas of change: transport, agriculture and industry. Now sort Sources 1-7 under these three headings. You should find that some sources come under more than one heading. For each source, say what it tells you about how industrialised Britain was around the middle of the nineteenth century.

For each source, use your own knowledge to say whether you think the source is likely to be accurate.

Do you think you have enough evidence here to reach a sound conclusion to the question: 'How far had Britain become an industrial country by the mid-nineteenth century?

Question Time

Now choose one area (transport, agriculture or industry) and answer this question: Industrialising Britain: how did people act and react? Use any or all of the sources in this Unit as well as the information in the text. Make your answer short and snappy: don't write out the Unit! Do remember to give the evidence which backs up your conclusions.

Unit 12: Snapshot 1900 – what was British middle-class life like?

WHAT THIS UNIT IS ABOUT

In this Unit, we are going to look at middle-class family life in Britain in 1900. Because so many different sorts of people made up the 'middle class', and because their lives were different in different parts of Britain, it's impossible to say 'This is what it was like for everyone'. So we are here going to look at one area of one British town, where middle-class people lived in 1900. We have chosen the Oldfield Park area of Bath, in Avon.

Some of you may want to look at your own local area. Suggestions as to how you could do this are included at the end of this Unit. But meanwhile, let's find out who the middle class were.

WHO WERE THE MIDDLE CLASS?

The Victorians defined the middle class as 'those who do not have to work with their hands' and the upper class (the aristocracy or gentry) as 'those who do not have to work'.

Question Time

Look at the twelve jobs that people could have done in 1900.

1. Who is in the upper class?
2. Who is in the middle class?
3. Who is in the working class?
4. Now explain how you worked it out.

a teacher

a railway guard

a shop assistant

Did you get it right? You should have found two members of the upper class, six from the middle class and four from the working class.

Now look at these occupations.

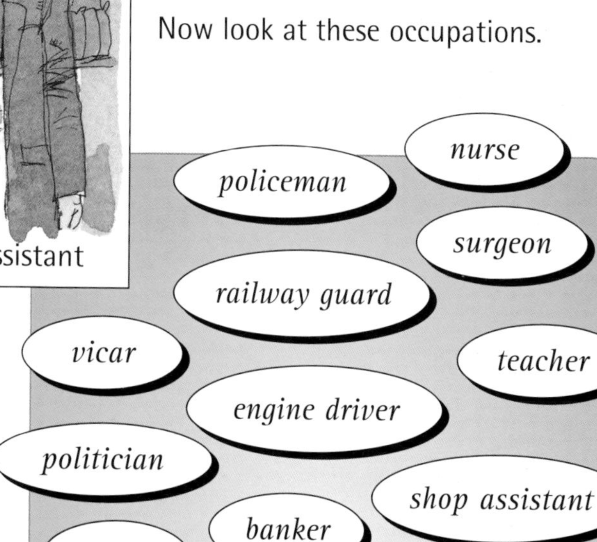

a telephonist

a farm labourer

a tramp

Which of these jobs would a person living in 1900 have thought of as being 'middle class'?

WHERE DID THE MIDDLE CLASS LIVE?

The years between about 1880 and 1910 saw an enormous growth in the sort of jobs people at the time regarded as middle class. Remember that people thought of the 'middle class' as those who had to work for their money, but who didn't earn their living by manual labour. As communications, trade and industry all grew at a great rate, so did the middle-class jobs and occupations. Women, too, came into the 'middle-class' workforce in a big way. People began to see it as quite respectable for women to work as, say, telephonists and shop assistants.

The clerks and postal workers, commercial travellers and teachers at one end of the scale, and bankers, merchants and lawyers at the other, all had to live somewhere. Some people liked to live near to where they worked and some had houses that went with their jobs. But mostly they wanted to live where the air was cleaner and the housing more suitable than that in the inner cities. So this is the time when solid, respectable houses with gardens and inside toilets were built on the outskirts of towns. These were the suburbs. Most of the houses were terraced or semi-detached, but others, smarter and more expensive, were detached and came with large gardens.

SOURCE 1

This is a photograph of the sort of housing that was built for middle-class Victorian families. It shows Oldfield Park, Bath, in 1905.

SOURCE 2

These are two maps of the city of Bath and the surrounding area. Where and in what directions did Bath expand? Where would you guess the middle-class people went to live?

Question Time

1. Find Oldfield Park on the more recent map of Bath.
2. Is it on the older map too?
3. Can you suggest reasons for this?

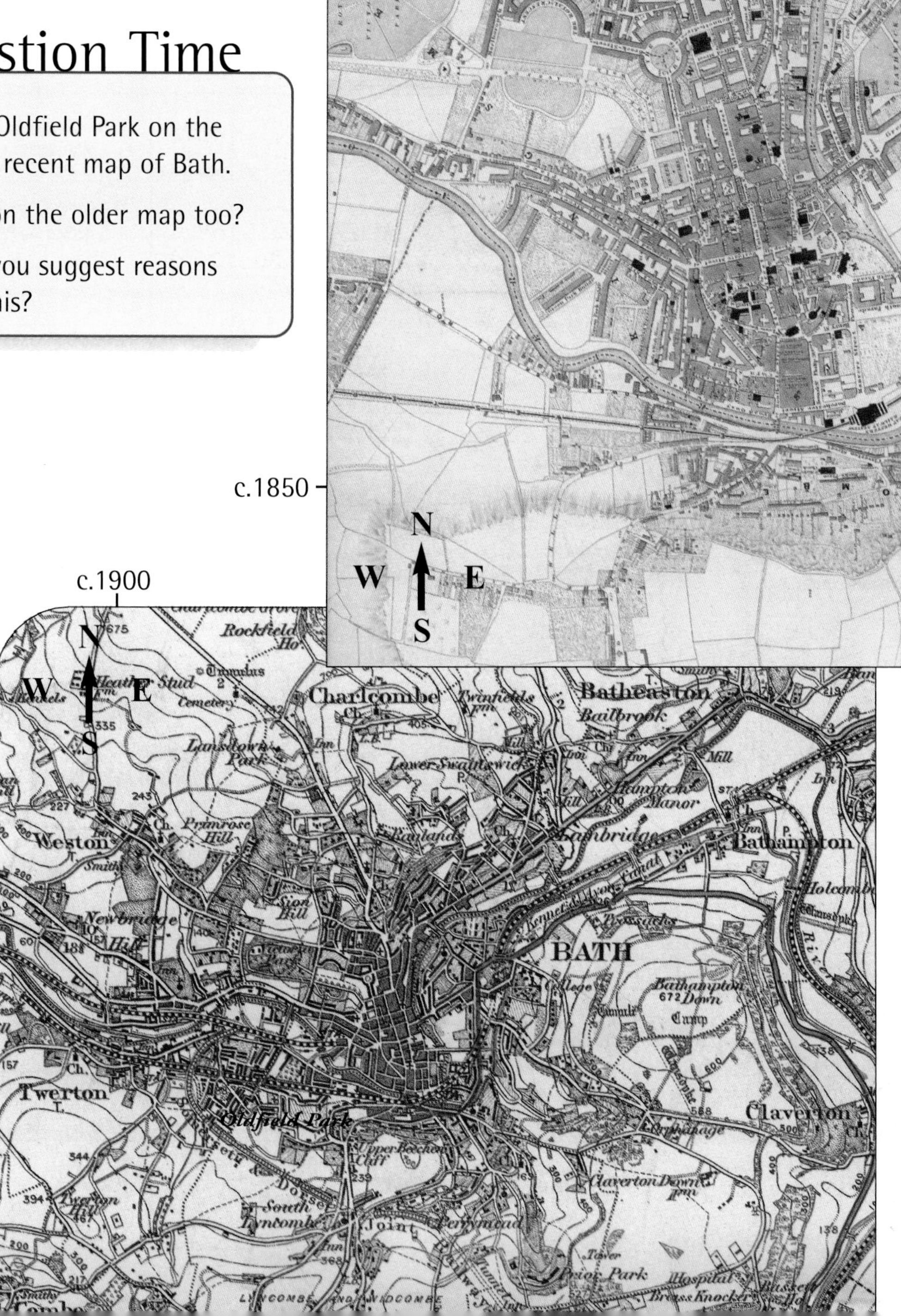

Now you are ready to get started on finding out who lived in Oldfield Park and what jobs they did.

SOURCE 3

This is a page from the 1891 census. It tells you about some families that lived in Oldfield Park, Bath. They would have lived in a house like the one in the photograph on page 136.

Administrative County of Somersetshire Bath — The undermentioned Houses are situate within the Boundaries of the

Civil Parish of Lyncombe & Widcombe | Municipal Borough of Bath | Municipal Ward of Lyncombe & Widcombe | Urban Sanitary District of Bath | ~~Town or Village or Hamlet~~ of | ~~Rural Sanitary~~ of

Cols. 1 No. of Schedule	2 ROAD, STREET, &c., and No. or NAME of HOUSE	3 HOUSES In-habited	4 HOUSES Uninhabited (U.), or Building (B.)	5 Number of rooms occupied if less than five	6 NAME and Surname of each Person	7 RELATION to Head of Family	8 CONDITION as to Marriage	9 AGE last Birthday of Males	10 AGE last Birthday of Females	11 PROFESSION or OCCUPATION	12 Employer
6 Cont^d					Lucy Compton	Serv	S		28	Housemaid (Domestic Serv)	
7	Rock Hall	1			William F. Gould	Head	M	41		Tailor & Outfitter	x
					Elizabeth Do	Wife	M		40		
					Mary S. Wills	2nd Cousin Visitor	S		33	Living on her own means	
					Gertrude R. Perrett	Niece Do	S		19	Do	
					Ellen Howard	Serv	S		23	Cook (Domestic Serv)	
					Annie M. Do	Do	S		25	Housemaid Do	
	St George's Lodge		1 U								
8	Oldfield Villa	1			Edward B. Titley	Head	M	37		Solicitor	x
					Arabella Do	Wife	M		34		
					Muriel H. Do	Daur			2		
					Kate Hulbert	Serv	S		26	Cook Domestic Serv	
					Annie Rawlings	Do	S		26	Housemaid Do	
9	Mount Rose	1			William E. Gkey	Head	M	48		Commercial Traveller	
					Jane Do	Wife	M		29		
					Edith M. Do	Daur	S		19		
					Amelia C. Do	Do	S		16		
					Eliza F. Do	Do			13	Scholar	
					Fanny L. Do	Do			12	Do	
					Dorothy G. Do	Do			1		
					Caroline Pickford	Serv	S		20	General Serv Dom	
10	Stow Villa	1			Frank Dolly	Head	M	58		Draper	x
					Ann F. Do	Wife	M		58		
					Llewellyn B. Do	Son	S	19		Accountant	
					Herbert Do	Do	S	29		Draper	x
					Delphine M. Do	Daur	S		18	Scholar	
					Noutteno H. Voss	Visitor	M	63		Retired Civil Engineer	
					Sophia Ball	Serv	Wd		32	Cook (Domestic Serv)	
					Emily Clarke	Do	S		28	Housemaid Do	
					Elizabeth Prot	Do	S		49	Nurse Do	
11	Southbourne	1			Sarah P. Roynon	Do	S		29	Cook Do	
5	Total of Houses and of Tenements with less than Five Rooms	5	1 U		Total of Males and Females...			7	23		

Page 2

Parliamentary Borough ~~or Division~~ of Bath	Ecclesiastical Parish or District of St Mark
15	16
WHERE BORN	If (1) Deaf-and-Dumb (2) Blind (3) Lunatic, Imbecile or Idiot
Somerset; Upton Noble	
Do Bath	
Gloster; Wootten under Edge	
Cornwall Kilkampton	
Gloster; Wootten under Edge	
Somerset Bath	
Do Do	
Somerset Bath	
Do Do	
Do Do	
Do Do	
Do Do	
Gloster; Marshfield	
Herefordshire; Hereford	
Somerset; Bath	
Do Do	
Do Do	
Do Do	
Do Do	
Lancashire; Manchester	
Kent; Margate	
Glamorgan; Swansea	
Somerset; Bath	
Do Do	
Do Do	
Glamorgan; Swansea	
Gloster; Marshfield	
Do Do	
Essex; Halstead	
London; Walworth	

Question Time

1. Look at the families in the census return. Work out who is the father and who is the mother in each family. What are the children's names and ages?
2. Now look at the occupations and make a list of them. Which occupations would people at the time have thought of as being 'middle class'? Remember that everyone who had to work for their living and wasn't involved in manual labour was called 'middle class'.
3. Find out what the school leaving age was in 1891. Do any of the children listed on the census pages work? What does this tell you about their families?
4. Do some research to find out which occupations were 'new' ones, in that they would not have existed before the nineteenth century.

SOURCE 4

This is a page from the 1900 Directory that lists some of the streets in the Oldfield Park area of Bath. Street directories can give a lot of useful information.

STREET DIRECTORY.

Oldfield Road, continued.

Sunnyside—Matravers Mrs. Ann
Lyncombe Vicarage—Müller Rev. James T., M.A.
Samford—Spear Mr. E. A.
Percy villa—
Belgrade—Palmer Mr. Edward W.
Dirleton—
Wade-Smith Rev. Thomas, M.A.
Maplethorpe—Sylvester Miss
Disbrowe Miss Harriet A.
Ilex villa—Taylor Mr. H. Stanley

Left-hand side from Wells Road.

Oldfield lodge—
Ellis Miss Mary E., ladies' school
Oldfield cottages—
1 Moon William, gardener
2 McLaren Ormiston G., gardener
Oldfield—Hunter Henry J., esq., M.D.
Rockhall—Gould Mr. W. F.
S. George's lodge—Collins Mr. J. J. S.
Oldfield villa—
Titley Edward B., esq., B.A.
Mount Rose—Ritson Capt. Raymond C., merchant mariner
Stow villa—
Southbourne—Hewitt Mrs. Augustus
Crowsmoor—Smith Miss Naamah
The Ferns—Matthews Charles J., esq.
Fern cottage—Elley William, gardener
Oldfield nursery—Kitley Thomas

Oldfield Park.

Left-hand side from Wells Road.

Hughenden—Tucker Mr. H. Bailis
Long Hope—Warden Capt. Frederick
Elmside—
Kidbrook lodge—Norburn Albert E., M.D., B.Sc., L.R.C.P., M.R.C.S.
Cheriton house—Long Mr. Jacob
Lynton lodge—Applegate Mrs. H.
The Hern—
Rivers—Hatt Mrs. T. J.
Westholme—Isaacs Mr. Fred. G., jun.
Oakleigh—Underwood Mr. E.
Rose bank—Fyson Mr. George E.
The Laurels—Dickinson Mr. G.
Fairfield—Chapman Mr. Isaac
Glenview—Young Mr. George C.

Oldfield Park, continued.

Benington house—Lyle H. P., esq.
Elburton villa—Ellery C.S., esq., C.E.
Blair Athole—Taylor Mr. James D.
Ellerslie—
Chalcroft—Hawes Mr. Alfred
Rose Dale—Colmer Mr. G. R.
Effingham house—Hill Mr. John H.
Charnwood—Fortt Mr. F. W.
Kingsley—Saunders Mr. H. J.
Stoneywood—Wood Mr. M. H. G.
Cromer—Harries Mrs. Elizabeth
Drachenfels—
Brynhyfryd—Lewis James W., esq.
Ashton house—Mills Mr. Ernest J.
Ravenslea—Stone Mr. Isaac John
Homestead—Barley Mr. Charles
Homeleigh—Bessell Mr. Charles W.
Morley villas—
1 Drummond Rev. H. Gordon
2 Bond Mr. H.
Fern Dene—Stephenson Mr. Robert R.
Fern lodge—Scudamore Mr. A. G.
Norwood villas—
1 Turner Mrs. Eliza
2 Adams Mr. William A.
Southwood villas—
1 Brown Harry F., lay reader
2 Woodrow Mr. Horace B.
Westwood villas—
1 Blackwood Mr. L.
2 Batten Mr. Edward
Bowood villas—
1
2 Snell Mr. James
Ashleigh villas—
1 Lewis William J., clerk
2 Burgess Mr. Thomas
Penrose—Goddard Mr. John R.

Right-hand side from Wells Road.

Elmsleigh—Andrews Mr. S. Fox
Badminton villa—
Marston villa—Moore G. P., esq.
Tremont house—Walker Mr. Samuel
Lyndhurst—Brettingham Chas., esq.
Ardenvohr—Walker Mr. Walter
Oldfield Park—Hatch Andrew D., esq.

Right-hand side from Lower Bristol Road.

Harben villa—Jenkin Mr. S. W.

* Thus denotes lodging-house keepers.

493

Question Time

1. Look at Source 4. In what ways is it more useful than the census?
2. In what ways is it less useful than the census?
3. Many street and trade directories were made up from entries submitted by the individuals themselves. Does this mean they are not reliable?

SOURCE 5

This is a street map of the Oldfield Park area of Bath in 1900.

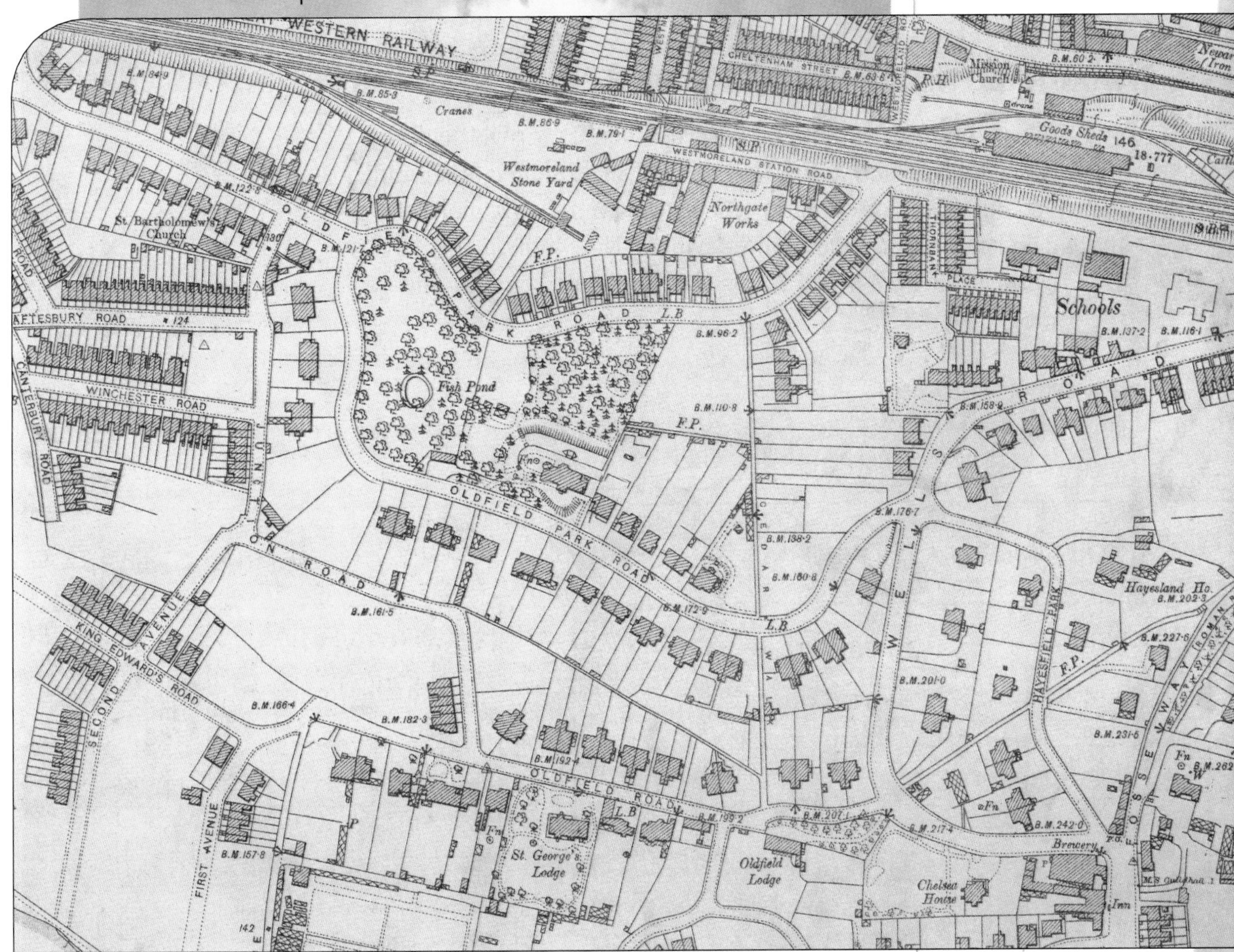

Question Time

1. Use all the information you have collected from the census and directory, and write information boxes for as many of the houses on the map as possible.

2. Make a wall display with the street plan in the centre and the information boxes arranged so that it is clear to which house they belong.

3. Can you draw any conclusions about what connections there might be between occupations and where people live? (For example, do all railway workers live near the railway?)

4. Write a description of the street as if you were an estate agent in 1900, trying to sell one of the houses. What might the owner of the house you are trying to sell say to a person thinking of buying the house? (Hint: the owner might talk about the neighbours, the garden, why they want to move.)

NEW JOBS AND NEW PEOPLE: WHERE DID MIDDLE-CLASS PEOPLE COME FROM?

WHAT HAPPENED IN OLDFIELD PARK?

Look back at the work you did on the 1891 census for Oldfield Park. There is a column 'Where born'. List all the places named, and work out which age groups were born where they were living in 1891 and which age groups were born elsewhere. Now look at the census data for the same area in 1871 and 1851 (Sources 1 and 2) and do the same.

SOURCE 1

This is part of the census for Oldfield Park in 1871.

[Page 2] The undermentioned Houses are situate within the Boundaries of the

Civil Parish [or Township] of	City or Municipal Borough of	Municipal Ward of	Parliamentary Borough of	Town of	Village or Hamlet, &c., of	Local Board, or [Improvement Commissioners District] of
Lyncombe & Widcombe	Bath	Lyncombe & Widcombe	Bath	Bath		Bath

ROAD, STREET, &c., and No. or NAME of HOUSE	HOUSES Inhabited	HOUSES Uninhabited (U.), or Building (B.)	NAME and Surname of each Person	RELATION to Head of Family	CONDITION	AGE of Males	AGE of Females	Rank, Profession, or OCCUPATION	WHERE BORN
Oldfield Villa	1		William Tilley	Head	Widr	53		Provision Merchant	Somerset Bath
Oldfield Road			Fanny Luisa Do	Daur	Unm		25	Office Clerk	Do Do
			Anna Maria Do	Do	Do		23	House Keeper	Do Do
			William Alfred Do	Son	Do	20		Commercial Traveller	Do Do
			Arthur Bussey Do	Do	Do	17		Ware House Clerk	Do Do
			Edward Bussey Do	Do	Do	17		Undergraduate Lon Univ	Do Do
			Walter Tilley Brown	Nephew	Do	17		Ironmongers Shopman	Wilts Warminster
			Wm Riggs Fuller	Visitor	Mar	37		Independent Minister of Congregational Chapel Winchester	Surrey Richmond
			Emily Josephine [illegible]	Do	Unm		30	Governess	Somerset Bath
			Helen Melissa [illegible]	Servant	Do		18	Cook	[illegible]
			Lydia Henrietta Vincent	Do	Do		18	Domestic Servant	Somerset Bath
Mount Rose	1		Colin Mitchell Shum	Head	Mar	34		Woollen Merchant	Do Do
Oldfield Road			Helen Shum	Wife	Do		26	Wife	London
			Helen Kathleen Shum	Daur			14		Somerset Bath
			Anna Volkmann	Sister in Law	Unm		22	Annuitant (already)	London
			Martha Maria Gane	Servt	Do		29	Cook	Somerset Bath
			Jane Hosey	Do	Do		21	Domestic Servant	Do Do
Stow Villa	1		Richard Chitty	Head	Unm	65		Lieut Colonel of Infantry H.M. Indian Army retired	Kent Deal
Oldfield Road			Henry Chitty	Sister	Do	27		[illegible] Unemployed	Do Do
			Elizabeth Moore	Servant	Do		20	House Maid	Somerset Coleford
			Emma Elizabeth Garland	Do	Do		30	Cook	Do Bristol
[illegible] Villa	1		Augusta [illegible]	Head	W		65	Gentlewoman	[illegible]
Old Field Road			Mary Do	Daur	Unm		51	Do	Somerset Bath
			Agnes Do	Do	Do		45	Do	Do Do
			Emily Snow	Sister	Do		57	Do	[illegible]
Total of Houses..	4		Total of Males and Females..			9	16		

* Draw the pen through such of the words as are inappropriate.

SOURCE 2

This is part of the census for Oldfield Park in 1851.

Parish ~~or Township~~ of Lyncombe Widcombe | ~~Ecclesiastical District of~~ Lyncombe Widcombe | City or Borough of Bath | ~~Town of~~ | ~~Village of~~

Name of Street, Place, or Road, and Name or No. of House	Name and Surname of each Person who abode in the house, on the Night of the 30th March, 1851	Relation to Head of Family	Condition	Age of Males	Age of Females	Rank, Profession, or Occupation	Where Born
Park View Lodge contd	Fanny Jolly	Wife	Mar		45		Kent - Deal
	William C Do	Son	U	24		Drapers Son	Do Margate
	Emily Do	Daur	U		17	Scholar at home	Do Do
	Fanny Do	Daur			15	Do	Do Do
	Thomas Do	Son		11		Do	Somerset, Bath
	Walter Do	Son		4			Do Do
	Arthur Do	Son		2			Do Do
	Harriett Osborne	Serv	U		36	Cook	Do Long Ashton
	Louisa Jane Parker	Serv	U		21	Nurse	Kent, Canterbury
	Anne Hall	Serv	U		25	Housemaid	Somerset, Timsbury
8 Oldfield Road	James Peacock	Head	Mar	46		Architect	Do Lyncombe & Widcombe
	Sarah Do	Wife	Mar		41		Wilts, Market Lavington
	Alfred James Do	Son		4			Somerset, Lyncombe & Widcombe
	Mary Griffiths	Serv	U		17	General Serv	Glamorgan, St Brides Major
9 St George's Lodge Oldfield Road	William Mitchell	Head	Mar	45		Maker Master Employing 11 men	Somerset, Bath
	William S Do	Son		11		Scholar	Do Do
	Eliza Watts	Serv	U		25	Cook	Do Do
	Mary Bristow	Serv	U		25	House Maid	Wilts, Chippenham
Oldfield Villa Oldfield Road	Richard Calthrop	Head	Mar	62		Landed Proprietor	Lincolnshire, Gosberton
	Elizabeth Do	Wife	Mar		57		Do Donington
I 3 U – B –	3	Total of Persons...		9	11		

Question Time

1. You now have a great deal of information about the movement of people into Oldfield Park. Can you spot any major differences between the places where people were born who were living in Oldfield Park in 1871 and 1891?
2. Work out, with your teacher and the group with whom you are working, the best way of presenting this information. It may be by using ICT, or a series of pie charts, or maps for each decade, using different-sized arrows to represent the different-sized groups of people.

WHAT HAPPENED NATIONALLY?

It would be interesting to see if what happened in Oldfield Park matched what happened nationally. Looking at Britain as a whole, historians and statisticians have worked out that there was a general movement of people from the countryside into the towns.

There were differences in the rates at which towns grew and in the towns that attracted people from different parts of Britain.

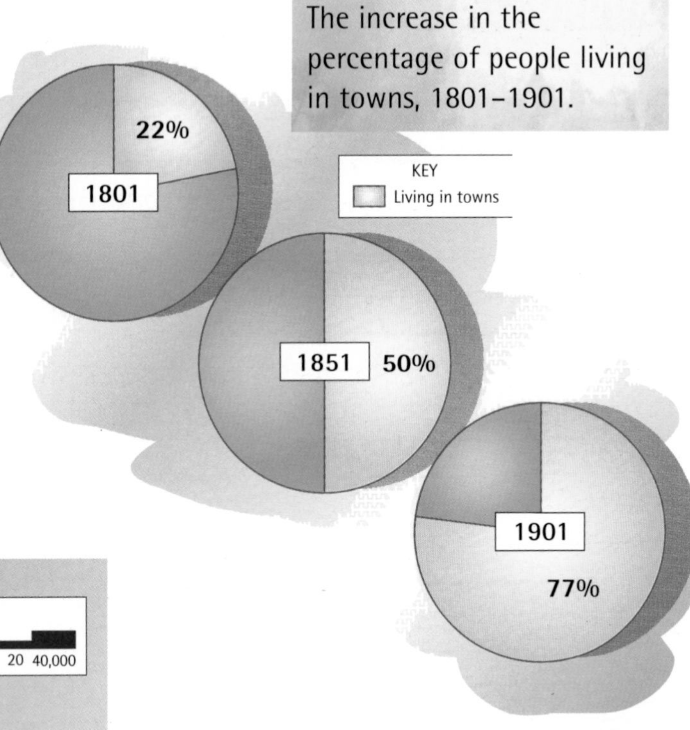

The increase in the percentage of people living in towns, 1801–1901.

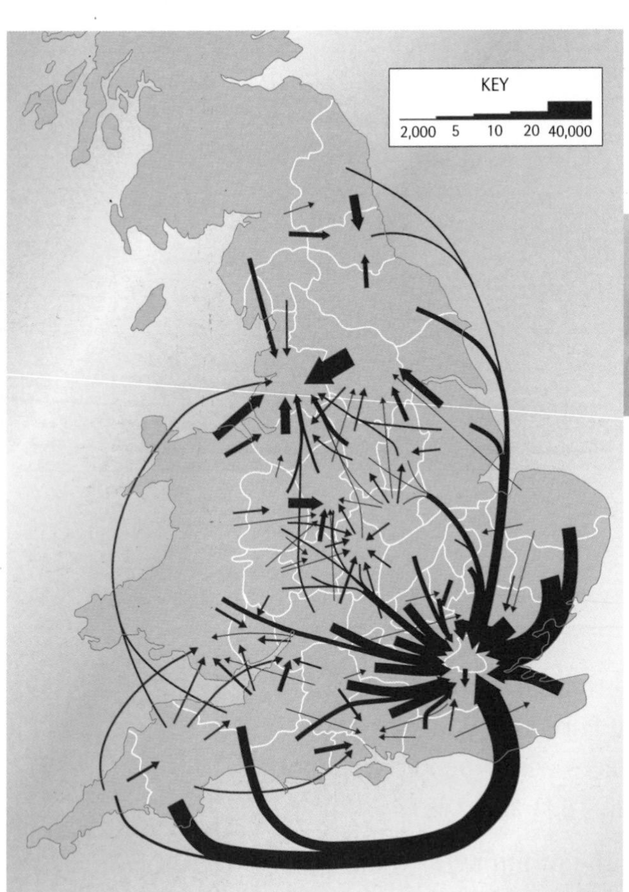

This map shows people on the move in Britain between the 1851 census and the 1861 census. The bigger the arrow, the more people were moving in that direction.

Question Time

1. Look carefully at the map on this page. Use a modern map to work out the main towns to which people were going.
2. Now look back at your data. How does what was happening in Oldfield Park compare to what was happening nationally?

WAGES AND PRICES: HOW WELL DID MIDDLE-CLASS PEOPLE LIVE?

You saw earlier how the 'middle class' ranged from ship owners and lawyers to clerks and postmen. Obviously there was a huge difference in their incomes. A successful lawyer could expect to earn around £1000 a year; a clerk around £250. So you can see that it is very difficult to generalise as to what the 'middle class' did with their money and the sort of standard of living they could afford.

THE MIDDLE CLASS IN YORK

Seebohm Rowntree was a Quaker, and as a young adult he managed the family's chocolate firm in York. He introduced schemes to help the poorer workers in the chocolate factory, and this inspired him to investigate poverty in York. He looked at the budgets and lifestyles of hundreds of families. He then extended his study to 'families who are comfortably off but live simply.' These were the tradesmen and cashiers, clerks and managers who made up most of the middle class in and around 1900.

Rowntree found that people in this 'class' lived in houses like the ones in Oldfield Park, Bath and which you can see in the photograph on page 136. Their children went to local private or grammar schools and every summer they had a holiday at the seaside.

SOURCE 1

According to Rowntree's investigation, these are three examples of meals a family with an annual income of £250 would eat.

	Wednesday	*Friday*	*Sunday*
Breakfast	*porridge, fried eggs, bacon and fried bread, toast, brown and white bread, marmalade, tea, coffee, milk and cream*	*porridge, fried bacon and eggs, toast, white and brown bread and butter, marmalade, tea, coffee, milk and cream*	*porridge, eggs, bread, butter, milk, coffee, cream, tea*
Dinner	*rissoles, poached eggs, potatoes, bread pudding, bread, butter, tea*	*mutton with haricot beans, carrots, potatoes, tapioca pudding*	*mutton, potatoes, cauliflower, bread sauce, rhubarb and custard, blancmange, oranges, biscuits, tea*
Tea	*bread, butter, tea-cake, porridge, milk, tea*	*brown and white bread, butter, cake, tea and milk*	*potted meat sandwiches, bread and butter, cake, marmalade, tea, milk*
Supper	*baked haddock, stewed plums, biscuits, hot milk*	*boiled chicken, white sauce, bacon, potato chips, stewed rhubarb, bread, butter, cocoa*	*potted meat, cornflour mould, bread, butter, cake, rhubarb and custard, cheese, hot milk*

WHAT ELSE DO WE KNOW ABOUT MIDDLE-CLASS LIFE?

Social investigators, like Seebohm Rowntree, found out that in 1900 middle-class families could afford to have at least one servant. The poorest could have a girl to help with the heavy housework and the washing; the richest could employ maids and a butler, as well as having gardeners and a groom.

When they shopped in 1900, they could buy, if they wanted to:

- pineapples and bananas
- tomato ketchup
- tinned food, especially Californian peaches (by 1914 Britain was the world's largest importer of canned goods)
- packets of baking powder, custard powder and blancmange powder
- breakfast cereals (new in 1890)
- cheap meat from Australia and the USA that had been transported in refrigerated ships.

The average middle-class family spent about 44 per cent of their income on food.

FACT FILE: THE COST OF SOME FOODS

Flour	*1s a stone*
Eggs	*1d each*
Potatoes	*1/2d per lb*
Cheese	*8d per lb*
Frozen beef and mutton	*4–5d per lb*
Sugar	*2d per lb*
Tea	*1s 6d per lb*

SOURCE 2

These are all advertisements that people in 1900 would have seen in their shop windows and pasted on walls.

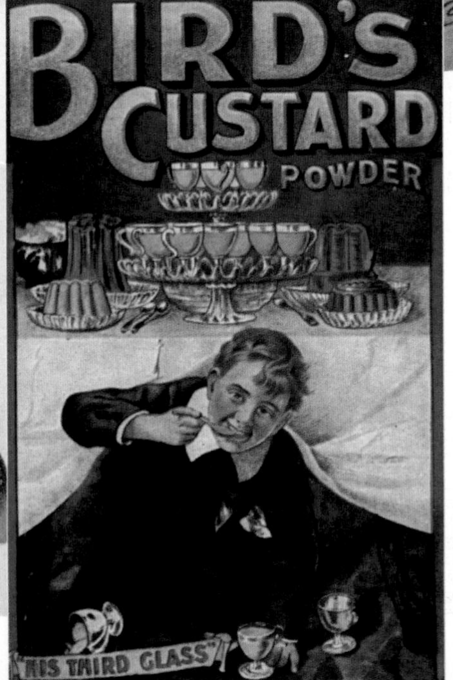

Question Time

1. Look at Source 1 on page 145. How would you describe the menus for these three days? How do they differ from what you eat? Why do you think this is?
2. Choose one middle-class family from the 1891 census for Oldfield Park and use all the information you have to work out what their weekly budget might have been. Is there anything left over? What might they have spent it on?

LEISURE TIME AND ENTERTAINMENT: WHAT DID MIDDLE-CLASS PEOPLE DO FOR FUN?

You can find out a lot about the sort of things people did for fun in 1900, but you must remember that Victorians often took their fun very seriously!

WHAT HAPPENED IN OLDFIELD PARK?

Go back to the 1900 maps and plans you used in the earlier work you did on Oldfield Park. Can you find anything that might suggest entertainment?

SOURCE 1

The opening of Innox Park, Bath in 1909.

SOURCE 2

An advert in a Bath newspaper publicising entertainment in 1903.

Public Notices.

THEATRE ROYAL, BATH
Acting Manager - Mr. WALTER D. HARTREE.

TO-NIGHT and during the week, at 7.30, and Matinee, Saturday, at 2.30,—

JIM THE PENMAN

By Sir Charles Young, Bart.

Private Boxes, 21s.; Balcony Stalls, 4s.; Grand Circle, 3s.; Upper Circle, 2s.; Pit, 1s.; Gallery, 6d. Box Office open from 11 till 4.30. Doors open at 7; commence at 7.30. Second price at 9. Children in arms not admitted.

THE LYRIC, BATH.
(OPPOSITE THEATRE ROYAL.)
General Manager - - MR. HARRY WILLIAMS.

TO-NIGHT and during the week, at 7.30. GRAND COMBINATION OF VARIETY TALENT. All Star Turns. First time in Bath of those Gladiatorial Marvels the THREE ROMAS in their Great Athletic Novelty. The original MUSICAL JAPS, in their grand Japanese Illuminated Bazaar. Special engagement of the Whistling Comedian, FRED MASON. Great success and Enthusiastic Reception of the Naval and Military Spectacle. QUEEN AND COUNTRY, in which 60 Bath Children take part. For other artistes see bills. Prices as usual.

ASSEMBLY ROOMS, BATH.

ONE WEEK ONLY, COMMENCING MARCH 5th.
Every Evening at 7.45.
SELECT MATINEES on WEDNESDAY, THURSDAY, and SATURDAY, at 3.
Doors open at 2.30 and 7.15.

Popular Prices ... 3s. (Reserved), 2s., 1s., and 6d. Children Half-price, except to 6d. Seats. Early Door to avoid crush, 3d. extra to all parts. Tickets and Plans at Usual Places.
Direct from Bristol after a Record Season, being visited by nearly 100,000 persons.

THE "CHAS. W."
POOLE'S WAR MYRIORAMA AND CIRCUS.

Magnificent Series of Scenes, showing all Events connected with
THE BOER WAR!
British Victories at Glencoe and Mafeking,
BATTLE OF ELANDSLAAGTE,
Terrific Charge of the Devons and Gordon Highlanders. The 5th Lancers charging.
LANDING THE NAVAL BRIGADE
at Durban. On their way to Ladysmith.
CAPE TOWN FROM TABLE BAY.
The "Dunottar Castle," with Gen. BULLER on board leaving for Natal.
GENERAL ROBERTS' DEPARTURE
From Waterloo Station—an impressive Tableau,
BOERS AT PRETORIA
The Burghers practising Shooting—Getting Ready for the "Rooineks." Johannesburg thirteen years ago and now.
BEFORE, DURING, and AFTER WATERLOO!
(Mr. Chas. Poole's Greatest Achievement. Produced after long and careful preparation, and with an extravagant outlay of money.
CAIRO TO THE CAPE.
POOLE'S PERFECT VAUDEVILLE ORGANIZATION.
POOLE'S EVENTOGRAPHE,
The Latest and Best of all Animated Picture Machines. Grand Series of Up-to-Date Films, Including the Pantomime of CINDERELLA.
GRAND ORCHESTRAL & MILITARY BANDS
The whole forming the most Elaborate Exhibition of its kind ever conceived.
Sole Manager (to whom all communications must be addressed),
MR. HARRY STEWART.

SOURCE 3

An extract from the bye-laws for Alexandra Park and Magdalen Gardens, Bath, in 1902.

Bye-laws made by the Mayor, Aldermen and Citizens of the City of Bath, acting by the Council with respect to the Pleasure Grounds known as The Alexandra Park and Magdalen Gardens, in the City of Bath.

1. Throughout these bye-laws the expression "the Council" means the Mayor, Aldermen and Citizens of the City of Bath, acting by the Council, and the expression "the pleasure ground" means each of the pleasure grounds known as The Alexandra Park and Magdalen Gardens respectively.

2. The pleasure ground shall be opened at the hour of 9 in the fore-noon of every day during the months of November, December January, February and March, and shall be opened at the hour of 8 in the forenoon during the rest of the year, and shall be closed at one hour after sunset on every day throughout the year:

   Provided always that this bye-law shall not be deemed to require the pleasure ground to be opened and closed at the hours hereinbefore prescribed on any day when, in pursuance of any statutory provision in that behalf, the Council may close such pleasure ground to the public.

3. A person, other than an officer of the Council, or a person or a servant of a person employed by the Council in or about any work in connexion with the laying out, planting, improvement, or maintenance of the pleasure ground, shall not

   (1.) On any day on which the pleasure ground may be open to the public enter the pleasure ground before the time hereinbefore appointed for the opening thereof, or enter the pleasure ground or remain therein after the time hereinbefore appointed for the closing thereof.

WHAT SORT OF ENTERTAINMENT DID PEOPLE LIVING IN THE REST OF BRITAIN ENJOY IN 1900?

All sorts! It really depended on where you lived and what you liked doing. There were big, spectacular outdoor entertainments like Derby Day, small, indoor family entertainments like magic lantern shows and street corner entertainments like Punch and Judy shows. There were daring pastimes, like motoring, which was considered by some to be highly dangerous, especially when the speed limit was raised to 12 m.p.h.

Sport was becoming an important feature of everyday life. The Football League was founded in 1888 and in 1890 the County Cricket championship began. In 1895 the Rugby Football Union refused to allow payments to members of northern clubs to compensate them for missed workdays and so the northern Rugby League was started.

HIGH DAYS AND HOLIDAYS

By 1900 there were 'official' holidays that meant most middle-class people, especially those at the 'lower' end, could afford to take time off work. Bank holidays, where banks, factories, shops and offices closed for a day, began in 1871. The bank holiday was usually a Monday. This gave families a long weekend so that they could get away to the seaside or the country or to visit faraway relatives. The rail network meant people could get to sporting events, the theatre or a music hall many kilometres from their homes. Gradually, employers began giving holidays with pay, which made holidays even more possible.

SOURCE 4

Cycling was a very popular pastime. Many cycling clubs grew up and members explored the countryside. This photo shows women and girls with their bicycles in 1900.

PLEASURE GARDENS AND PUBLIC PARKS

Pleasure gardens usually began as public house gardens. People could have a drink of beer, spirits or a cup of tea; they could eat sandwiches, pie and peas or potted shrimps. Some pleasure gardens were large and contained miniature racecourses or small zoos with exotic animals. People could listen to music or dance, have their fortunes told or watch a circus. But pleasure gardens were also the haunts of pickpockets, petty criminals and prostitutes. Although some were still flourishing in 1900, many had been closed down because of complaints from local people and the police.

Public parks were quite different. These were places owned by the local authorities, and local councillors took pride in them. These parks were laid out with lawns, flowerbeds and, often, a pond and a bandstand. The respectable middle class could walk here, push their perambulators and bring their toddlers to feed the ducks. On summer evenings the local band would play a selection of music – perhaps some Gilbert and Sullivan, Elgar or, very daringly, a selection of music hall songs.

SOURCE 5

A garden fête at Wood House, Bath, in the early twentieth century.

LIBRARIES, ART GALLERIES AND MUSEUMS

By the end of Queen Victoria's reign in 1901, nearly every town and city had its own art gallery, concert hall and museum. The demand from the middle class for this sort of entertainment was huge. In London, the National Portrait Gallery opened in 1896 and the Tate Gallery a year later. Work began on the Victoria and Albert Museum in 1899. Cities like Leeds, Birmingham, Manchester and Bristol quickly copied what was happening in London. Growing civic pride meant that, very quickly, nearly every town had its own museum and art gallery, and sometimes a concert hall. In 1892 the Public Libraries Act said that all local government areas could become 'library authorities' and spend 1d on books for every £1 collected in rates. Public lending libraries grew at a great rate.

AWAY-DAYS

For most middle-class people, holidays began at the local railway station. For Oldfield Park, in Bath, the local station was Oldfield Park Station.

SOURCE 6

An advert in a newspaper in 1903 advertising train excursions from Bath.

MIDLAND RAILWAY.

COOK'S EXCURSIONS from BATH :–

ON TUESDAY, June 30 to DUBLIN (for Motor Car Races), at 12.0 noon, 16 days.

To WORCESTER (Races) at 10.0 a.m. on July 2nd and 3rd.

On Friday, July 3,

To SCOTLAND, 3 to 16 Days, Glasgow, &c.

On Saturday, July 4,

To LIVERPOOL, Manchester, BLACKPOOL, SOUTHPORT, &c., 3 or 6 Days.

Tickets, etc., at the Midland Station.

1760 JOHN MATHIESON, General Manager.

SOURCE 7

A timetable for trains from Bath in 1900.

Public Notices.

MIDLAND RAILWAY.

☞ EXPRESS TRAINS BETWEEN BATH AND BIRMINGHAM, DERBY, MANCHESTER, LIVEPPOOL, LEEDS, BRADFORD, AND THE NORTH.

The DIRECT ROUTE TO AND FROM SCOTLAND is via SETTLE and CARLISLE, and includes the BEST PARTS OF THE LAND OF "BURNS"; THE HOME & HAUNTS OF "SIR WALTER SCOTT"; THE "FORTH" BRIDGE, &c., &c.

IMPROVED NIGHT SERVICE from the WEST OF ENGLAND to the NORTH. The 1.3 a.m. Mail from Bristol to Derby, in connection with trains from Penzance, Plymouth, Exeter, &c. has been extended to Sheffield; with connections to York, Newcastle, Leeds and Bradford, thus giving an improved service for the conveyance of passengers, parcels, and perishable traffic from the Scilly Isles, and the West of England to the North.

DINING CARRIAGES TO AND FROM THE NORTH. The 9.0 and 9.45 a.m. and 12.20 p.m. EXPRESSES from BRISTOL and 8.42a.m. and 12 noon from BATH, run in connection with EXPRESS trains from LONDON (St. Pancras) to SCOTLAND to which FIRST & THIRD CLASS DINING CARRIAGES are attached.

The MORNING EXPRESSES between LONDON (St. Pancras), and EDINBURGH; and the AFTERNOON EXRESSES between LONDON (St. Pancras) and GLASGOW are composed of New CORRIDOR CARRIAGES of the most Modern Type.

† EXPRESS TRAINS between BRISTOL and BRADFORD, to which DINING CARRIAGES, first and third class, are attached.

PILLOWS IN NIGHT EXPRESSES.—Pillows may be hired by Travellers (first and third class) in the night mail and express trains from Bristol and a few other towns. Charge 6d. each, prepaid.

Passengers should be careful to ask for *"Midland tickets"* when booking. *These tickets enable passengers to travel by* THROUGH TRAINS *thereby avoiding the inconvenience of changing at Birmingham.*

DOWN TRAINS.—WEEK DAYS.

Bath ... dep	p.m 11 0	a.m 8 42	a.m 8 4?	a.m 10 0	p.m. 12 0	p.m 1†12	p.m 3 5	p.m 4 5	p.m 6 30	7
Bristol	a m 1a3?	9 0	9 45	1015	12 20	2 *5	3 15	4 15	7 0	7 50
Glo'ster .arr	2a 3	9 54	—	1122	1 w13	2 56	4 12	5 18	8 6	8 47
Cheltenham	2a30	1010	1038	1138	1 30	3 12	4 28	5 33	8 26	9 5
Worcester...	8a10	11 0	—	p.m 1220	3k35	4 45	5 25	6 33	9 6	9 36
Birmingham	1 a5	1120	1142	1 15	2 38	4 20	5 35	6 45	9 56	1022
Leicester ...	9 20	p.m 1238	—	3g10	4 12	6 0	—	8 25	—	a.m 1q40
Burton-on-Trent ...	5 0	1214	p.m 12	2 25	3 24	5 8	6 24	7 38	—	p.m 1110
Derby	5 20	1236	1248	2 55	3 45	5 30	6 46	8 0	—	1130
Nottingham	6 35	1 18	1 55	3 42	4 42	6 4	7 43	8 45	—	a.m 1 30
Lincoln	9 50	—	3 20	—	6 12	7 40	—	1010	—	4 50
Manchester Central	10 0	—	2 30	5 0	5b35	—	8 20	9 47	—	2†20
Manchester Victoria	10 2	—	3 2	—	6 25	—	8 52	9 50	—	—
Bolton	1045	—	3 27	—	6 51	*	9 16	1033	—	5†46
Blackburn...	p.m 1218	—	3 58	—	7 23	—	9 50	1123	—	6†20
So'thpt(L.S)	12 0	—	4 20	6 0	7b 1	—	1025	1155	—	8†35
Liverpool, Cen.......	a.m 10 0	—	3 43	5 20	6b25	—	9 40	1045	—	4 55
Sheffield.......	7 0	1 40	1 55	4 15	4 52	6 23	8 15	9 35	—	1230
Hull (N.E.)	10 2	4 15	5 53	—	7 2	9 42	1110	p.m 1255	—	4 42
York	9 15	8 5	4 8	5 50	6 5	8 50	10 5	a.m 1140	—	3 36
Scarboro' ...	1115	5 16	6 0	—	7 5	—	1125	—	—	5 35
Darlington...	105?	4 21	6 41	7 7	8 30	—	1129	a.m 2 8	—	4 47
Durham.......	1133	4 54	7 28	7 59	9 28	—	a.m 12 3	—	—	5 28
Sunderland..	p.m 1213	5 36	7 38	—	8 38	1052	1242	—	—	5 49
Newc'stle-on-Tyne	1 2?	5 19	7 57	8 2	9 2	1115	1233	1†32	—	5 53
Hudd'rsfield	a.m 9 46	—	4 12	—	7 7	8 33	p.m 1025	—	—	5† 5
Halifax	1011	—	4 23	—	7	8 45	1056	—	—	4†10
Leeds	9 12	—	3 20	5 40	6 2	7 25	9 35	p.m 1050	—	1 35
Bradford ...	9 52	—	3 50	6 20	6 4	7 50	1018	1120	—	3 0
Carlisle	p.m 1 5	5 50	5 50	—	8 55	—	—	—	—	4 5
Glasgow.......	3 53	7y3	—	—	11y2?	—	—	—	—	7y35
Edinburgh...	3 5?	—	8 30	—	11j30	—	—	—	—	9 48

* The time from Bristol to Bradford will not apply on Bank Holida

UP TRAINS.—WEEK DAYS.

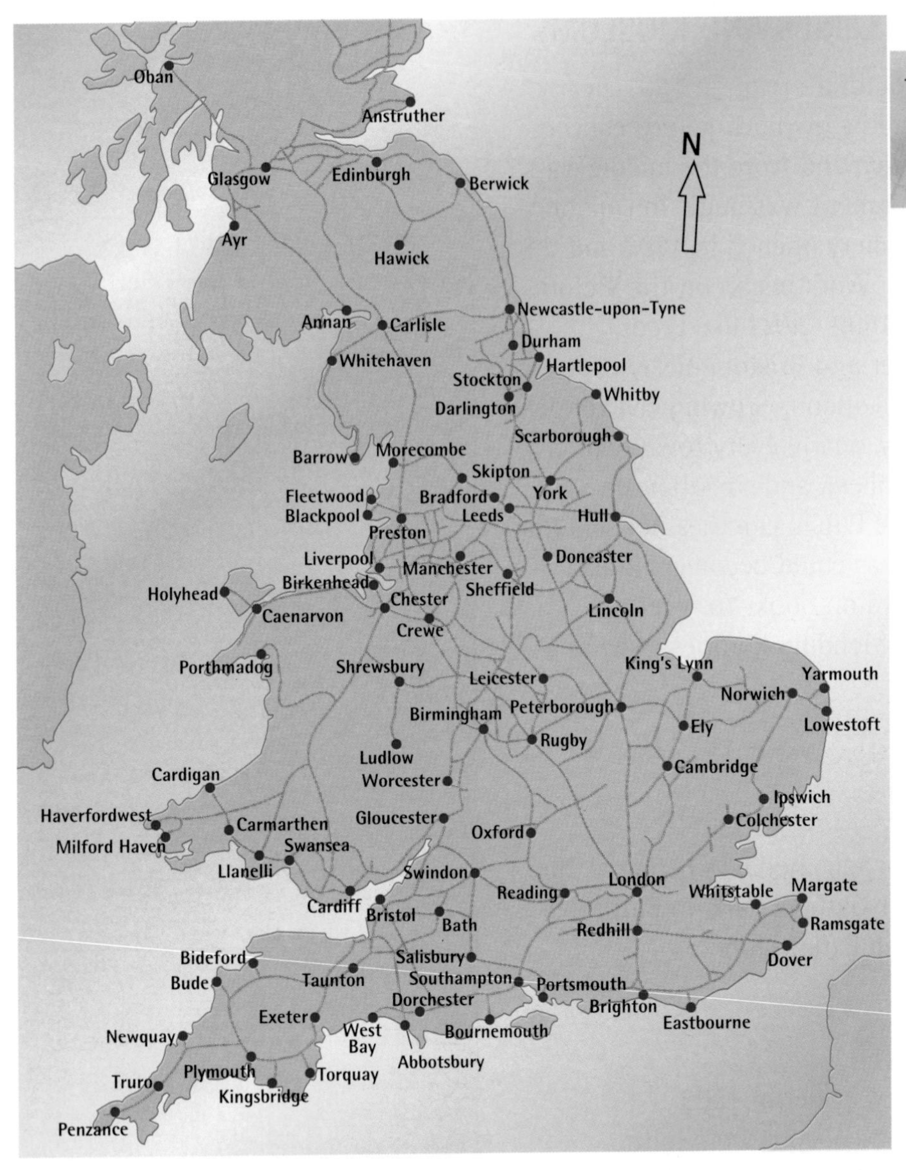

This map shows the British rail network in about 1900.

Question Time

1. What can you find out from Sources 6 and 7 about the ways in which people from Oldfield Park could have used the railways for holidays and excursions?
2. Using the map of the railway network in 1900, work out where Oldfield Park families were likely to have gone on their holidays.
3. Work with a partner and choose ONE leisure activity: for example, music halls, organised sport, circulating libraries or concert halls. Do some detailed research into what, where, how and why your chosen leisure activity operated. Find out, too, who supported it. Then plan how you will present your findings to the rest of your class.

REPRESENTATIONS OF VICTORIAN MIDDLE-CLASS LIFE: HOW ACCURATE ARE THEY?

Sources 1 and 2 give two representations of family life in 1900.

SOURCE 1

Mr Gradgrind's Country

There was a dining-room, there was a drawing room,
There was a billiard-room, there was a morning-room,
There were bedrooms for guests and bedrooms for sons and daughters
In attic and basement there were ample servants' quarters
There was a modern bathroom, a strong-room, and a conservatory.
In the days of England's glory.

There were Turkish carpets, there were Axminster carpets,
There were oil paintings of Vesuvius and family portraits,
There were mirrors, ottomans, * *wash-hand-stands and tantaluses,* **
There were port, sherry, claret, liqueur, and champagne glasses,
There was a solid brass gong, a grand piano, antlers, decanters, and a gentlemen's lavatory,
In the days of England's glory.

There was marqueterie and there was mahogany,
There was a cast of the Dying Gladiator in his agony,
There was the 'Encyclopaedia Britannica' in a revolving bookcase,
There were finger-bowls, asparagus-tongs, and inlets of real lace:
They stood in their own grounds and were called Chatsworth, Elgin or Tobermory,
In the days of England's glory.

This poem by Sylvia Townsend Warner (1893–1978) is called 'Mr Gradgrind's country'. Mr Gradgrind is a character in Charles Dickens' novel *Hard Times*, where money and usefulness are the measures of everything. These are the first three verses of the poem.

* an *ottoman* is a low sofa
** a *tantalus* is a tray for bottles of whisky and brandy which can be locked

SOURCE 2

In 1999 Channel 4 put a modern family into a house that had been restored to the way it was in 1900. Paul and Joyce Bowler, with their children Kathryn, Ruth, Hilary and Joe, lived for three months as if they were living in 1900. This is a still scene from one of the broadcasts.

Question Time

1. Read Source 1. Explain whether or not you think it gives a good idea of what life was like for middle-class people in the last years of the nineteenth century.
2. Now look carefully at Source 2.
   a How could the programme makers be sure that the house and its contents were just as they would have been in 1900?
   b The Bowler family dressed in 1900 clothes, lived in a 1900 house in 1900 ways and ate 1900 food on a 1900 budget. Do you think they would have thought, felt and behaved like a 1900 family?
3. Which interpretation of middle-class life in 1900 is better? Why?

WHAT WAS IN LIKE IN YOUR OWN AREA?

You may be lucky enough to live in, or near to, a town that had a growing middle class at the end of the nineteenth century. You can, however, only really study how middle-class people lived there if you can find and use the sort of material – maps, plans, photographs, census data – that we found and used with the Oldfield Park area of Bath. To do this you need a good local studies department in your local library; a record office that has, and will let you use, this sort of material; and a local archivist who will help you find the material you are looking for. You will also need a lot of time!

In case you have all of this, and a teacher who can help you, too, we are going to suggest how you might use your own area instead of, or as well as, Oldfield Park.

WHO WERE OUR LOCAL MIDDLE CLASS AND WHERE DID THEY LIVE?

What about the area where you live and go to school? Who were the middle class and where did they live?

In order to answer these questions, you will need to use the sort of source material we used for Oldfield Park. You may know the answers to some of the questions already!

Activity Time

1. Where did the middle classes live? It may be absolutely obvious, but if you are at all uncertain about where your town's new, middle-class housing might have been built, work with a map or plan that was made in about 1900 and compare it with one made about fifty years earlier.
2. What does the earlier map tell you about where people were living?
3. What does the later map tell you about how your town grew? You should be able quickly to see where, and in which direction, your town grew.
4. If you can, go and check out where you think the 1900 middle-class housing would have been. Were you right? You should find the sort of houses you are looking for. Note down the road names because you'll need to use them later on.

WHAT JOBS DID LOCAL MIDDLE-CLASS PEOPLE DO IN 1900?

You may live in a country area where the market town will be where you are looking for people with middle-class occupations; or you may live in a town that was, in 1900, dominated by heavy industry like coal, steel, iron or shipbuilding. Or your town may have been a thriving port or a growing business centre in 1900. If your town was focused in this way, then you would find a fairly narrow range of middle-class jobs.

So, let's get on with seeing what people did! You will need to work with local street directories and census returns. You will also need to have a large street map of the area in your town on which you are working. Ideally, this should be a 1900 street map, enlarged to make it big enough for everyone to see quickly and easily, and it should be pinned up on the wall of your classroom. If you have census returns for families living in several streets, you can work in groups. Your teacher will tell you what to do.

Activity Time

1. Look at the families in the census returns. List all the occupations of the fathers and mothers. Which occupations would people living in 1900 have thought of as being middle class?
2. Make a whole-class list of the middle-class families living in your town in 1900. These are the families you will be concentrating on.
3. Divide the families between you, working either individually or in groups. Find out, using directories and census data, as much as you can about 'your' families. You will need to find out the names of parents and children, and their ages; and whether any other relatives live with them, and their ages and occupations. Remember that you will already have the occupations of the parents. Do any families have lodgers? Do the children go to school?
4. On the big street map on the wall, find the house where 'your' family lived. Either enter this information directly on to the map (if it is big enough) or pin it separately on the wall, with some wool or string linking the people with their house.

Now let's think about where these middle-class families came from. Were they all born in your town, or did they move in from outside?

5. Go back to the census data and work out where the adults were born. How many were *not* born in your town?
6. How are you going to show this movement of people? You could use maps and arrows, pie charts or graphs, for example. Work out which way would be best with your data and make a wall display.

WHAT DID LOCAL PEOPLE DO IN THEIR TIME OFF?

It's very tempting to say 'Much as they do today', and in some ways that would be true. They dug their gardens, went down to the pub, joined the local amateur dramatic society, played with their children, went to the library and worshipped at the local church. But we want to find out a bit more detail about the middle-class families in your area.

Activity Time

1. Go back to the large street map of the 1900s middle-class area in your town. Can you find anything on it that could have been connected with leisure? The sorts of things you are looking for are parks, dance halls, music halls and libraries. If you can't find anything, you'll have to extend your search and use a map that covers a larger area. Make a list of all the leisure activities in which your middle-class families could have taken part.
2. Your local archivist may have been able to give you, or lend you, all sorts of different material to do with leisure – programmes and posters, photographs and invitations, newspaper reports and reviews, for example. Sort these by activity and, working in groups, divide the different activities among the groups. Each group should write up their particular activity and what was happening locally. Put them all together and you will have a local directory of leisure activities in 1900.
3. Middle-class people went away on holidays. Use your local maps to find out where their local rail station was. Use any rail excursion posters and timetables your local archivist may have been able to find for you and the map of the rail network on page 152. Where would your middle-class families have gone on holiday?
4. Many middle-class Victorians took their leisure time seriously! A lot of them were very proud of their own town. This is called civic pride. What examples of civic pride are there in your town? This may be a town hall, art gallery, library, statues of mayors and other dignitaries and foundation stones. What do these tell you about your neighbourhood in 1900?

AND NOW?

You have got a lot of information about your town and the middle-class families who lived there in 1900. How can you best present it?

You could:
- plan a wall display
- put together an exhibition
- design a web-site
- a combination of all three!

Now set to, as a class, and work out what you are going to do and who is going to do it. Who are you going to invite to the final display?

Unit 13: Mughal India and the coming of the British 1526–1857 – how did the Mughal Empire rise and fall?

HOW DID THE MUGHAL EMPIRE BEGIN?

About one-seventh of the population of the world today live in India. It is a varied place with fourteen different official languages and several major religions. However, most people today in India are Hindu. In neighbouring Pakistan and Bangladesh, the majority are Muslim. Until the middle of the nineteenth century all these people were part of the Mughal Empire. When this empire ended, it was the British who took over ruling India.

Who were the Mughals? To begin with, they were a family who had ruled areas that today we call Afghanistan and Uzbekistan. They invaded India and eventually ruled an area as big as all of Europe. They ruled almost nonstop from 1526 until 1857 – a period much longer than most ruling families in the world.

The Mughal Empire became famous not only for covering so much land for so long, but also for its excellent organisation and brilliant painting and architecture. What made the Mughal Empire so successful and why did it eventually decline? We will begin by looking at two powerful emperors.

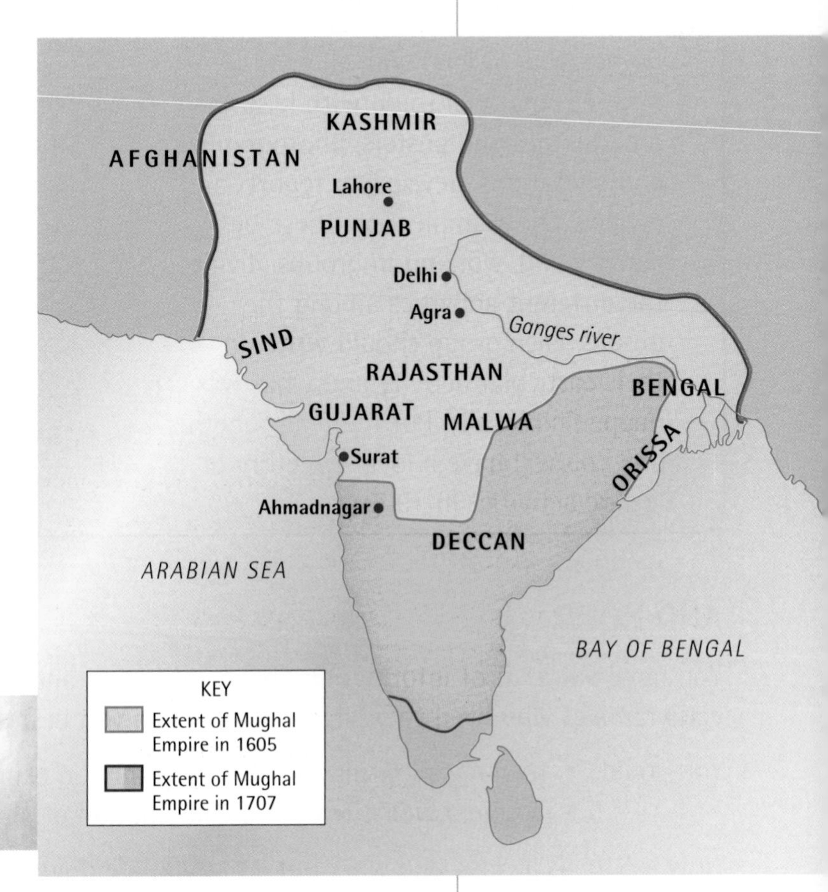

This map illustrates the location and expansion of the Mughal Empire.

Babur the Conqueror (1483–1530)

The name Babur means 'lion' and it was a good name for the first Mughal Emperor of India. He was a Muslim from Turkestan and had ruled there from the age of eleven when his father had died. He came from a very successful warrior family. He was related to Timur, a famous Turkish conqueror on his father's side, and to Genghis Khan, the Mongol conqueror, on his mother's side. The word 'Mongol' is 'Mughal' in Persian. Babur wanted to expand his land and when he was asked to come and overthrow the leading king in India, he couldn't miss such an opportunity. So in 1526 he brilliantly beat the Emperor of Delhi, Ibrahim Lodi, at the Battle of Panipat. Although he was outnumbered by Ibrahim's men ten to one, he had much better weapons and tactics. He used new light guns, as well as cavalry and archers, and surrounded the enemy so that they died either from the gunfire or from arrow shots. He was also clever enough to send his men after any of the enemy who escaped. This victory meant that although there were other kings and princes in India, he still gained a lot of power for himself. He captured the towns of Delhi and Agra and began to settle in the area. Unfortunately he died after only four years of being such a good emperor.

SOURCE 1

God made the victory easy for us! The battle was over in half a day; 5-6 thousand men were killed close to King Ibrahim. We counted at least another 15 or 16 thousand dead elsewhere on the battlefield ... Those who fled the battlefield were followed; our men captured nobles of every rank. During the afternoon Ibrahim's body was found in a heap of the dead. His head was brought to my court.

This account is from Babur's memoirs, written down by his scribe.

Question Time

1. The work of the historian should be based on fact rather than opinion and should not really exaggerate the evidence. Can you spot any opinions or exaggeration in the text entitled 'Babur the Conqueror'? Explain your answer.
2. Why do you think that Babur would have been pleased when Ibrahim's body was found after the Battle of Panipat?
3. Do you think that we can rely on Babur's count of the number of Ibrahim's men who were killed in the battle?

TAKING CONTROL OF INDIA

Winning the Battle of Panipat was a turning point for the Mughals, but they still had to take full control of their new land. India was made up of many different tribes and they were mainly Hindu, unlike the Mughals. Despite these problems the Mughal Empire soon expanded and became strong and wealthy. How did it achieve this?

AKBAR 1542–1605 – THE GREATEST OF ALL MUGHAL EMPERORS

Akbar's father, Humayun (Babur's son), had not managed to expand Mughal lands in his time as emperor. In fact he lost land to an Afghan leader and had to spend the rest of his life getting it back again. So it was up to Akbar to establish the Mughals as the rulers in northern India. He had plenty of work to do, as not only was the majority of India a different religion to the Mughals, but there was a lot of infighting between different princes and local leaders. Akbar was able to expand the Mughal Empire so that it stretched from the Hindu Kush area in the north, to the Bay of Bengal in the south, and from the Himalayas in the east, to the Arabian Sea on the west coast. However, there were still many different tribes that he had to keep under control. A Dutch trader called Pelasaert commented that there were nearly as many rebels as loyal subjects in the empire.

AKBAR'S RELIGIOUS FREEDOM

Akbar was a very religious man, but he was more of a free thinker than a strict follower of Islam; he even developed his own religion. He showed that he supported all religions by banning the traditional Muslim tax on non-Muslims, the *jizya*, as well as the tax on Hindu pilgrimages. This did not always make him popular with strict Muslims, but helped to keep peace in the empire. He also put money into religious buildings for different religions. Hindus were able to keep their own laws and courts as long as they were loyal to Akbar's government. He employed a Hindu minister in charge of his taxes. Akbar had over 300 wives and 5000 women in his harem, but his favourite wife was a Hindu princess. He married most of his wives to make alliances with rebel leaders.

AKBAR'S ORGANISATIONAL SKILLS

Because Akbar had introduced a lot of religious freedom to keep people happy, he had to make sure that everyone was still under his control. He did this by introducing a new system of army officials, called *mansabdars*, and made all the appointments himself. This meant that every official, even those in small towns and country areas, had to answer directly to Emperor Akbar. They felt that they had to be loyal as they could be sacked for any small problem if necessary. Akbar let the *mansabdars* take taxes from the local peasants, but he gave them new jobs every few years to make sure that they did not become too powerful in one place. He employed Hindus in top jobs, which meant that they co-operated with the Mughals even more. He also gave top jobs in his army to Rajput princes, who had been rebel leaders in the north.

AKBAR'S TAX SYSTEM

Akbar reorganised the tax system. His new system was seen as being fair as all people paid the same amount, 30 per cent of their profits. He also let people pay less when harvests were bad, and keep any extra when crops were especially good. This encouraged people to take on more and more land, and trade as much as they could. This in turn meant that more markets and towns grew up, making the Mughal Empire a profitable place to live in. Akbar was able to spend the taxes on building towns and palaces and sponsoring artists and craftsmen.

AKBAR'S DETERMINATION

Although he ruled very fairly, Akbar was not afraid to resort to tough measures to keep control. This was especially true in the early years of his reign. He removed his power grabbing chief minister by sending him on a pilgrimage to Mecca, where he was killed on the dangerous journey. He also dealt harshly with his foster brother, who had murdered another of Akbar's ministers.

SOURCE 2

When he was nineteen years old, Akbar had his foster brother, Adham Khan, thrown from the top of the palace walls.

OTHER FAMOUS EMPERORS

Akbar laid the foundations for other emperors to expand the successful empire south to its greatest size. This was mainly done by Shah Jahan and his son, Aurangzeb. Shah Jahan (1592–1666) is also famous for building the beautiful Taj Mahal as a tomb for his wife, who died giving birth to her fourteenth child. We will look at the achievements of Aurangzeb (1618–1707) in more detail later.

Activity Time

Write a report on the state of Mughal India when Aurangzeb took over in 1658. Mention the strengths of the empire, including its organisation, size, wealth and tax system and how the population were kept loyal. Also mention what could go wrong for any new emperor and how you would advise Aurangzeb to rule.

WHAT WAS LIFE LIKE DURING THE PERIOD OF THE MUGHAL EMPIRE?

Would you like to have been one of the Mughal emperor's courtiers, or perhaps one of his officials, called *mansabdars*? We will now find out what it was like for many different groups to live under Mughal rule.

WHAT WAS LIFE LIKE FOR COURTIERS?

There was a strict hierarchy (ranks of different levels) at the court of the Mughal emperors. Courtiers had to be careful to stand in the correct places and stick to the strict rules of behaviour for people of that rank. The more important the courtier, the closer he stood to the emperor's throne. Mistakes could offend people and your job could be at risk. Visitors could get to see the emperor, but had to bring him gifts of coins and jewels or even animals. If you worked hard for the emperor or were loyal to him, you might receive a gift of beautifully decorated robes as a reward.

The emperor's courtiers also had to be ready to move from place to place. The early courts, especially, moved to different cities for battles, hunting sessions or to crush a rebellion. It is said that the emperor would go hunting in any area which was considering a rebellion. Any rebels

SOURCE 1

Akbar's court with visitors paying him respect, bringing presents with them.

would be so scared by the strength and wealth of the emperor's party that they would change their minds about disloyalty straight away. Moving was not easy, however, as between 200,000 and 300,000 men were involved. It took 1000 men alone just to put up the emperor's tents.

WHAT WAS LIFE LIKE FOR TRADERS?

Traders spent most of their time on the roads travelling from ports to markets. They travelled in caravans or groups as it was safer. Some smaller roads were very narrow, muddy and difficult to pass. There were also imperial highways which were much bigger and better. They included inns called *sarai* and watering places along their routes. Business for merchants under Mughal rule was good. A great profit was to be made. Foreigners wanted luxury goods, such as silks, and precious stones, such as diamonds. Copper, iron and salt were also popular. Foods were exchanged for silver bars. Most merchants were Muslims. They hired ships going to China, other parts of India and East Africa. However, the Portuguese and the Dutch began to challenge Indian traders' positions and take over the trade routes.

WHAT WAS LIFE LIKE FOR THE RICH?

Just like those at the imperial court, the rich in the Mughal Empire led a luxurious life. They could spend money on the arts, on paintings, pottery and luxurious clothes. They wore silks and good quality cottons. Men and women both wore jewellery. Foods were imported from all over South Asia. One friend of Emperor Akbar is said to have ordered at least 100 courses at each meal. The rich ate from gold or silver plates and drank coffee, wine or sherbet from goblets. Another expensive part of the rich man's life was his harem, the part of the house where his wives lived. (Remember that Muslim men could take more than one wife.) Money would be spent on each wife and her servants. The rich would also spend money on various animals. Nobles needed to have several elephants, camels, mules and carts ready in case the emperor demanded that they go into battle.

SOURCE 2

Inside a good house the whole floor is covered with a fine cotton mattress four inches in thickness, over which a fine white cloth is spread during the summer, and a silk carpet in the winter. On one side of the room are one or two mattresses, with fine covers decorated with delicate silk embroidery, laced with gold or silver. These are intended for the master of the house, or for important visitors. Five or six feet from the floor the sides of the room are full of shelves, in which are seen porcelain vases and flower pots. The ceiling is gilt and painted, but without pictures of man or beast, such representatives being forbidden by the religion of the country (Islam).

François Bernier, a French doctor, writes about the inside of a noble's house, in his *Travels in the Moghul Empire, 1656–68*.

Question Time

1. Read Source 2 carefully and make a sketch of how you imagine this room in a rich man's house to look. Label as many features as you can.
2. Where did the rich get all their money from?

WHAT WAS LIFE LIKE FOR THE POOR IN THE COUNTRYSIDE?

Life in the countryside was very different. Some peasants owned or rented land, but some had no land at all and just worked for other people in the village. Most peasants lived in mud huts with thatched roofs. They had little furniture and very few possessions, perhaps just a mat to sleep on. The material used for their basic clothes was coarse cloth. Few had shoes. One meal per day would be the average diet for most people in the countryside. They ate rice, millet and grass roots, but no beef or pork for religious reasons. Meals would be flavoured with cheaper spices, like cumin and coriander, and a little salt would be used to preserve some foods. Although wheat was grown, families would usually sell it rather than eat it themselves. Fruit such as mangoes, melons and coconuts would be more common and would vary according to time of year.

Although this lifestyle seems very basic to us, Mughal farmers were quite advanced. They built dams and canals and also used wells and water tanks to irrigate the land. They also rotated the crops they grew on each area of land to keep it as fertile as possible. The biggest problems for the peasants were the taxes that were often forced on them by the *mansabdars*, and were collected by the *zamindar*. He was usually the largest landholder in the area and was the given the job of tax collector. The other threat to people's lives was the weather. Floods and droughts could ruin entire crops and lead to famine.

SOURCE 3

This scene shows houses near Calcutta drawn by an Englishman in 1813.

SOURCE 4

15 per cent of the population lived in towns and cities in India by the end of the seventeenth century. In England at that time, 13 per cent was to be found in towns. Nine Indian cities had populations of 200,000 or more, including Delhi, Agra and Surat. In the whole of Europe, there were only three cities with such large populations – London, Paris and Naples.

A modern historian, Paul Goalen, describes the population of India.

WHAT WAS LIFE LIKE IN THE TOWNS?

The Mughal period is famous for building many new towns in India. The buildings were often grand and beautifully decorated. Some emperors built completely new cities. Old Delhi was built by Shah Jahan as his new capital. Akbar built the Red Fort at Agra and he also built a fabulous new city called Fatehpur Sikri. It included his palace, a huge mosque, many towers and other different buildings. The architecture combined Muslim and Hindu styles, with Hindu decoration and Muslim arches. Akbar built it in honour of a holy man who had successfully predicted that Akbar would eventually have three sons to secure the Mughal family line.

Under the peace of Mughal rule, trade was less disrupted and so flourished. Selling goods at markets in towns was an important way of making money to pay taxes in cash.

SOURCE 5

In among these different houses is a great number of small ones, built of mud and thatched with straw, in which live the common people, and all that great number of servants and camp followers who follow the court and the army.

It is as a result of these thatched cottages that Delhi has such frequent fires. More than 60,000 roofs were destroyed by three fires during the last windy season. So rapid were the flames that several camels and horses and poor women were burnt.

François Bernier, a French doctor, wrote this in his *Travels in the Moghul Empire, 1656–68*.

Question Time

1. In groups, research different aspects of Mughal life. Your teacher will tell you which aspect to find out about. Each group should find evidence about what it was like to live there, explaining the good points of Mughal civilisation and also whether the benefits of living under the Mughals were greater than any problems.
   See if you can find any extra information by searching in your library, in encyclopaedias or on the Internet. Make a list of key search words before you start.
2. Compare the information that you found in this book with the new information and discuss these questions as a group:
   a Was all the information the same?
   b What new things did you learn?
   c Which source was most useful for your topic?
   d Which source was easiest to use?
3. If you were living in Mughal India, who would you rather be: a courtier, trader, rich or poor person? Explain your decision carefully. You could think about food, housing, luxuries, work and freedom when making your decision.

DID AURANGZEB'S REIGN MARK THE BEGINNING OF THE END OF THE MUGHAL EMPIRE?

Aurangzeb ruled from 1658 to 1707. He became emperor by imprisoning his ill father and executing his elder brother, who also wanted the position. The Mughals believed that whoever God wanted as emperor would get the job, so there were no strict laws about who should take over when an emperor died or became ill. This did not help keep the peace and meant that Aurangzeb often had to bribe people to support him in the early years of his reign.

AURANGZEB'S RELIGIOUS INTOLERANCE

Aurangzeb was far less tolerant of other religions. This meant that he did not want them to exist. He sacked Hindus from jobs as public and military officers and reintroduced the taxes on their religion. He wanted everyone in the empire to be Muslim and destroyed many Hindu temples to get his way. He introduced Shari'ah, which is Islamic law, covering all aspects of life. This meant that Hindus and Sikhs had to live according to laws based on the Qur'an (the Islamic holy book) and go to Islamic courts. This did not make him popular.

SOURCE 1

This painting shows Aurangzeb on horseback. It was painted in 1680.

SOURCE 2

Aurangzeb keeps the fasts on Fridays and other sacred days and he reads the Friday prayers with the common people. He fasts during the whole period of Ramadan (when Muslims fast for a period during daytime each year), says the prayers for the month and reads the Holy Qur'an. He does not eat forbidden meats, does not listen to music or wear forbidden clothes. In his court, no wicked talk, no backbiting or lying is allowed.

This extract is from the *History of Aurangzeb* written by Mohammed Kazim in 1668.

SOURCE 3

Aurangzeb says 'My kingdom is now full of mosques instead of the most hideous temples. Instead of poisonous inns and brothels we find groups of holy men.' But despite what Aurangzeb says in India every day there are committed the most monstrous crimes in the world.

Nicolao Manucci, an Italian visitor, wrote about Aurangzeb in his book *History of the Mughuls, 1653–1708*.

TOO MUCH LAND TO CONTROL?

Under Aurangzeb the empire was at its greatest, but it was difficult to control and the number of rebellions increased. The Sikhs and the Marathas caused the most problems. The Marathas were a Hindu tribe based in the south, in the Deccan mountains. The Sikhs had been a minority under earlier Mughal emperors, but now wanted their independence. Fighting against these powerful enemies cost Aurangzeb a lot of money.

AURANGZEB'S MONEY PROBLEMS

Shah Jahan (Aurangzeb's father) had already increased the tax rate to 50 per cent. Aurangzeb had to spend more money controlling rebellions, but spent most of his income on luxurious palaces. Even the famous Pearl Mosque at Delhi was built as a place for his private prayers. Aurangzeb's popularity began to fade.

Trouble for Aurangzeb: Shivaji's rebellion

Shivaji was a Hindu and chief of the Maratha tribe. He had taken over more and more Mughal land and had created his own kingdom within the Mughal Empire by 1646. His rebellion was crushed by Aurangzeb, but Shivaji was not killed and continued to fight, using tactics of guerrilla warfare. This is where the soldiers do not fight face to face, but prefer to carry out raids and then hide from the enemy. Over the next 100 years, the Marathas took control of more land than the Mughal emperor.

Activity Time

1. What might have happened if a European had been given the chance to interview Aurangzeb about his time as emperor of the most powerful empire in India. Make a list of questions to ask him, including ones about why he took the actions he did.
2. Copy these headings and fill in a chart to show Aurangzeb's strengths and weaknesses as emperor.

Aurangzeb is a good leader	Aurangzeb is a foolish leader

3. Do you think that Aurangzeb's strengths outweigh his weaknesses? Explain your answer.
4. Shivaji's army sent a spy to report on Aurangzeb's power. Write a report that could have come from the spy, recommending that now would be a good time to attack. Provide evidence that the Mughal Empire was weakening because Aurangzeb was:
   a undermining Akbar's system of government
   b making lots of his own mistakes.
   Include evidence on money matters, religion, expansion, rebellions and popularity.
5. Try to find out what happened to Mughal rule after Aurangzeb's reign. A clue is to look at how many emperors followed in the next ten years and what the nobles began to do with their taxes.

TIMELINE – MAIN EVENTS IN SHIVAJI'S LIFE AS A REBEL

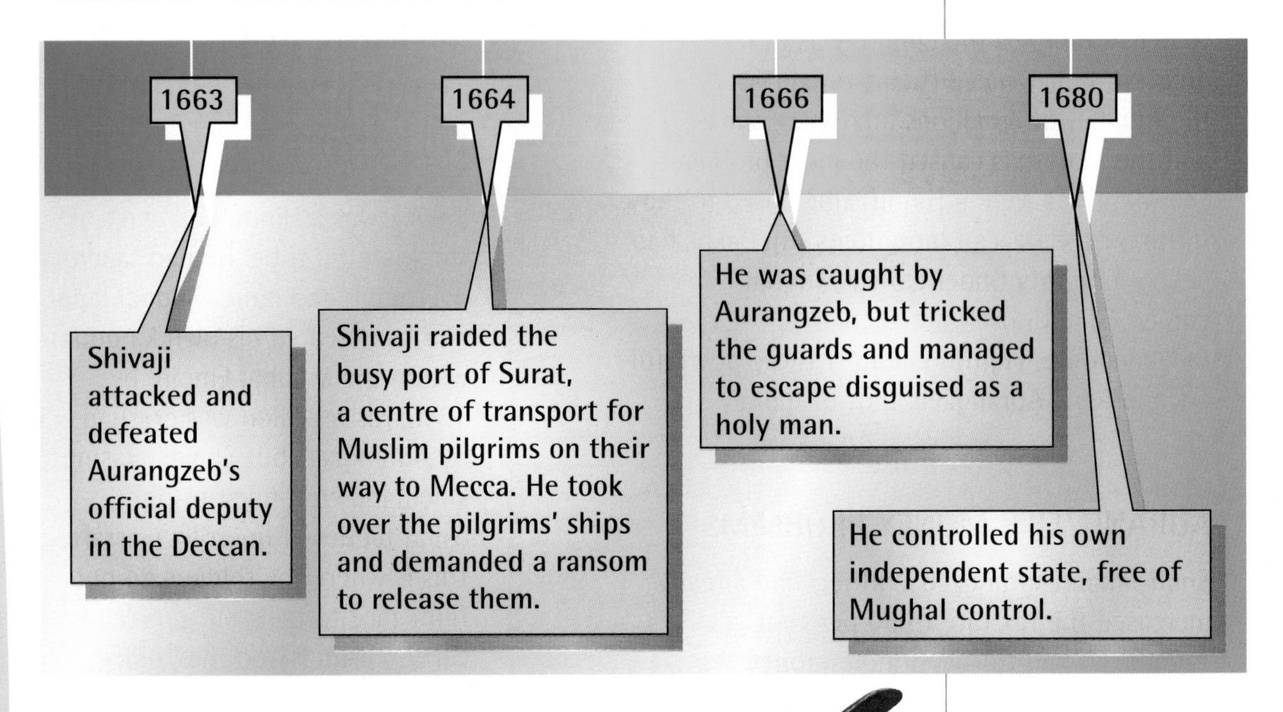

SOURCE 4

Shivaji wore this tiger claw on his hand as a weapon. He is said to have ripped out the stomach of an enemy general with it. The general had met Shivaji to talk rather than fight, but was tricked and killed.

SOURCE 5

Whenever Shivaji heard of a populated and rich town he attacked it, robbed it and took it over for his people ... He collected a large number of specially chosen robbers from the Marathas and prepared to capture the well-known Mughal strong forts.

Shivaji is descibed by a Muslim historian, Khafi Khan, in *The History of Alamgir*, written in 1680.

SOURCE 6

The rise of the Maratha power was because ... it was the first experiment of its kind after the disastrous period of foreign Muslim (Mughal) invasions. It was a national movement or upheaval in which all classes of people co-operated.

An Indian nationalist (someone who is proud of India) wrote in 1900 about the power of the Marathas.

Question Time

1. Give two reasons why Aurangzeb would have been furious when Shivaji attacked the port of Surat.
2. Is the author of Source 5 praising Shivaji or just describing his success? Explain your answer by looking at who the author is as well as what he says.
3. a How does Source 6 make Shivaji seem less important in the story of the defeat of the Mughals?
   b Are you surprised that this author describes Mughal rule as 'disastrous'?
4. Make two lists of evidence, one including reasons why Shivaji could be seen as a troublemaker, and one with reasons why he could be seen as a hero. Compare your lists with your partner or another group.
5. Make the reasons into speech bubbles to show what Aurangzeb would say about Shivaji, and how the Maratha tribe would describe him.
6. Do you think that Shivaji was more a hero or a troublemaker? Think about these aspects when making your decision: his aims, his methods, his support, Aurangzeb's rule.

HOW DID BRITISH POWER IN INDIA EXPAND DURING THE EIGHTEENTH CENTURY?

PROBLEMS FOR THE MUGHALS

After Aurangzeb, the Mughal emperors became weak and divided. Twelve different emperors followed in the next ten years. To make matters worse, Persia invaded and captured Delhi in 1739, stealing vast amounts of Mughal treasure. Although the Persian leader, Nadir Shah, did not have enough support to take over as ruler, he had damaged Mughal pride and showed how weak they had become. Their weakness was made worse by 1756 when Bengal became a sort of independent kingdom ruled by a young leader called Siraj ud-Daulah. Other regions became independent, too, ruled by local leaders called *nawabs*.

Another reason that the Mughals were losing power was foreign competition. They had gained their wealth through farming and they could not compete with the trading experience of countries like Portugal, Britain and France, as they fought over control of trade routes in the East.

THE EAST INDIA COMPANY

This famous trading company was set up as early as 1600 by merchants living in Elizabeth I's reign. It was given the monopoly in trade between England and the Far East, which means that no other English company could trade in that area. The company traded silver, spices, silks and cottons from India and began to take over control of trade routes from the Portuguese. The city of Calcutta was founded in 1690 as a trading post for the company, and it grew to have a population of 100,000 in just 100 years. The East India Company employed many Indians in its own huge private army to protect its factories. Once established in many of India's ports and trading posts, the company came to take over large parts of Bengal and Mysore, ruling with a committee set up by the British Parliament.

PUNJAB
Delhi
OUDH
SIND
Calcutta
MARATHA STATES
ORISSA
BAY OF BENGAL
KEY
British possessions in India up to 1765
British possessions in India, 1857
Main centres of rebellion

This map shows how British rule expanded in India and the main towns which rebelled in the Indian Mutiny of 1857.

HOW DID THE BRITISH TAKE OVER BENGAL AND MYSORE?

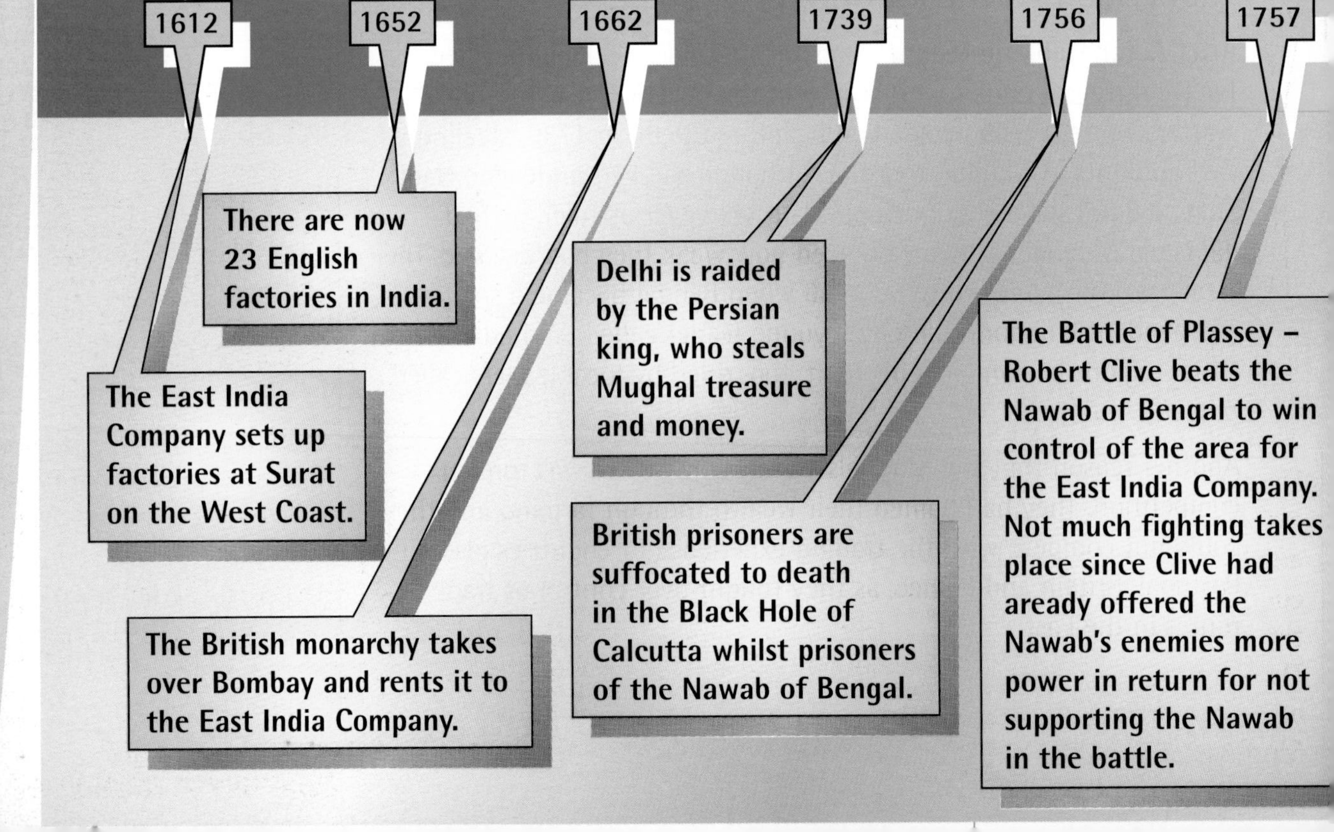

Question Time

1. Each event on the timeline below is a step towards British rule of India. Discuss each event with a partner and explain to each other how each event gave the British more power.

2. a The British did not just use force to take control in India. Trade links, wealth, making deals and the weaknesses of the Mughals are other reasons for the British conquest. Use each of these five reasons as a heading and list the events from the timeline underneath each one if it matches. Each event may fit under more than one heading.
   b Which type of reason has the most events underneath it?
   c Does this mean that this is the biggest reason for the British conquest?
   d How could the banning of *sati* be said to be a way of taking control?

3. Design a poster to show how the British took over rule in India. You could design it like a cartoon or film strip, or have different sections for the different types of cause. Mention specific events and use captions to show how each event increased British power.

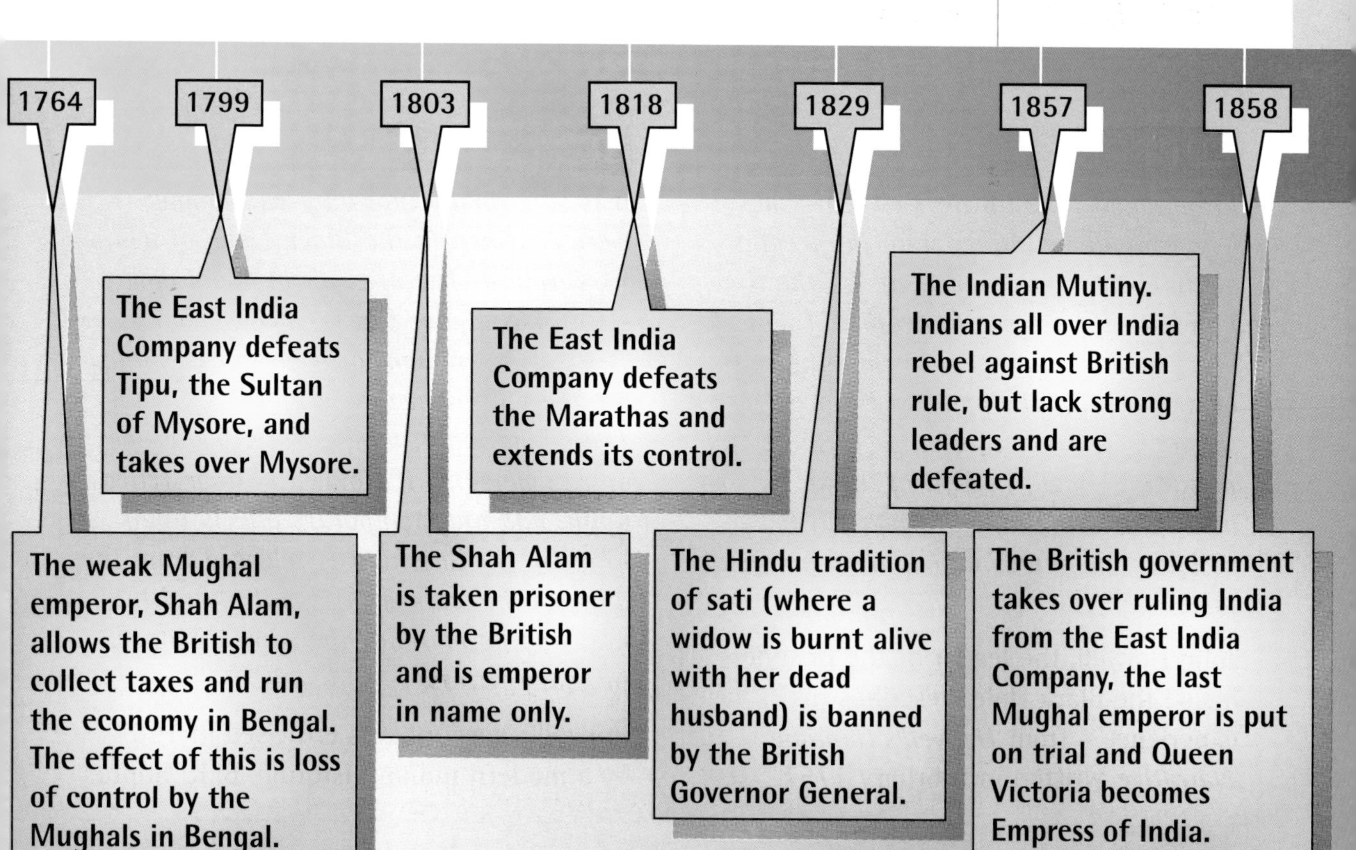

BRITISH PROPAGANDA – THE BLACK HOLE OF CALCUTTA

This is also studied in Unit 14, on pages 187–9. You might want to look at the sources on those pages to help you understand what is said here.

In 1756, Siraj ud-Daulah, the Nawab of Bengal, attacked Calcutta. The story goes that his soldiers kept 146 British prisoners locked up for a night in one tiny prison cell, called the 'Black Hole'. It was a hot night in June and only 23 of the men survived.

SOURCE 1

The barracks at Fort William, Calcutta. This is an artist's idea of what the Black Hole might have looked like. The Black Hole itself is behind the barred windows. This sketch was drawn in 1882.

SOURCE 2

From about nine till near eleven ... my legs were almost broke with the weight against them (of other men). By the time I was nearly pressed to death ... I moved over the dead and went to the other end of the room ... The moment I moved from the window my breathing grew short and painful ... I had, in a fit of thirst, attempted drinking my urine, but it was so bitter, there was no enduring a second taste.

John Holwell, the leader of the prisoners inside the Black Hole, describes his experience – from *Holwell's Genuine Narrative* written in February 1757.

SOURCE 3

It is safe to say that only 64 persons were confined in the Black Hole, of whom 21 survived. The area of the room gave about 4.2 square feet to each person. This seems enough for a person to stand up and sit down, though not comfortably. The whole night, which claimed the lives of 123 persons, if Holwell is to be relied upon, had only temporary effects upon him. On the day he was released from the dungeon he walked three miles, and the next day he marched the same distance, in heavy fetters.

Holwell's account was criticised in 1962 by a modern Indian historian, B. K. Gupta.

SO WHY ARE THE STORIES SO DIFFERENT?

Although we know that some men did die in the Black Hole, it seems likely that Holwell and the British exaggerated the event to discredit the Nawab of Bengal. They used the story as a form of propaganda against their enemy. People who produce propaganda do so for a reason. It might be to win an election or a war by getting people on their side. The 'Black Hole of Calcutta' is one example of an event that was exaggerated for propaganda purposes. In the following year, the British plotted and overthrew the Nawab, using a combination of bribes and force. The plot was funded by the East India Company.

TIPU, SULTAN OF MYSORE'S TERRIBLE REPUTATION

Here is another example of British propaganda. Stories of the feared Tipu, Sultan of Mysore, were spread to help the British. Here we will see how his reputation was exaggerated and how the British used such stories.

WHY WAS TIPU SUCH A THREAT TO THE BRITISH?

Mysore was a large province in central India. Tipu, which means 'tiger', ruled there as sultan. He made the province wealthy and strong and became famous for his determination to defeat the British. He bought weapons from France to be able to fight the British in their own style of warfare. These included 50 cannons, 100,000 cannon balls and 10,000 muskets. He had rockets and handguns made in Mysore.

The British hated Tipu because he stood up to them. He tried to prevent them from controlling all the trade by building trade links with Persia and Arabia himself. Tipu's army was so strong that he won two wars against the British.

Question Time

1. Look at Source 1. Why do you think that artists were still drawing pictures of the 'Black Hole' 125 years after the event took place?
2. How does Holwell in Source 2 try to convince the reader that his story is true?
3. Is there anything about his story which you find hard to believe?
4. What new evidence has Gupta used in his account (Source 3) to challenge the traditional story?
5. Does he suggest that Holwell was making up the whole story?
6. What do you think would have been the effect of news of the events in the Black Hole on
   a British soldiers working for the East India Company
   b wealthy bosses of the East India Company?
7. Try to find an example from the news or a newspaper this week that might have been exaggerated for political reasons.

The British were particularly annoyed that Tipu had help from the French. Remember that England was concerned that revolutionary ideas from France would spread there. Tipu called himself 'Citizen Tipu', in the revolutionary way, which gave the British more reasons to hate him.

WAS HE REALLY A TYRANT?

The British called Tipu a 'monster' and a cruel tyrant. They described how he mistreated his prisoners and his own people.

SOURCE 4

The main features of his character were vanity and arrogance; according to Tipu no human being was ever so handsome, so wise, so learned or so brave as himself. He murdered his English prisoners because he hated their bravery. He insulted his Hindu subjects, because he hated their religion.

This account is by Colonel Wilks in his historical *Sketches of the South of India*, 1810.

SOURCE 5

The British claimed that Tipu was a Muslim fanatic. In fact Tipu made offerings in the Christian churches and Hindu temples of his loyal subjects; he only destroyed the places of worship of his enemies!

This account is by a modern historian, Paul Goalen, writing in 1992.

THE TIGER INCIDENT

In 1891 Tipu's army was beaten by the British, who were led by Sir Hector Munro. Eleven years later Munro's only son was mauled and killed by a tiger. Tipu saw this as revenge and had a giant working model of a tiger attacking a British soldier made, just for fun. The image of the tiger was used as a traditional royal symbol in Mysore and was painted on uniforms and swords as well as household decoration. You can imagine what the British thought of this.

WHAT HAPPENED TO TIPU?

Tipu lost the third war against the British and had to pay compensation. He also had to give up half his land and all his prisoners, and his sons were taken as hostages. He died of battle wounds in 1799. Mysore was then taken over by the East India Company.

SOURCE 6

A painting showing Tipu's sons being handed over as hostages to Lord Cornwallis in 1792.

WHY DID THE BRITISH EXAGGERATE HIS CRUELTY?

Tipu stood up to the British for over twenty years before he was beaten by Governor General Cornwallis in 1792. He had not shown them respect or agreed to pay money to the East India Company for protection. He was open in his hatred of the English. He thought that they were invading his country. The East India Company wanted to improve its army so that it could defeat any enemy and protect its trade. To do this, it needed funds and support. The creation of an exaggeratedly strong enemy meant the company could justify its demand for more money and support.

Question Time

1. Source 4 is an example of propaganda against Tipu. What can it tell us about him?
2. How does Lord Cornwallis seem to be treating Tipu's sons in Source 6?
3. How could this source be called propaganda against Tipu?
4. Why do you think that the British exaggerated stories about Tipu?

WHY WAS THERE REBELLION AGAINST BRITISH RULE IN INDIA IN 1857, AND WHAT WERE THE CONSEQUENCES?

In 1857 uprisings against the British took place all over India. This event has been called the Indian Mutiny or Rebellion, or the First War of Independence. It took the British army several months to regain control, and after this date the East India Company's rule over its provinces was taken away by the British government. We are going to investigate why it happened and what it tells us about Mughal rule in India by this time.

June 1857

Delhi has been captured by Indian mutineers for a month now. There were no British soldiers in Delhi to stop the murder of British officers, workers and their families in the city. The East India Company has sent Sir Henry Barnard with 6000 troops to take control again, but he has as yet been unsuccessful. His men are outnumbered by seven to one.

THE GREASED GUN CARTRIDGES

Most of the soldiers in the East India Company's army were actually Indian. They were Muslims and Hindus and were called sepoys. In 1857 the sepoys rebelled when they heard that the gun cartridges that they used were filled with grease from the fat of cows and pigs. Muslims consider pigs to be unclean and Hindus consider the cow to be a holy animal. To use the cartridges, the sepoys would have to bite off the ends with their teeth and this would be sinful. This was seen as an insult. Three regiments refused to use the cartridges and were punished, causing the rebellion. The greased cartridges turned out to be just a rumour.

TAXATION

High taxes were another cause of concern, especially in the countryside. Peasants and small landowners found it hard to pay the increasing taxes. Some tax collectors were corrupt, taking money just for themselves. The British had come to rely on the income from Indian land and made sure that taxes were collected.

SOURCE 1

British rule is for the lasting benefit of millions of the human race.

This was said by the Marquess Curzon, Viceroy of India from 1898 to 1905.

LOCAL PRINCES AND NOBLES WANT INDEPENDENCE

Local leaders resented British rule. In Delhi nobles supported the last Mughal emperor, Bahadur Shah, and plotted to restore his power as emperor. One woman, Raji, the widow of the king of Jhansi, hated the fact that the East India Company now ruled her husband's land and she led an army against the British. She died fighting in 1858.

BRITISH CHANGES TO INDIAN LIFE

Indians began to think that the British were trying to remove their customs and beliefs. When a Hindu man died, it was traditional to burn his wife on his funeral pyre. This was called *sati* and brought great respect on the woman's family. When the British Governor General banned *sati* in 1829, some Hindus welcomed the ban because they thought the custom was cruel – widows were sometimes forced to commit *sati*. Other Hindus were angry about the ban and the custom continued in parts of India for many years.

Indians also began to resent the education system that was set up. Persian was replaced by English as the official language in India. Western-style schools were run by Christian missionaries who thought that it was their duty to convert the Indians to Christianity and 'civilise' them. Indians working for the British were encouraged to give up their religious traditions. The British also built roads and railways across India.

SOURCE 2

A watercolour painting showing a woman commiting *sati*.

Question Time

1. The use of cow or pig fat as grease in the army cartridges was only a rumour, so does that mean that it was not a real cause of the uprising?
2. Why do you think that Marquess Curzon thought that millions of people would benefit from British rule?
3. Does the support for the Bahadur Shah during the rebellion suggest that people wanted the Mughals to take full control of India again?
4. The rebellion is called the Indian Mutiny in many British history books, but the First War of Independence by some Indians. Why are there different names for this event?
5. Your teacher will act as Bahadur Shah, the last Mughal emperor. Prepare a list of questions to ask the emperor about the causes of 1857 rebellion and what happened as a result of the rebellion.

THE CAWNPORE MASSACRE

During the rebellion violent acts and murders were carried out by both sides. One example of an atrocity was in Cawnpore in 1857.

The city of Cawnpore was a base for the British army and the East India Trading Company. As part of the rebellion, Indians massacred the families of British troops who had been granted a safe passage away from the city. Two hundred women and children were shot at and later killed with butchers' knives. In revenge, anyone who was suspected of sympathising with the mutineers was executed by the British. Similar atrocities were carried out by both sides.

SOURCE 3

British officers and their wives are shown trying to escape from Cawnpore in 1857, from a book published in 1858.

SOURCE 4

British officers are shown killing sepoys, who had mutinied, by blowing them apart with large guns. This was, according to the sepoys' own religious beliefs, to prevent them from having any peace after death as their bodies were incomplete. This picture is from a book published in 1858.

OTHER EFFECTS OF THE REBELLION

- The rebellion shocked the British government, which took away the East India Company's right to rule, and sent a viceroy (governor) from Britain to rule in 1858.
- Bahadur Shah (the last Mughal emperor) was put on trial for the rebellion and sentenced to life imprisonment. He was sent to live in Burma in 1858.
- Queen Victoria became Queen and then Empress of India, replacing the last Mughal emperor.
- Cawnpore stayed a centre for anti-British protests into the twentieth century. It changed its name to Kanpore in 1948.
- Bitterness between India and Britain continued as a result of the atrocities. Campaigns for Indian independence continued, too.

SOURCE 6

Pea fowl and partridges and mutineers rose together: the latter giving the best sport.

This account is from a British gunner officer talking about hunting out rebels from a field of wheat, as if they were animals.

SOURCE 7

The British magazine *Punch* published a series of cartoons after the Cawnpore Massacre. This is one of them, from September 1857.

JUSTICE.

SOURCE 5

Whilst it is true that large numbers of European men, women and children were murdered with great brutality by the mutineers ... some of the stories of torture and rape have been grossly exaggerated or totally untrue ... The British forces felt that every Indian male capable of carrying arms (weapons) was guilty of such crimes. Hundreds were killed in the days following the recapture of Delhi, either by shooting or by slow strangulation.

A modern historian, R. Perkins, describes the Indian Rebellion.

Question Time

1. Study Sources 3–6. How much do they tell us about British attitudes towards the Indians?
2. In pairs, see if you can find proof of the following statements in the cartoon in Source 7:
   - Britain and British soldiers are taking revenge against the Indians.
   - British soldiers are sparing women and children.
   - There are dead British bodies on the battlefield.
   - Scales of justice are on the shield of the woman. She represents Britain.
3. Does the cartoon prove that the Indians deserved to be killed?
4. Do you think that people who commit atrocities during a war should be put on trial?
5. Write a paragraph explaining the effects of the Indian Rebellion. Try to write different sections for the short-term and long-term effects, those which happened shortly after the rebellion and those which lasted longer.

HOW DID THE MUGHAL EMPIRE RISE AND FALL?

We have seen how the Mughal emperors took over India and made it into a wealthy, powerful empire. We have also investigated how they gradually lost control to the British and to rival leaders in India. Your final task is to design and make a big timeline for a display. Work as a group or in pairs. The timeline will help to answer the big questions of this Unit: How did the Mughal Empire rise to power in India? How did the power of the Mughal Empire decline?

Activity Time

1. Copy the timeline on the next page. Some of the main events in Mughal history have been included. The events that increased Mughal power are above the line and those that decreased power below it. Fill in the remaining labels to show how events increased or decreased power.
2. Add more examples of events from this book or your notes. Remember to add labels to explain.
3. Some events may have increased power in the short term, only to decrease them in the long term. See if you can find any of these special examples and label them to explain.
4. Can you find a turning point on your timeline, after which Mughal power was not the same again? Discuss your ideas with the rest of your class.
5. Decorate your timeline with sketches of the events and things which you have learned in this Unit.

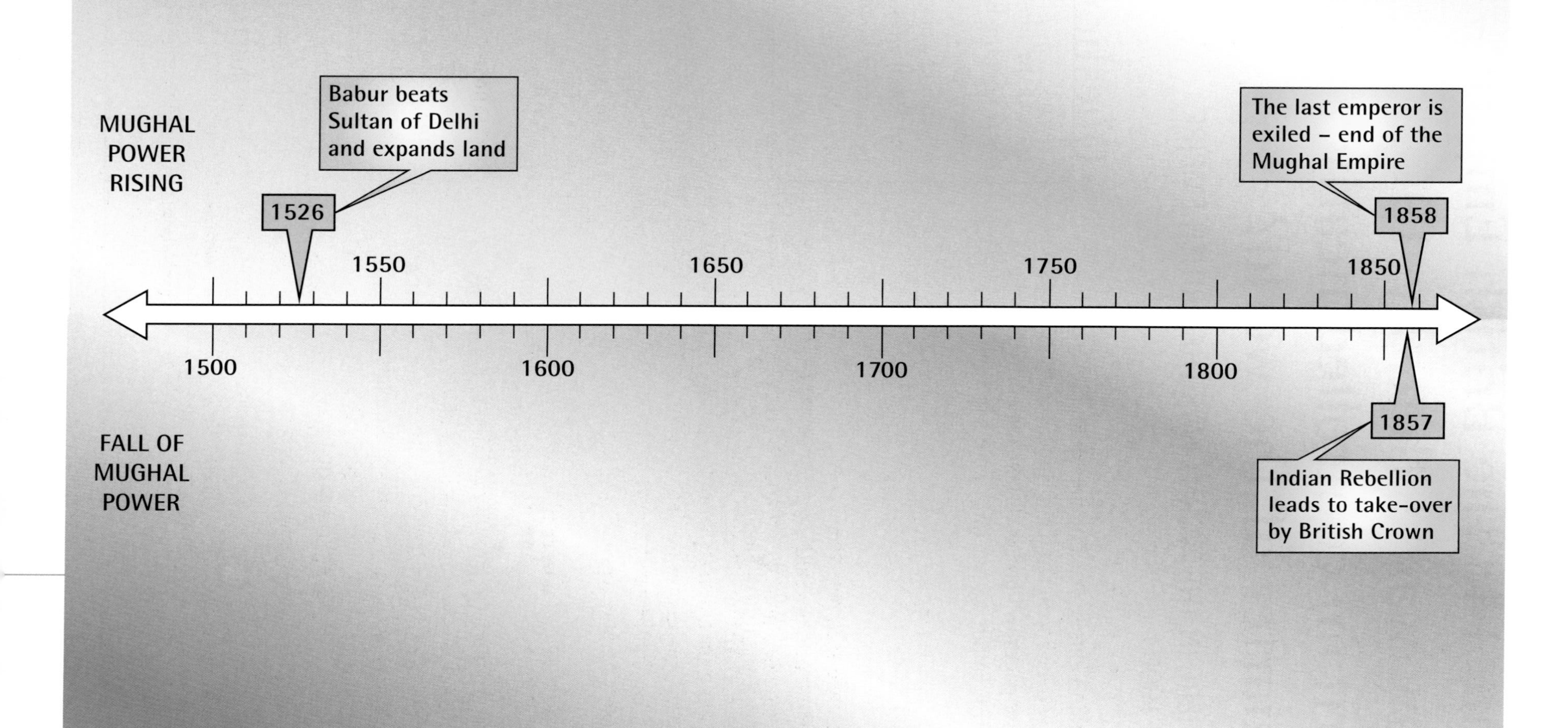
MUGHAL POWER RISING
FALL OF MUGHAL POWER
1526
Babur beats Sultan of Delhi and expands land
1500
1550
1600
1650
1700
1750
1800
1850
1857
Indian Rebellion leads to take-over by British Crown
1858
The last emperor is exiled – end of the Mughal Empire

Unit 14: The British Empire – how was it that, by 1900, Britain controlled nearly a quarter of the world?

WHERE IN THE WORLD WAS THE BRITISH EMPIRE BY 1900?

Britain's empire was not gained all in one go, but grew over a long stretch of time. The three maps on these pages will give you some idea of where the British Empire was at three points in time.

Question Time

Look at the three maps, which show how the British Empire grew between 1765 and 1900. At each key point (1765, 1800 and 1900) work out what had been gained and what had been lost. You might need a modern atlas to help you.

This is a modern map showing the extent of the British Empire in 1765.

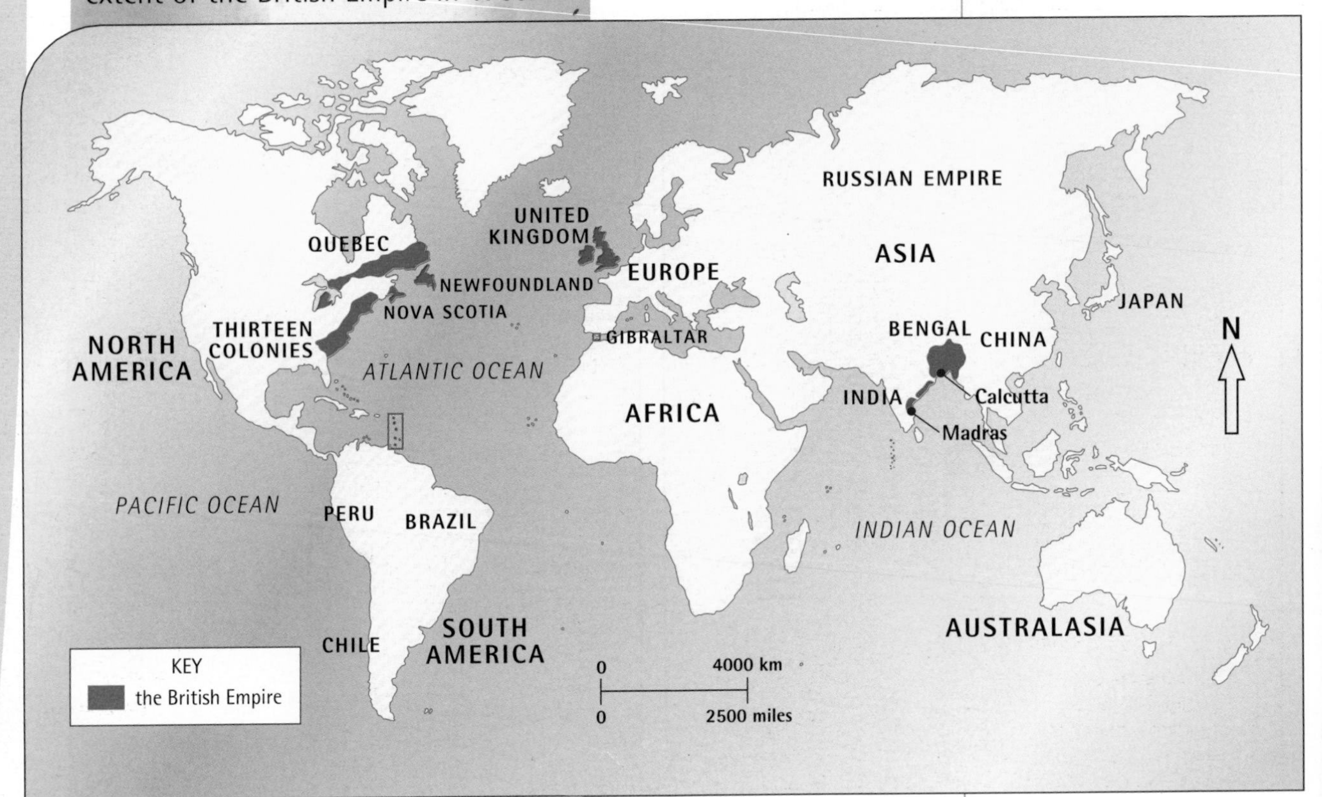

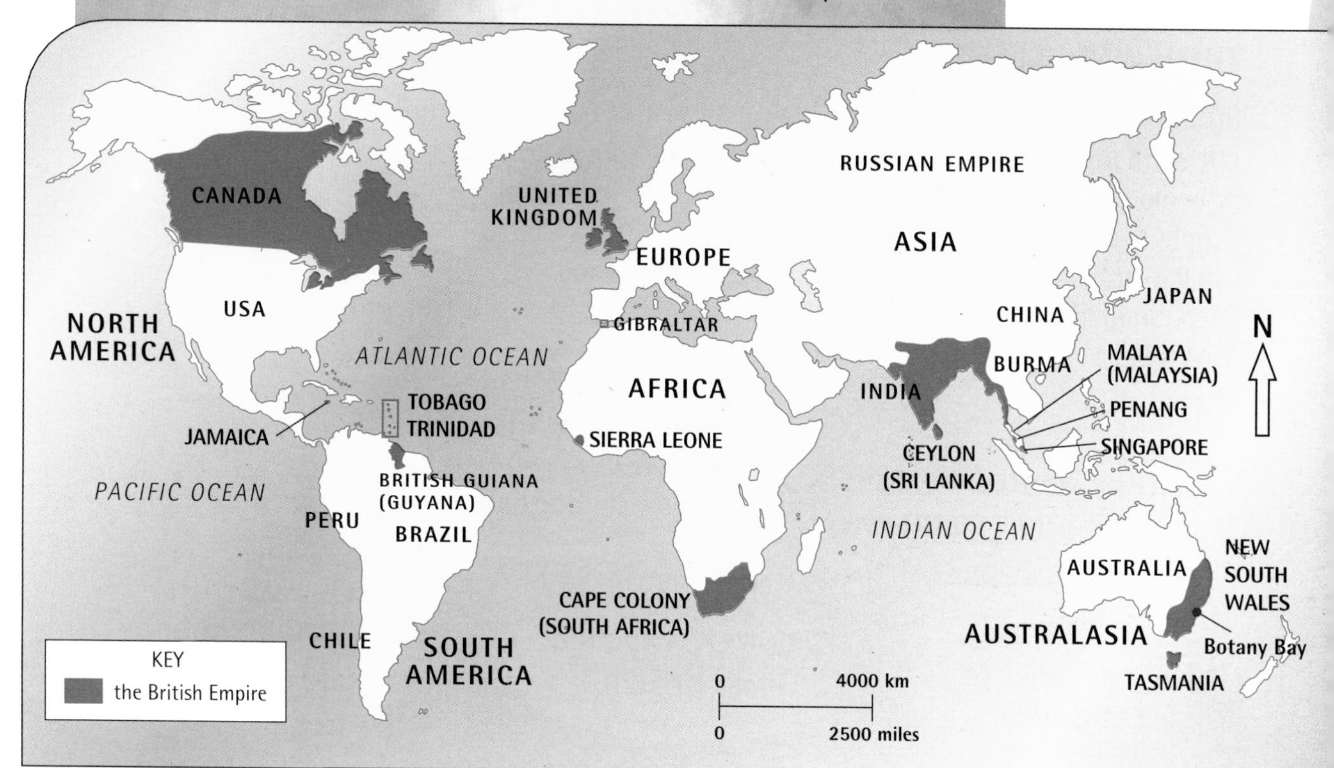

This is a modern map showing the extent of the British Empire in 1800.

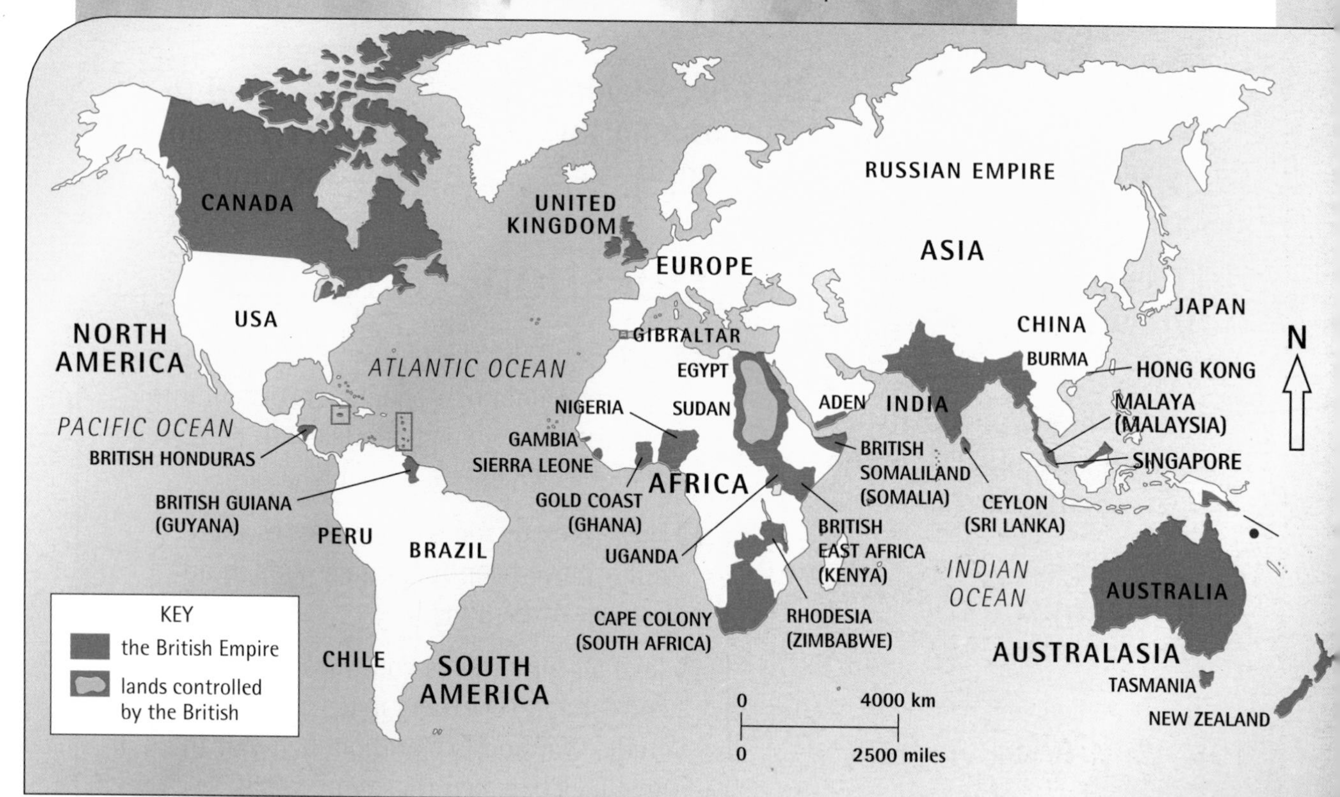

This is a modern map showing the extent of the British Empire in 1900.

WHY DID PEOPLE LIVING IN BRITAIN END UP CONTROLLING LAND MASSES FAR GREATER THAN THEIR OWN ISLAND?

Britain is a small island off the north-west coast of Europe, so it does not seem a likely candidate for control of a widespread empire. Why did it happen? There could be many reasons. Individual people and governments would have had different reasons, some of them private and secret, and others public and open. Some of these reasons would have changed over time.

They wanted to conquer the world

They wanted to trade with other countries

They wanted to teach everyone to speak English

They decided to emigrate

They were expelled from Britain

They wanted to start package holidays abroad

They wanted to visit their relatives

They won land in war

They were explorers and claimed new lands for Britain

They wanted to civilise the world

They liked sailing ships around the world

They wanted to teach everyone about Christianity

They had a strong army

They wanted to find raw materials for British industry

It happened accidentally

It was carefully planned

Question Time

1. Look at all the reasons the British might have had for gaining an empire. Sort them into two lists: ones which are likely to be correct and ones which are probably wrong.
2. Now think of some other reasons there might have been for Britain gaining an empire at this time.
3. Take all the reasons you think are probably correct and sort them under three headings: Trade, War and Exploration. Can you think of any links between these three lists?

HOW DID OVERSEAS TRADE LEAD TO BUILDING A POWERFUL EMPIRE OF COLONIES?

In 1900, British merchants imported goods worth thousands and thousands of pounds: gold and wool from Australia, meat and cheese from New Zealand, tea and jute from India, cotton and corn from India, fish and wood from Canada and cotton and sugar from the Caribbean.

SOURCE 1

These are labels and packaging from goods that a family living in 1900 might buy in a grocer's shop.

Question Time

1. Look carefully at the labels and packets in Source 1. Make a list of the countries from which they came.
2. Use the lower map on page 183 and work out which countries were in the British Empire in 1900. Then, work out by which shipping routes the goods would have travelled to Britain. (Hint: you will need to find out whether the Suez and Panama Canals were open by then.)

HOW WAS TRADE WITH OVERSEAS COUNTRIES ORGANISED?

There were some British merchants who were lone traders. They owned their own ships, made their own contacts overseas and shipped raw materials and goods themselves. But traders like this were few and far between. Most traders worked in, and for, large companies, like the East India Company (set up in 1600), the Hudson's Bay Company (set up in 1670) and the Royal African Company. These companies were formed to trade with certain parts of the world, as you can tell from their names. They owned fleets of ships, employed hundreds of people (merchants, sailors and warehousemen, for example), negotiated with overseas suppliers, arranged importing and exporting, paid customs duties – in fact, did everything connected with trade to 'their' part of the world.

DID THESE TRADING COMPANIES SET UP COLONIES?

No, they didn't. The trading companies set up trading posts overseas. Some of them were more like forts; others were like small towns. British merchants lived, or lodged, there when their ships were moored offshore to trade, and when suppliers came to negotiate rates for the goods and raw materials they had to sell. The East India Company, for example, had trading posts (called 'factories' in the early days) on the Indian coast at Calcutta, Madras, Bombay and Surat. They were there to trade with the East, not to conquer India.

WAS THE EAST INDIA COMPANY THE ONLY TRADING COMPANY IN INDIA?

The British government gave the East India Company sole rights to trade in India. In return, the company gave the British government a share in its profits. No other British merchants could trade in India, but what about merchants from other countries? The French set up their own East India Company with trading posts just like the British East India Company. Both companies kept private armies to protect their trade in India. Both companies worked with and against the local *nawabs* (rulers) who often played the British and French off against each other. Then, thousands of miles away in Europe, Britain and France went to war in what is now called the Seven Years War. Immediately, the situation between them in India became more tense.

THE BLACK HOLE OF CALCUTTA, 1756

The new, young ruler of Bengal in 1756 was Nawab Saraj ud-Daulah. He believed that the growth of Calcutta and British trade was a threat to his power. He also felt quite insulted because the British hadn't sent him the traditional gifts he expected, as a mark of respect, when he had become ruler earlier in the year. With French encouragement, he attacked the British base at Calcutta. No one is really sure what happened next. The official story is that Saraj ud-Daulah and his soldiers captured the English settlement of Calcutta in 1756. They threw 146 English prisoners into a small cell in the Fort William Barracks. The cell measured about 8 by 6 metres. By the next morning, 123 prisoners were dead, suffocated and dehydrated in the hot, airless 'hole'. But was this true?

SOURCE 3

Of 140 prisoners, 123 were smothered in the Black Hole prison in the night of 20 June 1756. From about nine till near eleven my legs were almost broke with the weight against them. I moved over the dead and went to the other end of the room. The moment I moved from the window my breathing grew short and painful. I was seized with a pain in my chest and palpitation in my heart. I had, in a fit of thirst, tried drinking my urine. From half past eleven till nearly two in the morning, I sustained the weight of a heavy man, with his knees in my back, and the pressure of his whole body on my head.

Eight months afterwards, John Holwell wrote about his experiences in the 'Black Hole'.

SOURCE 2

This is a drawing of the Fort William Barracks, Calcutta, showing the barred windows behind which was the Black Hole. The drawing was done in 1882 and the artist never visited Calcutta.

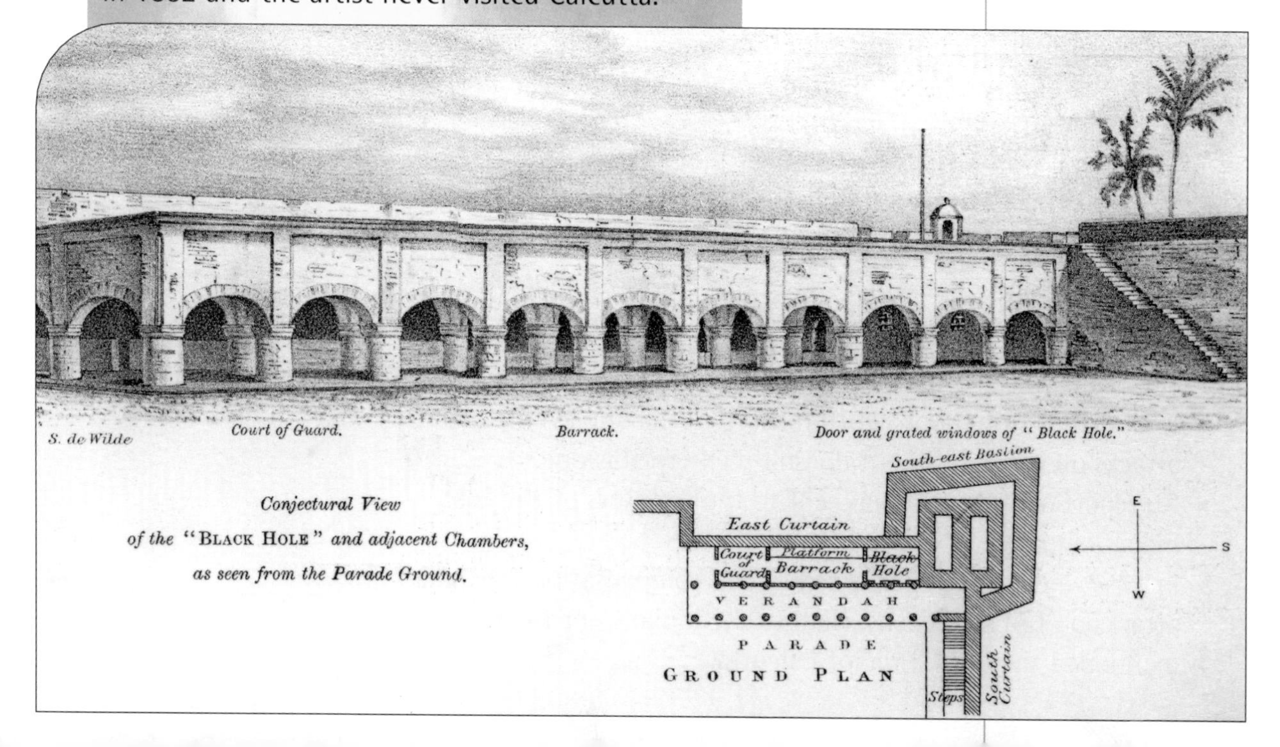

SOURCE 4

If among those builders of empire there are any who especially deserve commendation, it must be those martyrs whose fate I remember and whose names I revive on this site. If there be a spot dear to an Englishman in India, it is that below our feet which was stained with the blood of the victims of that night of June 1756.

In 1902, Lord Curzon, who governed India 1899–1904, unveiled a memorial to the people who died in the Black Hole. This is part of what he said.

SOURCE 6

The campaign against this monument has to be started at once. The 3 July 1940 is going to be observed in Bengal as the Saraj ud-Daulah Day, in honour of the last king of Bengal. The monument is not just an unwarranted stain on the memory of Saraj, but has stood at the heart of Calcutta for the last 150 years or more, as the symbol of our slavery and humiliation.

Subash Chandra Bose was an Indian nationalist. He didn't want the British to be in India at all. One of his campaigns was to get rid of the Black Hole memorial. This is part of what he wrote in June 1940.

SOURCE 5

It is safe to say that only 64 persons were confined in the Black Hole, of whom 21 survived. The area of the room amounted to 267 square feet, giving about 4.2 square feet to each person. This seems enough for a person to stand up and sit down, though not comfortably. At six o'clock in the morning, Holwell was found 'under the dead', but the fresh air instantly revived him. The whole night, which claimed the lives of 123 persons, if Holwell is to be relied upon, had only temporary effects upon him. On the day he was released from the dungeon he walked three miles, and the next day, in spite of the boils that covered him from head to foot, he marched the same distance, in heavy fetters, 'under the scorching beams of an intense hot sun'.

In 1962, an Indian historian, B. K. Gupta, challenged John Holwell's account.

As well as the accounts in the sources, think, too, about the following points:

- The cell was called the 'Black Hole' before the events of 1756.
- An Indian history book, written shortly after the event, lists attacks on the English but doesn't mention this one.
- No report of the event was sent to the directors of the East India Company.
- In 1757, Indian *nawabs* agreed to pay compensation for Indian attacks on British citizens. Neither the Indians nor the British mentioned the Black Hole of Calcutta.

Question Time

1. Read Source 3. Do you think this is likely to be a reliable account of what happened in the Black Hole?
2. Study Sources 2 and 3. How far does Source 2 help you understand what happened in Source 3?
3. Look at Source 4. What is a martyr? Why do you think Lord Curzon said that those who died in the Black Hole were martyrs? What does this tell you about British attitudes to India?
4. Read Source 5. The historian B. K. Gupta disagrees with John Holwell's account of what happened in the Black Hole. Does this mean that John Holwell was lying?
5. Why did Subash Chandra Bose want the Black Hole memorial pulled down?
6. Look back to the official story. Write your own account of what happened, using the sources in this section.

ROBERT CLIVE AND THE BATTLE OF PLASSEY, 1757

The East India Company sent Robert Clive, in command of a force of 3000 Indian sepoys (soldiers) with British officers, to Bengal to sort things out. Clive plotted with the enemies of Saraj ud-Daulah. In a skirmish outside the town of Plassey, Saraj's soldiers were quickly defeated and he was killed.

HOW DID THE BRITISH GOVERNMENT BECOME INVOLVED?

The British government became involved in India because of the East India Company. By 1763 the company had driven the French from India and took more and more of India under its control. In 1784 Parliament, worried by the power of the East India Company, passed an India Act which set up a Board of Control in London to supervise its activities. In 1857, sepoys in the British army in India mutinied. The British government then took direct control of India, instead of allowing the East India Company to run the country's affairs.

This map of India shows the stages by which Britain gained control of India.

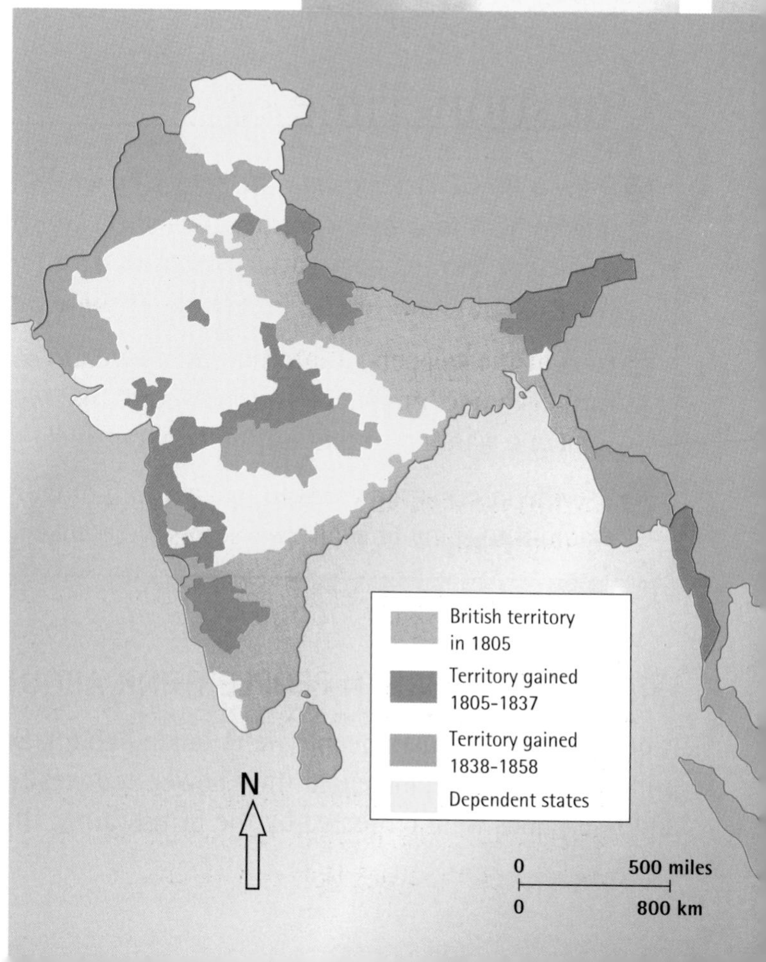

HOW IMPORTANT WAS INDIA TO BRITAIN?

Immensely. By 1900 India was a source of such wealth to Britain that people called it the 'Jewel in the Crown' . How had it come about that, by 1900, India was the most important part of the British Empire?

The Indian handweaving and craft industries collapsed

Queen Victoria became Empress of India

The Suez Canal was opened

Britain exported one-fifth of its cotton goods to India

'Viceroy of India' became a top administrative job

India exported rice, tea and raw cotton to Britain

British upper-class parents sent their younger sons out to India to learn how to run government departments

British upper-class parents send their daughters out to India to find suitable British husbands

Question Time

1. Draw a flow chart showing the stages by which the British government took over control of India. Do you think there was a particular 'turning point' after which the East India Company was going to have to give up control at some time?
2. Look at the snippets of information above. Do some research and turn each one into an 'information card' that would be useful to someone wanting to find out more about India.
3. Use the information cards to make a web of causation/spider diagram to show how all the factors were linked together.

WHAT DID THE INDIAN PEOPLE THINK ABOUT ALL THIS?

It depends which Indian people we're talking about. Some Indian princes, for example, increased their power and wealth because they and their lands were protected by the British army. Others lost everything they had. Some Indian merchants and bankers prospered because they did business with the British, who were running their country. Others went bankrupt. Some Indian workers found jobs as engine drivers, guards and track layers on the railways. Others were forced to beg because their handloom weaving was no longer wanted. Of course, these are only examples and they are extreme examples. In between come all sorts and conditions of Indian people, some of whom did well out of the British, some of whom did badly and most of whom just got through as best they could.

HOW ELSE DID THE BRITISH TRY TO DOMINATE INDIA?

Most British people in the nineteenth century believed, quite simply, that their way of living was the best. Because it was the best, they believed they had a duty to bring this way of living to all the less fortunate people in the world – whether they liked it or not.

Administration

Administration of this vast continent had to be efficient, and so the British threw out any Indian princes they thought were lazy and inefficient.

Language

The British encouraged everyone to speak English. In order to provide an incentive, no one could rise above a certain grade in the Indian civil service unless they spoke English.

Communications

The British introduced a railway network into India and brought British engineers over to build it, and they introduced cheap postal and telegraph services. They built a road network and set up a system of elementary schools for Indian children.

Traditions

The pace of change was too fast, and the British took it for granted that the Indians wanted to be westernised. They ignored many Indian customs and religions. They tried, for example, to do away with certain Indian customs, like *sati*. Hindus did not bury their dead; they burned their bodies on funeral pyres. It was the custom, in many parts of India, for Hindu widows to throw themselves into the burning timbers of their husbands' funeral pyres and so die as well. The British in India tried to stamp out this and other customs of which they disapproved.

India was going to be the 'Jewel in the Crown' of Britain, whether the Indians liked it or not!

SOURCE 7

This painting is called *The Jewel in the Crown.* It was used in the television series of the same name.

Question Time

1. Make three headings: Political, Social and Economic. Under each heading, list the ways in which the British tried to dominate India. Use the examples in this section and try to discover others. Which of the ways do you think would have been the most effective? Which might have angered the Indians the most? Why?
2. Find out about the Hindu religion. How might a Hindu have explained why *sati* was the right thing to do?
3. Look carefully at the painting (Source 7). What is the artist 'saying' about British people? What is the artist 'saying' about Indian people? Do you think the painting would have been popular at the time? Why?
4. People have argued for a long time about whether or not British rule benefited India. What do you think? Try to argue as someone living in the nineteenth century might have argued.

WHAT PART DID EXPLORERS, ADVENTURERS AND MISSIONARIES PLAY IN CREATING THE BRITISH EMPIRE?

The eighteenth and nineteenth centuries were times when the last remote coastlines of the world were mapped by Europeans and when Europeans explored the interiors of huge land masses, like the Great Plains of North America and the deserts and jungles of Africa. It was a time of adventure and greed, of courage and cowardice, of exploitation and empire. Few of the places that the Europeans explored were empty.

Some had held vast civilisations that were far more sophisticated than existed in Europe at the same time. In some, people lived who had values and attitudes that were quite different from those of the Europeans. Often, what the Europeans didn't understand, they destroyed and tried to replace with European values. Sometimes explorers claimed the land they explored for their home country and extended that country's empire. Europeans sometimes used this land in great power struggles between themselves and sometimes they mined gold, tin and precious metals to increase their own wealth.

WHO WERE THE BRITISH EXPLORERS, ADVENTURERS AND MISSIONARIES?

There were many: some were famous and some were known only to their families. Some died of exposure, typhoid, malaria or snake bites, or were torn to pieces by tigers or trampled to death by elephants. Some lived to tell the tale.

WHAT WAS THE 'SCRAMBLE FOR AFRICA?'

In the last years of the nineteenth century, many of the European states raced each other to get control of as many colonies as possible. In this way they would appear strong and powerful. One of the last places in the world to be claimed as 'theirs' by Europeans was Africa. As they scrambled for control, fortunes were made and lost, men and women were killed and maimed, and European rivalries and tensions were brought to Africa.

Activity Time

A Look at the biography boxes. They are just making a start: they need finishing! Find out as much as you can about these people and finish the boxes.

James Cook 1728–79
Explorer and navigator

Where did he explore? Why?
What did he do?
How did he die?
How did he add to the British Empire?

Cecil Rhodes 1853–1902
Explorer and politician

Why did he go to Africa?
How did he amass a fortune?
What was his vision for the British Empire?
What did he do to try to achieve it?

Mary Kingsley 1862–1900
Explorer and novelist

Where did she explore? Why?
What did she do?
How did she die?
What was her importance in the growing British Empire?

Mungo Park 1771–1806
Explorer and doctor

Where did he explore? Why?
What did he discover?
Did he succeed at anything?
What was his importance in the growing British Empire?

David Livingstone 1813–73
Explorer and missionary

Where did he explore? Why?
What did he discover?
What happened when people thought he was lost?
What was his importance in the lands he explored?
How did he add to the British Empire?

This map shows European possessions in Africa in 1914.

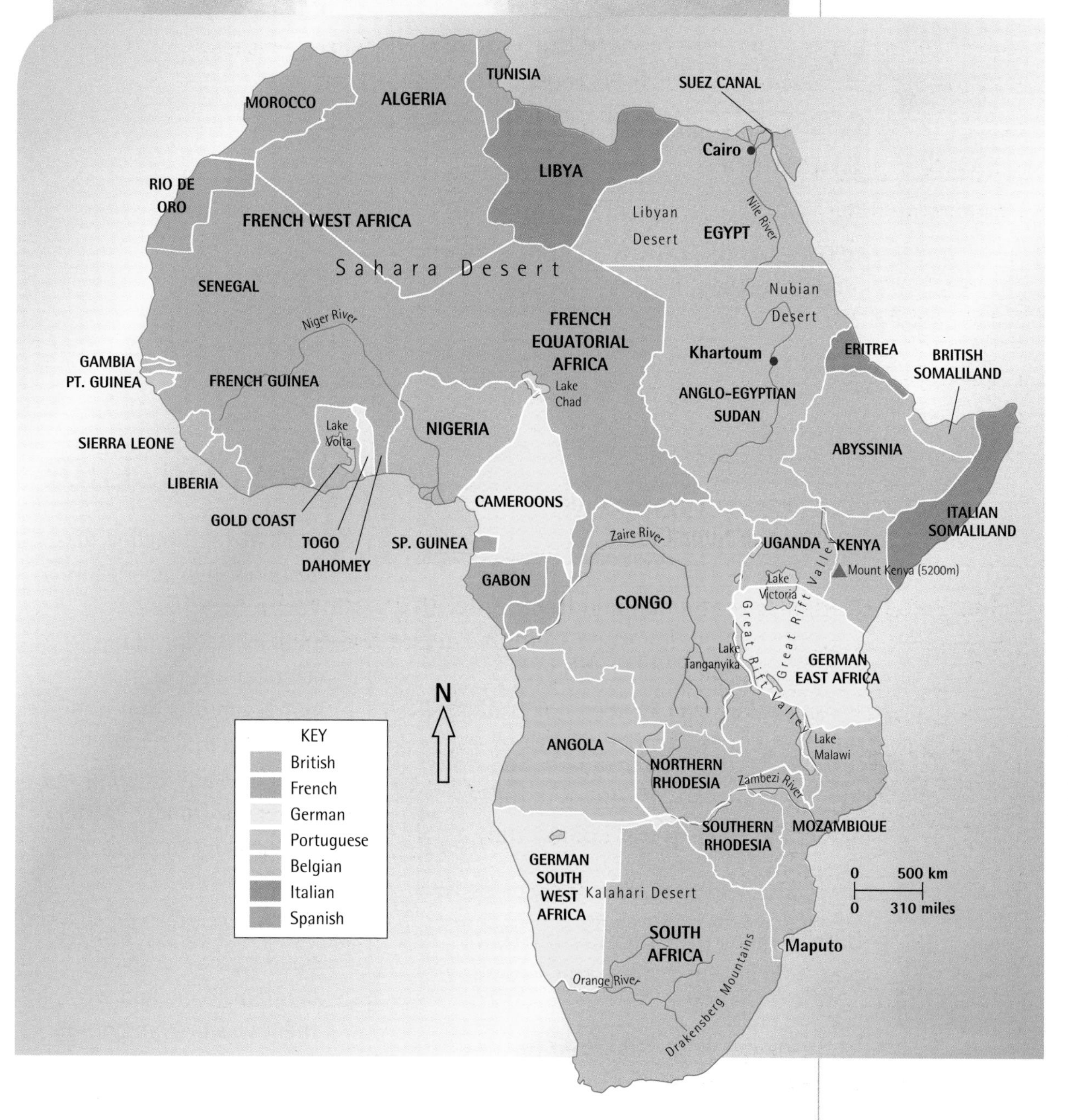

Question Time

1. When you have done your research and answered the questions in the biography boxes, work out how you are going to present them to the rest of the class. You could work with a group of friends on a wall display, or mock interviews, or a mini-drama.
2. On the map of Africa, plot where each of the explorers went.

TIMELINE

1869	Suez Canal opened.
1870s	Gold and diamonds discovered in South Africa.
	Twenty years of on/off fighting between Zulus, British and Boers (Dutch settlers) begins.
1874	Britain takes over the Gold Coast for trade and to keep out France and Germany.
1882	Britain seizes Egypt in order to control the Suez Canal.
1884	Britain seizes Somaliland in order to control the Red Sea route to India.
1885	Britain takes over Nigeria for trade and to keep out France and Germany.
	Britain takes over Bechuanaland for trade and to keep out France and Germany.
1890/4	Britain takes over Uganda for trade and to keep out France and Germany.
1893	Cecil Rhodes joins Rhodesia to the British Empire and dreams of a 'Cape to Cairo' railway.
1899	Britain gains control of Sudan after an army of Dervishes attacks Khartoum and kills the British governor, General Gordon.
	British and Boers go to war in South Africa over Britain's claim to rule there. Britain wins the Boer War in 1902.

Question Time

1. Look at the timeline of Britain's involvement in Africa. Sort the events under these headings: keeping out European powers; protecting trade routes to India; trading with Africa; obtaining raw materials. Do any events come under more than one heading?
2. Use the sorting you have done to draw a spider diagram to explain why there was a scramble for Africa.

WHAT DID BRITISH PEOPLE THINK ABOUT 'THEIR' EMPIRE IN AFRICA?

Nowadays we know that no race, nation or people is in any way superior to any other. In 1900 it was different. Many British people believed they had a duty to spread their sort of civilisation throughout the world. Because they believed this was their duty, they thought they had a right to take over any country that, in their view, needed 'civilising'. It didn't seem to matter whether the people living in those countries had customs and laws, traditions and systems of government of their own. They had to be 'civilised' into the British way of life.

SOURCE 1

This cartoon was published in the magazine *Punch* on 30 September 1882. The lion represents Britain.

THE LION'S JUST SHARE.

SOURCE 2

I say that we are the best race in the world, and that the more of the world we inhabit the better it is for the human race. To bring the greater portion of the world under our rule simply means the end of all wars. To bring the whole uncivilised world under British rule! What a dream! But yet it is possible.

Cecil Rhodes wrote this in 1881 in a letter to a friend.

SOURCE 3

They are just like children. They are always either laughing or quarrelling. They are good natured and passionate, lazy but will work hard for a time; clever up to a certain point, densely stupid beyond. The intelligence of the average negro is about equal to that of a European child of ten years old.

G. A. Henty wrote a lot of adventure books for children. Most of the adventures were set in the British Empire. This comes from one of his stories called *Sheer Pluck*, which was set in Africa. He wrote it in about 1884.

Question Time

1. Look carefully at the cartoon (Source 1). What 'message' is the cartoonist giving out?
2. Read Source 2. What was Rhodes' dream? From what you know about Cecil Rhodes, how did he set about achieving his dream? Did he achieve it?
3. Read Source 3. Why do you think that books that told this sort of thing to children were immensely popular?
4. Look at Source 4. What attitude to empire is the cartoonist showing?

SOURCE 4

This advertisement was published in about 1900.

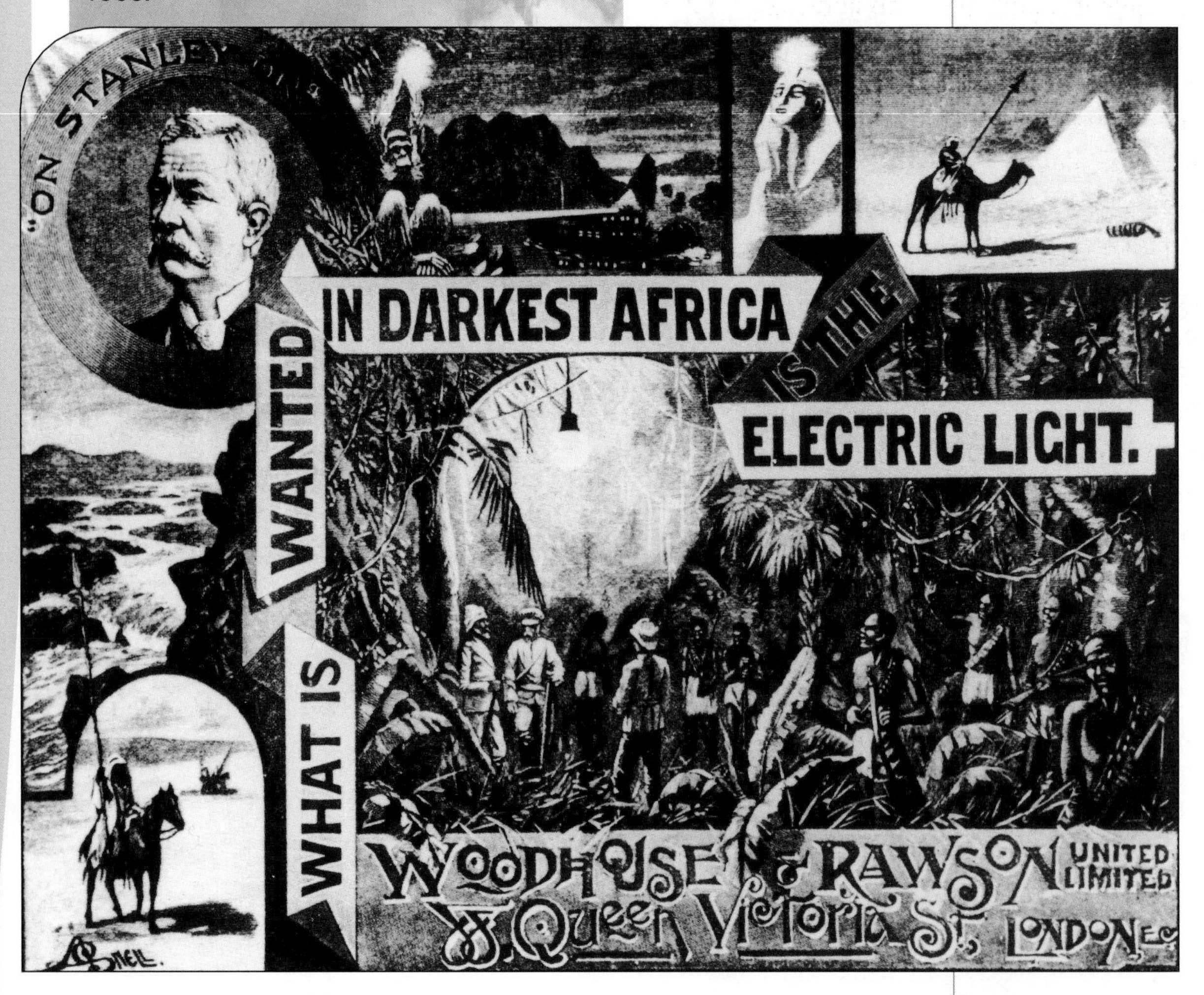

WHAT DID THE MISSIONARIES DO?

You have seen how many British people believed that it was their right and duty to bring the British way of life to all parts of their empire, whether the people living there wanted them to or not. Part of this British civilisation was their religion, which was Christianity.

Christian missionaries set out from Britian to spread the word of the Christian gospel in Africa, as well as in other parts of the British Empire. Men and women travelled willingly into the unknown because of their religious beliefs and their conviction that they should share these with those people who did not know anything at all about the Christian God and Jesus Christ. Remember that Africa was called the 'Dark Continent' by many people in the nineteenth century and that the first missionaries had little or no knowledge about the continent to which they were going. They knew nothing about the climate, the jungles and deserts, huge rivers and vast waterfalls, the wild animals and snakes. They knew nothing, either, about the people they were determined to convert to Christianity.

SOURCE 5

1 *From Greenland's icy mountains*
From India's coral strand,
Where Afric's sunny fountains
Roll down their golden sand,
5 *From many an ancient river,*
From many a palmy plain,
They call us to deliver
Their land from error's chain

What though the spicey breezes
10 *Blow soft o'er Java's isle,*
Though every prospect pleases
And only man is vile:
In vain with lavish kindness
The gifts of God are strown
15 *The heathen in his blindness*
Bows down to wood and stone

Can we, whose souls are lighted
With wisdom from on high
Can we to men benighted
20 *The lamp of life deny?*

This is part of a Christian hymn written by Bishop Heber (1783–1826).

Most missionaries were sponsored by organisations like the British and Foreign Bible Society which equipped them and supported them as best they could. Missionaries in Africa usually lived and worked in small settlements, which they set up close to African villages. They encouraged the Africans to come to them for basic medical help, sometimes for food, often for lessons in reading and writing and always to learn about the Christian religion.

SOURCE 6

A photograph of missionaries in the Lower Congo in Africa in the late-nineteenth century.

Question Time

1. Read the hymn (Source 5) carefully. It tells us a lot about nineteenth century British people's attitudes to Christianity and to other people's religions.
   a How do lines 1–4 and 9–11 describe lands beyond Britain?
   b What do lines 12 and 19 say about the people living there?
   c How do lines 15–16 explain this?
   d What do lines 13–16 say about British attitudes to the religions of non-Christian people?
   e How do the last four lines explain why most British people believed they should convert non-Christian people in their empire to Christianity?
   f Read lines 7–8. What are these two lines saying about people living in lands beyond Britain?
   g How might British missionaries use this idea to justify what they were doing?
2. How useful is Source 6 as evidence of the success of missionaries in Africa?

DID THE BRITISH FIGHT WARS TO GAIN COLONIES?

The answer to this question is both yes and no. Britain did fight wars against various European countries, but not really in order to gain colonies. Britain gained colonies as a result of the peace conferences after these wars. At other times, Britain fought wars against the rulers of states that seemed to be threatening the British in an existing colony. In this way, they gained more and more of the land surrounding the colony.

GAINING LAND IN CANADA AND NORTH AMERICA

Look back to the map of the British Empire in 1765 (page 182). In 1763, Britain and France finished fighting a series of wars against each other. The British won and, in the peace treaties, gained French-held land in Canada and India to add to their empire. Remember that Britain already held land in North America (the original thirteen colonies) and in the Caribbean.

GAINING ISLANDS

Now look back to the map of the British Empire in 1800 (page 183). Between 1783 and 1815, Britain and other European countries were fighting the French armies of Napoleon. It was during this time that Britain gained the Caribbean islands that had been held by France and Spain, as well as Ceylon (now Sri Lanka) and Cape Colony (now South Africa) from the Dutch. The East India Company, as you have read, was gradually extending its control in India, often by fighting, and was doing the same in Burma and Malaya (now Malaysia).

LOSING LAND

But as well as gains, you will see that some land has been lost. In 1776, the thirteen colonies on the east coast of America fought a successful war of independence against Britain and became the United States of America.

If you look at the lower map on page 183, you will see that by 1900 Britain controlled nearly one-third of the world. Minor skirmishes had added more land in India, Burma, Malaya and the Pacific Ocean, but it was in Africa that Britain took control over vast lands while France and Germany were also battling to build up large empires.

Question Time

1. Make a timeline of the wars and peace treaties that added lands to the British Empire.
2. Choose one of the generals or admirals involved and research his life. Then write an obituary for him, remembering to praise what was good and gloss over with clever phrases his bad points.

THE CAPTURE OF QUEBEC

In 1759 British soldiers captured the French-Canadian city of Quebec. This ended French control over Canada, and brought Canada into the British Empire. The major-general leading the British troops was James Wolfe, who was then aged thirty-two. He was killed in the fierce battle to take the city. His youth, and the fact that he was killed in a battle of such importance, meant that all kinds of myths would grow up around his death.

SOURCE 2

This picture of the death of General Wolfe was painted in 1763 by Edward Penny.

SOURCE 1

Then up comes the Captain and tells me to take a message to the General to say our line had held and the enemy was put to flight. I was tired at all we had done last night and this morning. But I obeyed and ran over the field stepping through blood and faces upturned in death. But the General was nowhere the Captain had said and I was making to go back down our line when suddenly I saw him. He was lying on a mound behind a sad little bush, looked after by just two men, one leaning over and supporting Wolfe by his arm. Mr Browne, for that was his name, shouted at me to come fast and help. I approached Wolfe and saw that his face had gone stiff and greenish and his red hair glistened with sun and sweat. Blood had matted his belly where another ball had struck him and now more was oozing through his shirt and coat, so seeing he would not live, I told him our news and in a groaning gurgling sort of way I could hear him praise God for it.

In 1991 the historian, Simon Schama, wrote about the death of General Wolfe. He used accounts from soldiers who were there at the time. This source is part of what he wrote.

SOURCE 3

This picture, called *The Death of General Wolfe* was painted by Benjamin West in 1770.

Think about these points when you look at the West painting of General Wolfe's death:

- Benjamin West said 'Wolfe must not die like a common soldier under a bush.'
- Look at the people close to Wolfe. Monckton, standing at the left, had played an important part in the battle. But he had been badly wounded and wasn't there when General Wolfe died.
- The Ranger, in the green jacket on the left of the picture, wasn't there either when General Wolfe died.
- Indians fought with the French against the British in the battle for Quebec. Wolfe thought American Indians were cruel barbarians. It is very unlikely that Wolfe would have tolerated an Indian being there when he died. It is equally unlikely that an Indian would have wanted to be there.

Question Time

1. Read Source 1. Is this a reliable source of evidence about how General Wolfe died?
2. Look at Source 2. How likely is it that a general, in the heat of a battle, would die like this?
3. Study Sources 1 and 2. What are the similarities between these two sources? What are the differences?
4. Look at Sources 2 and 3. What are the differences between these two sources? What are the similarities?
5. Look at Source 3 again. Read the 'Think about' points. How reliable is this source as evidence of the way General Wolfe died? Why do you think Benjamin West painted the picture in this way?

HOW WAS IT THAT, BY 1900, BRITAIN CONTROLLED NEARLY A QUARTER OF THE WORLD?

This is the question with which we began. You have thought about, and worked through, the three main ways in which Britain gained control of nearly a quarter of the world. These were trade, exploration and war.

SOURCE 1

In June every year, British people celebrated 'Empire Day'. Villages, towns and cities put on shows, exhibitions, plays and entertainments to show their appreciation of their empire. These pictures show Empire Flag Day in 1922 (below), a poster for the 1924 British Empire Exhibition (right) and, on page 205, a photo from Empire Day in 1934.

Question Time

You are going to plan a presentation to your class to show them how people living in 1900 might have celebrated Empire Day. Choose trade or exploration or war as your theme. Working in groups, plan your presentation to the rest of the class in order to explain how important your theme was to the growth of the British Empire. Your presentation could be, for example, a decorated float, a wall display or a series of mini-dramas. Remember, too, that you are showing what British people living in 1900 would have thought and believed about the empire.